An Education for the People?

A History of HMI and Lifelong Education 1944–1992

An Education for the People?

A History of HMI and Lifelong
Education 1944–1992

KT Elsdon and others

Published by the National Institute of Adult Continuing Education
(England and Wales)
21 De Montfort Street, Leicester, LE1 7GE
Company registration no. 2603322
Charity registration no. 1002775
The NIACE website on the Internet is http://www.niace.org.uk

First published 2001
© NIACE

CATALOGUING IN PUBLICATION DATA
A CIP record for this title is available from the British Library
ISBN 1 86201 110 9

Typeset by The Midlands Book Typesetting Co., Loughborough
Cover design by Boldface, London
Printed in Great Britain by Hobbs

Contents

Contents

Preface

This book is dedicated to the memory of our friend and colleague Edwin Sims. He made long, greatly valued and important contributions to most aspects of Other Further Education (OFE) before he joined HM Inspectorate in 1962, during his service in it until 1980, and continued afterwards until his very end.

The idea of this study originated with Harold Marks, who felt that the Inspectorate's contribution to the development of OFE should be put on record while memories lasted and led to obtainable source material. As this idea took some shape he sought the co-operation of Konrad Elsdon and Edwin Sims in an enterprise which he felt unable to carry through on his own. Long delays meant that, sadly, Edwin died suddenly and prematurely before he was able to do more than write about the early history of the Youth Service and HMI's organisation. Chapter 5 has been largely completed by Tom Wylie and David Rees, with assistance from Alan Gibson. Our friend and colleague Eric Sudale, another important contributor to the field, also died suddenly before completion. His was a major creative influence on the development of Liberal and General Studies, and he was the main author of Chapter 7, which was completed by Fred Parrott. Harold Marks contributed particularly and largely to Chapters 1, 3, 4 and 5. For the section on Penal Education in Chapter 3 he must acknowledge the great help of Alan Baxendale, sometime Chief Education Officer in the Home Office. Harold Marks is the sole author of Chapter 6 on Careers Education and Guidance. He, Alan Gibson and Fred Parrott gave much help with general editing.

Other surviving HMI, including particularly Joe Barks, Alan Gibson, Joan McDonald, Jean McGinty, Kay Tobin, and others too numerous to mention individually, have contributed helpfully from their experience. All main authors listed, several other former HMI from other sections than OFE, and Peter Baynes, Alan Parrott and Susan Stewart, have read the text in draft. Their extensive critical comments and numerous constructive suggestions have been in the very best tradition of HMI and their friends and colleagues. The main responsibility for doing justice to so much, and such invariably punctual help, of shaping and editing the whole of the material, as well as making substantial contributions of his own throughout the text, rested on Konrad Elsdon, under whose editorship the book appears.

Inaccuracies, omissions and doubtful interpretations are inevitable in the task of compiling and integrating the work of so many and such different hands. We apologise for them and shall be happy if the text stimulates considered criticism, corrections and additions, which we shall be glad to receive.

Finally, we are particularly grateful to the Association of HMI for their generosity in supporting the cost of publication. Mindful, however, of HMIs' traditional obligation we delight in exonerating both the Association and the employers of serving HMI from complicity in the origins or outcome of our work.

HESM
KTE
6.IX.1999

Introduction

This study attempts an historical account of a unique educational endeavour, and of the organisational relationships which played a large part in its development. Other Further Education (OFE) comprised all the institutions, organisations, movements and activities of post-school and out-of-school education, other than the work-related provision of the Colleges of Further Education. Our account relates the ways in which OFE on the one hand, and a small and arguably unique sub-section of a public service, the OFE section of HM Inspectorate of Schools (HMI)[1] on the other, developed and influenced each other in political contexts which were variable but never supportive over a period of some 40 years following the 1944 Education Act. The character of the relationship varied between the poles of formality and interdependence. The service of HMI as a whole was unique to Britain. It was admired and sometimes envied in other countries, and it was first attenuated and then abolished in its established effective form. Whether Government has become wiser and education better as a result must be judged by others than the authors.

Institutions such as all the different kinds of schools and colleges are complex but people have always had a reasonable basic understanding of what they are, and are for. The 1944 Education Act's intentions towards them were equally intelligible. However, this Act differed from its predecessors in that it proclaimed *a duty* to provide not merely schools for children and colleges for those who had recently left them, all pursuing their studies in formal and accepted frameworks, but *education for 'the people of England and Wales'*. By its wording the Act extended the concept of education in Britain; it implied that adults and young people out of school are people, who have educational needs beyond those which are defined by traditional institutions and curricula or the interests of employers. Government accepted that there was a duty upon it to meet these needs.

The educational frameworks and pursuits developed for these newly admitted beneficiaries of the education system were exceedingly varied. They included community centres and later related developments, village halls, sport and physical recreation, evening institutes, adult education centres or educational settlements as they were then named, youth work, university extramural and WEA classes, the few day continuation schools set up following the Fisher Act of 1918, and related provision in some institutions and by some employers. Careers education and guidance, liberal or general studies in vocational Further Education (FE), second chance, and adult basic education were shortly added, or their existence recognised as significant elements in public educational provision. So were old-established educational work in HM Forces and penal institutions.

With the exception of careers guidance, all these were Further Education in the sense of the Act since they were and are undertaken after the completion of compulsory schooling or at least out of school. However, they had or at least seemed to have nothing in common with formal college-provided examinable courses intended to qualify students to earn their living in standard occupations. It seems that nobody could think of a positive and meaningful label to attach to this newly recognised gallimaufry of educational provision. It was named simply after its *otherness* from what had always been known and respected. It became, perhaps ominously, *Other Further Education (OFE)*, an absurd term scorned by HMI at the time, but unfortunately accepted. It was provided in due course with its own section of the inspectorate, namely Other Further Education HMI (OFE HMI). After initial reliance on interested members already in post they had to be drawn mainly from what was, and remained, the exiguous number of full-time professionals who ploughed that alien furrow.

At the time of the 1944 Act HMI had, already, more than a century of history behind it. Because it was unique to Britain and no longer exists in its original form, some readers may want the briefest possible explanation of what it was, of whom it consisted, and what were its fundamental role, working principles and relationships. It will be found in Appendix 1.

For reasons which will no doubt become clearer as confidential files are opened, HMI in its final years became increasingly preoccupied with large scale surveys. Consequently, and because the growth in educational institutions far outstripped HMI numbers, its deep knowledge of individual institutions on the ground and its intimate and regular contact with them were attenuated. As a body whose *raison d'être* was to provide well-grounded evidence and unbiased advice it had not uncommonly been an irritant to governments. If the inspectorate was becoming less able to provide reliable answers in its latter days it was, perhaps, not surprising that a government which believed itself in *a priori* possession of them, felt able to dispense with its services. Moreover, it desired a service that would deliver straightforward monitoring and control to meet the needs of market forces, rather than continuity of evaluation and policy advice. Ofsted and its current inspectorate are clearly designed to provide this with a high degree of efficiency. It intends, with its reduced HMI numbers, and the aid of new agencies, to provide some continuing concern for certain aspects of what used to be comprised in OFE.

OFE HMI as a separate section within the service had ceased to exist over 20 years before the original inspectorate as a whole was wound up, and replaced by different arrangements. They were few in number and their brief was seen as marginal by many of their colleagues, not least those who coveted the additional manpower for rapidly changing and expanding work-related FE. In the Department and among politicians OFE carried little weight because the greatest pressures upon them came necessarily from the big battalions of the schools and FE colleges. The 255 pages of John Dunford's (1998) history of HMI from 1944 to the present include three passing references to the youth service and no other mention of OFE, or its inspectorate. We understand that MacLure's (forthcoming 2001) general history does not pay much more attention to it. The justification for this present account is that OFE, at its peak, was indeed an education service for 'the people of England and Wales': it involved more of them at any one time than all the rest of the education system put together, albeit mainly part-time. It also rests on the fact that, in some of the most substantial parts of OFE, England[2] led the world for perhaps half a generation, and the part played by OFE HMI in these developments was not without significance. Much of the work in their purview was itself eroded from the mid-1960s on and largely lost in the 1980s, by successive governments' abandonment of the 1944 Act's concern for spreading socially valuable and culturally valid education based on liberal principles. It was replaced by concentration on whatever is considered to have a clear primary economic value.

The plan of the book

The span from the 1944 Act to the end of OFE HMI as a separate section in 1967 will therefore take up most of our space. Before this we trace the origins of, and the later involvement of, HMI in those activities which were later to constitute OFE, prior to the 1944 Act. (Chapter 1).

In Chapter 2 we trace the early development of policy on OFE, the setting up of an OFE Inspectorate, its structure, composition, relationships to other HMI tasks, the characteristics of its members, their working methods and approach to their task *vis-à-vis* the Office and the field. The Chapter ends with some account of the dissolution of the OFE section and its consequences.

These two generic Chapters are followed by a series in which the development of particular areas of work within OFE and their interaction with HMI are described.

Chapter 3 deals with all the more institutional forms of Adult Education, including penal and Forces education, basic education, Access courses, disadvantage, research and training. Chapter 4 covers work with voluntary organisations, including community centres, village halls and community development. Chapter 5 addresses the Youth Service; Chapter 6 careers guidance, and Chapter 7 liberal and general studies in FE institutions.

It used to be customary for HMI's formal reports to end with 'conclusions'. Earlier in our story it might have seemed possible to round the book off in a similarly considered way, but it is certainly impossible to do so now: the whole of education remains in too much turmoil. We have tried to present as carefully factual *a history* as seems possible now. 'History' *tout court* will be the work of another day. The envoy which can be framed now, and only now, is a contrast, rather than a conclusion, to the preceding text. Chapter 8, an epilogue, is no less factual, but its facts, presented as a composite picture, are the personal views, experiences and arguments of many contributors who participated in the events described in the preceding chapters. Its impression of what it was, and felt like, to be an OFE HMI, or to work (and live) with them, derives from personal statements and private communications of former OFE HMI, members of their families, members of other sections of HMI, and non-HMI. It seeks to identify some of the important strands in the characteristics of both the OFE field and of the specialist HMI working in it, and trace their effects.

We describe this book as *a history.* As such we have made it as fair and complete as enquiries, memories and above all research in voluminous records – many of them unpublished – permit. But this book neither is, nor claims to be, a definitive history of OFE or any of its constituents. Moreover, not all of its authors would agree with every one of each other's conclusions or attitudes: the same careful reflection on given evidence can and does point different individuals in their own directions. We trust the book will be the more useful to those who will till this field in the future.

Two short passages, which are integral parts of the text, appear as Appendices because they would disrupt the flow elsewhere. Appendix 1 is addressed to the many readers who will be unfamiliar with the structure and role of HM Inspectorate as it used to be. Its arcane hierarchy of acronyms, the principles upon which individual assignments and responsibilities were organised, and the functions of various HMI play an inevitable part in the text. Readers to whom this is unfamiliar territory are urged to look *now* at Appendix 1, which explains the essentials very briefly. Appendix 2 is addressed to those who may wish to have an exceedingly modest historical context suggested to them as background to a story which will, by now, seem remote to some.

Throughout the text, passages in inverted commas and without a given source are quoted verbatim from the written communications or verbal statements of individual informants.

All substantial published sources are listed in the Bibliography. We have, however, refrained from burdening this with material whose provenance is given in the notes, or passing references to publications which may have played a part historically but have not been used as sources.

The Glossary explains such technical terms as are essential, and the common acronyms. A very few need explanation now. *The Department* refers invariably to the Department of Education and Science, before its amalgamation with Employment after the end of our period. Before the 1944 Education Act was passed education was in the charge of a *Board*; subsequently this became a *Ministry. The Office* is the short-hand term by which HMI usually referred to the administrative apparatus of the Department and the officials who worked there, as opposed to Ministers, and themselves. OFE inspectors normally linked up with one, sometimes two, Further Education Branches of the Office, and occasionally others. A *Branch*, throughout our period, would have been led by an Under Secretary; and its sections variously by Assistant Secretaries, Principals and sometimes Senior or Higher Executive Officers. HMI in the field operated outside this hierarchy and cultivated egalitarian functional relationships with all its members. HMI themselves usually referred to their own functional divisions into those specialising in primary or secondary schools, vocational further education (usually referred to as TCA), teacher education and training, and OFE, as branches. To avoid confusion with those just explained, we shall usually call them *sections* in this book. A *district* is the territory of a single LEA, and HMI charged with overall liaison with it (for OFE, or FE, or Schools) would be its *district inspector.*

Notes

1. The common acronym HMI will be used both for the service and for its members. It will be clear from the context which is intended.
2. The reference to England is deliberate. Scotland and Northern Ireland had, and retain, their own systems. Wales was administered under the same Act, but both the actual provision of OFE under that Act, and the practice of Welsh HMI, differed too much from those in England to be easily accommodated in an account such as that offered here. However, Welsh OFE development paralleled English in many respects during the period surveyed.

1 Prelude: Before the 1944 Education Act

The 1944 Act broke new ground in requiring the newly-styled Minister to promote the education of *all* the people of England and Wales. It initiated notable developments outside formal school education and vocational provision by colleges and extended the system into leisure-time provision. All this involved an enhanced role for HMI at the very time when it was least able to take it up. Like many other professional groups, they had on the outbreak of hostilities in 1939 been largely diverted to a multitude of other tasks, and their numbers were rapidly depleted. Before the war, however, a few of its members had played a formally established part, and more had been regularly but less formally involved since the latter part of the nineteenth century, in activities which were later to become part of OFE. In this chapter we examine these activities and the gradual establishment of formal relationships in the course of the preparations which led to the passing of the 1944 Education Act.

Adult education

The values and attitudes of senior officials of the Board of Education, and of HMI both before and after World War I, were powerfully informed by the English Christian humanist tradition and its peculiarly nineteenth-century offspring, Christian Socialism. Both were central to the development of adult education. They strongly influenced university extension and expressed themselves in the settlements, the working men's colleges and, from 1908, also in the educational settlements (later centres). From 1903 developments in university extra-mural and WEA work added a powerful new impetus, which sprang from the belief of the growing trade union and co-operative movements in the possibility of emancipation through higher education. Board officials and HMI had played an important part in fostering education for adults since at least 1908. Their vital support in the development of university extra-mural and WEA provision is well documented. By the 1930s three HMI (T Jack, WF Dann and H Grierson) were travelling the country full-time, looking at extra-mural and WEA classes provided mostly from these sources, the so-called Responsible Bodies for Adult Education (RBs), and consulting with their heads. They were assisted part-time by DH Lawton from the, then, separate T (technical) section of the inspectorate; his involvement continued for some time after the war.

Less well known is the part played by a number of HMI from the T Branch in supporting and extending the non-vocational AE developments with social education objectives which had been initiated by a small number of LEAs after the 1902 Act. The leading pioneer among them was the London County Council (LCC). Developments there and elsewhere owe much to the Board of Education Adult Education Committee's 1933 report on the LCC's efforts to improve the situation of working class students through men's and women's institutes, and on analogous work in a few other LEAs. This report also looked at the so-called pre-vocational work which was the bread and butter of thousands of small evening institutes scattered around the country, working mostly in school buildings and with part-time staff. The very few day continuation schools which had been set up in the wake of the Fisher (Education) Act which was passed at the end of World War I, and analogous work sponsored by far-sighted employers such as the Post Office and social pioneers like Rowntree's and Cadbury's, were also considered.

Steered by its energetic and imaginative Secretary, (Sir) William Emrys Williams, the British Institute of Adult Education advocated tirelessly throughout the pre-war decade the need for more adult education: it should be extended beyond the three-year tutorial class model, and also into film and radio. The educational settlements idea received new impetus from the problems of the 'Special' Areas depressed by structural unemployment, and was influenced from 1924 by Henry Morris's pressure for village college provision to meet the need for rural regeneration.

As early as 1936 the Board had requested LEAs to survey their provision in adult education. Their disappointing response led to the establishment during the following years of an internal Adult Education Committee of the Board.[1] This would consider the whole field of AE, including the role of the LEAs which were expected to shoulder the main financial burden, and that of the Rural Community Councils. By 1939 the Committee's work was sufficiently advanced, and well supported, for it to envisage the publication of a pamphlet on AE. However, the Board's concern for the widening of post-school educational opportunities was swamped by the urgent issues and new requirements which the conversion of the government apparatus to a war footing imposed on it. The AE committee was suspended.

During the war there were no further developments of note in general AE, except for the steep increase of public participation in its provision. Together with wartime conditions and concerns, and cultural initiatives such as CEMA (the Council for the Encouragement of Music and the Arts, the predecessor to the Arts Council) this may well have resulted partly from the first raising of the school leaving age by the Fisher Education Act, which had followed World War I. It was also stimulated by concern with the wartime context, and the growing ferment of ideas about post-war development.

Penal education

Penal education is said to be a misleading term, but it happens to be the one that is normally used for the education of those in prisons and other penal establishments. HMI concern for the practice began even before their interest in what later became known as the Service of Youth. Education in local prisons, run in the later nineteenth century by local Justices, was the responsibility of prison chaplains. With some of these HMI, then largely clerical, had some natural affinity. Literacy work had long-standing connections with the religious character of educational efforts such as the Adult School movement. A new era started with the notable contribution of the Rev TW Sharpe, CB, who was HMI from 1857 to 1897, the last seven years as Senior Chief Inspector (SCI). When the Prison Commission was established to take over from the Counties in 1878, he was a member of the committee which prepared an educational scheme for inmates. Subsequently, in 1896, he gave evidence to an enquiry into 'Educational and Moral Instruction in Local and Training Prisons'. This also covered the Convict Prisons Directorate establishments, responsibility for which the Commission was to assume in 1898 (cf Kekewitch 1920). He doubtless greatly influenced other HMI. They helped to develop not only literacy teaching for Bible reading, but also endeavours to relieve the tedium of incarceration with lectures and other educational group activities. All these were, at that time, provided by the responsible chaplains with the help of volunteers.

Education provision was encouraged by the Prison Commission and developed, if patchily, after 1910 (Baxendale, 1993; Ferguson, 1981). It was, of course, central to thinking about the treatment of young offenders, which was then encapsulated in the Borstal system. As Secretary to the Board of Education, Sir Robert Morant had been influential in this development. HMI were called on officially to advise on both the 'school' and 'vocational training' elements of the new regimes. These were developing to include general education and even 'club' activities by the mid-twenties. HMI sometimes also formally inspected Borstal education.

After the hiatus in the development of penal policy caused by World War I the Commission, supported by the British Institute of Adult Education, also encouraged further educational activity in its adult institutions. In 1923 the Board of Education Adult Education Committee, on which the Institute was represented, proposed that an education adviser be appointed to every penal institution. With such voluntary help many prisons, as well as the borstals, developed educational programmes. In the latter it was mainly prison staff without educational training who were responsible for the work. Annual meetings for the growing number of honorary advisers started in 1929. Weekly news sheets, radio-based discussion programmes, lectures and classes were provided by volunteers. A private member's bill, which might have led to more systematic development was sadly blocked by the Home Office and the Board of Education in 1927. However, in the same year the Commission invited some HMI together with SH Wood (then in the Office as an Assistant Secretary), who had a background in boys' clubs, to examine Borstal education unofficially and to advise on its development. By 1938 they proposed that the Board should second an HMI to their service to run penal education, but war intervened. Up to the end of World War II prison chaplains remained responsible for the growing but still modest and patchy educational provision in prisons. Following the nineteenth-century settlement tradition, some HMI who were personally concerned with prison conditions gave major assistance to them, but the Board was not involved.

Armed services education

Adult Education has had a long history in the armed services, from the nineteenth-century in particular, but with relatively little connection with the Education Department, except for some help given to the YMCA in its efforts to provide adult education during World War I. All three services, however, had their own variously developed educational organisations to meet their perceived needs.[2]

Much of the army educational effort was devoted to running children's schools in its widely scattered garrisons, as well as to a system of general adult education linked to promotion and also to technical studies of military import. Work in the RAF was more heavily weighted towards technical studies.

It was typical of the erroneous expectations in 1939 of what kind of fighting would ensue that the army education scheme was suspended and the Army Education Corps moved to other and supposedly more pressing duties. With the introduction of national service a little earlier, however, some unsuccessful efforts had been made to introduce a statutory requirement for educational provision. Further pressure came primarily from the YMCA and from university Responsible Bodies (RBs). Dr Basil Yeaxlee of the YMCA and the Master of Balliol College, later Lord Lindsay of Birker, as chairman of the Oxford Delegacy for Extra Mural Studies, played major roles in a widespread campaign. Lindsay was professionally briefed for this by George (later Lord) Wigg, who had been a regular soldier before becoming a WEA District Secretary.

As a result of all the pressures, a Central Advisory Council for Education in HM Forces was set up with a regional organisation. Through this the RBs and many LEAs provided a considerable volume of adult education. In spite of all this powerful support, some AE circles expressed a good deal of doubt about the idea that the army itself should provide more AE; proposals that it should be compulsory as a part of training met with particular scepticism. However, in 1940 a War Office committee chaired by the Adjutant General, Sir Robert

Haining, saw the need – given the prospect of a prolonged war – for establishing army education more substantially. FW Bendall, a divisional HMI, was
seconded to become civilian Director of Army Education. The Army Educational Corps was gradually returned to educational duties, and enlarged. A
theoretically entirely voluntary scheme of adult education was developed. This
was closely linked with the civilian providers, but an education officer was to
be nominated in every unit to encourage activity. Later the RAF was also to
find time for a general AE scheme. A considerable volume of work was
developed.

In September 1941 the volume of services education was greatly increased
and the atmosphere generally changed by the introduction of a separate ABCA
(Army Bureau of Current Affairs) scheme with WE Williams as its director.
Compulsory further education activity based on discussion of a series of
pamphlets on current affairs, led by unit regimental officers, was introduced in
spite of reported opposition by the Prime Minister.

In 1942 Bendall retired and was replaced by the more imaginative Cana-
dian educationist, JB Bickersteth, as director of army education. The
introduction of a new 'Winter Scheme' followed in November of that year.
According to this, three hours a week of training and working time were to be
devoted to education, including one hour for 'citizenship education'. The
scheme was so successful that its development and extension 'without terminal
date' was decided by Christmas 1942. A remarkable series of booklets by independent experts was commissioned and distributed as the basis of the
citizenship education discussions, and in 1944 these, together with documents
on post-war reconstruction issues, were issued in collected form (Directorate
of Army Education, 1944).

The scheme marked the beginning of remarkable further growth in
services education, and this continued into the demobilisation period. Discussion groups flourished, the need of many servicemen and -women for basic
adult education was recognised, and special units were created to provide it.
Women had been conscripted since 1941, and literacy and citizenship education for the ATS (many of its cooks and orderlies largely illiterate) played an
important part. Wide-ranging provision was made in the substantial 'Formation Colleges' and the even more numerous local education centres which
were established. Altogether, army education (cf Chapter 3) in particular was
the most substantial and arguably the most successful effort to provide citizenship education for adults that has ever been made in Britain.

One reason for this success was that the need for systematic training for
AE teaching was for the first time recognised and met with seriousness and
determination. ABCA in particular pioneered a variety of new AE and teacher
training techniques (including 'microteaching', a wheel to be reinvented under
its present title 20 years later), and also approaches to social groups previously
and (too often subsequently) unaffected by AE offerings. Not surprisingly, as

early as 1943 the White Paper on *Educational Reconstruction* referred to educational developments in the services as showing AE to be the place where 'an ultimate training in democratic citizenship must be sought' and 'likely to produce a much larger public anxious to pursue a variety of subjects on informal lines'.

A former naval education officer recalls that, other than technical training, AE hardly existed in the navy. Unaware of the faithful pioneering of the Seafarers' Education Service, the Admiralty assumed that it must be quite impossible to create an organised system in ships. Most were very small units and seagoing conditions were supposed to preclude continuity. Nevertheless some shore establishments and a few capital ships made some provision, which was largely based on army materials. Only in 1944 education officers (such as the informant) were designated in all ships of destroyer size and above, and provided with postal back-up resources – but not East of Suez. 'The Royal Navy could not be described as enthusiastic – the Reserves were more friendly'.

The early HMI contribution to service educational development was minor and had been less than positive in the immediate past. The development has been outlined at some length because a few *future* OFE HMI contributed directly to its pioneering work, and a larger number of them became enthusiastically involved in the practice of tutoring and leading discussion groups while serving in the Armed Forces. Their own educational development benefited greatly. It had a notable effect on the atmosphere in which post-war development was planned, and laid the foundations for their future practical involvement in OFE, and OFE HMI.

Community provision

Like so many other forms of OFE, the community association and centre movement had its origins in the residential settlement philosophy, and especially in those educational settlements which were established in the 1920s in order to meet some of the problems of the inter-war 'depressed areas' of major unemployment. These organisational patterns were now adapted in an effort to meet some of the social problems arising from defective town planning. The huge post-war municipal estates on the edges of towns were perceived to be in most need of assistance because, although intended to improve working class housing conditions, they lacked all social amenities.

The National Council of Social Service (NCSS; now the National Council for Voluntary Organisations) played a major part in securing finance from trusts for experiments in social education; subsequently it supplemented and brokered expenditure for the purpose from local authority housing accounts. The Council also played a notable part in developing a rationale for such community work and in spreading knowledge of research enquiries. It was primarily instrumental in helping spontaneous efforts by community associations and centres to develop into a movement with its own organisation, the National Federation of Community Associations (now Community Matters). Its development is charted in Clarke (1990) and other publications listed there.

After private trusts had shown the way, some financial assistance towards provision of local centres was made available by local authorities under their housing powers. The Board of Education was also modestly involved in the early stages through direct grant to the NCSS as the central body, and indirect aid via LEA finance towards salaries of community centre wardens. It also helped, under the Evening Institute Regulations, with AE activities in the centres. However, very few LEAs seem to have been interested at this stage, and HMI involvement, though possible, appears to have been slight.

The Board's involvement grew greatly with the passing of the 1937 Physical Training and Recreation Act. Under this it assumed the task of improving community facilities by grant-aiding capital projects for community centres, youth clubs and playing fields. At this point it also replaced trusts as the major source of finance for the community centre work which was being done by the NCSS.

A greater number of NCSS organising staff now worked to meet the increasingly vocal local demands from a variety of neighbourhoods beyond the new housing estates. However, the outbreak of war temporarily put an end to aid before more than a very few of the applications for it could succeed. Before the outbreak of war 304 community associations were reported as active or 'in the pipeline'. In 1940 just 220 were still active, a few of them in their own premises. These were very rarely purpose-built, more often borrowed or rented, and almost always inadequate. The number of premises grew during the 1939–45 period by the addition of a number of 'war workers' clubs' established from public funds to promote the social and educational wellbeing of workers in armaments factories.

The NCSS was active in a further area which did not at the time attract HMI interest but was to do so in later years. With grant from the Development Commission (not the Board of Education) it promoted Rural Community Councils, and these were active in developing social and other facilities in the countryside. They were particularly energetic in stimulating the foundation of parish councils and all their activities and facilities, including village halls. These, in turn, became central to the development of arts and other community activities in the countryside. The Women's Institutes in particular were much involved in these. Neither they nor other active women's organisations received aid from the Board.

Youth work

More than any of the other future constituents of OFE, the Youth Service had by the time the 1944 Act was drafted already reached a degree of coherence and official support which adult education never succeeded in achieving. Since the 1840s it had grown both from large national movements and from individual boys' and girls' clubs serving mostly young people from the poorest parts of the big cities, although later on Scouts and Guides and the cadet forces cast their nets more widely.

The popularity of youth movements grew rapidly in the twentieth century, and organisations like the Scouts and Guides aimed at wider and deeper levels of personal development. The World War I years, and those that followed, exacerbated the social and economic stresses which had stimulated the work previously. New movements were called into life, especially girls' clubs, since work with girls had hitherto suffered from comparative neglect. As early as 1919 the Youth Hostels Association, the National Federation of Young Farmers' Clubs, the National Associations of Boys' and Girls' Clubs, and others, had come into being as part of reconstruction activities, and Government grant-aid (from the Home Office, not the Board of Education) had started to become available. These grants were intended to help local authorities to assist juvenile organisations; they continued on a very small scale until the 1930s. The Ministry of Labour, through its regional staff, also showed active concern for the welfare, including leisure activities, of young people. The NCSS dates from 1919 and its youth department played a major part in building good relations between organisations and establishing national co-ordinating bodies.

Until the 1930s the provision of recreational and social activities for young people was thus still entirely located in the voluntary sector. HMI had no official links with it at the time, though some took a personal and tangential interest in much the same way and for the same reasons as took them into penal education. No major pressure came from HMI. Prior to 1935, the active centre in the inter-war years was the NCSS and, growing out of its work, the Standing Conference of National Voluntary Youth Organisations (SCNVYO), the progenitor of the current national body. To this was added, in 1935, a trust to celebrate the jubilee of King George V, which published a survey, *The Needs of Youth*, by Dr AE Morgan. Between 1935 and 1944 the King George's Jubilee Trust was, with SCNVYO, the active centre of research as well as pressure towards creating an effective youth service.

The nascent Youth Service heralded a change of attitudes from comparatively narrow and somewhat patronising aims to a wider recognition of the contribution that could be made to the needs of a society in depression, poverty, and fear of social upheaval. Moreover, in a 1936 report the British Medical Association emphasised the grim effects of deprivation on the nation's health and especially that of the young. Yet out of four million between the ages of 14 and 20 only half a million (based on doubtful statistics) were reached by the voluntary organisations. These, and the likelihood of war, were among the pressures which moved government to take an active role in something called officially the Youth Service for the first time.

The 1937 Physical Training and Recreation (PT&R) Act – already mentioned in its relation to community centres and village halls – brought with it official HMI involvement in Youth Service activities. There was concern for the welfare of young people during the social disruption inevitable in war-time conditions, and this brought with it policy decisions and greater official involvement by HMI, though not yet at the rate which developed subsequently. The Board's Circular 1456 of 1939 records its decision to take responsibility for youth welfare as part of the national system of education. A National Youth Committee – later the Youth Advisory Council – was created, and a separate branch was established in the Board to administer grants. The Circular urged LEAs to set up youth committees representing both statutory work and voluntary organisations, and a comprehensive Youth Service, and to report action within three months. Central grants enabled the appointment of LEA youth officers, and thus the skeleton of a national service came into being. A further Circular (15/6) on *The Challenge of Youth* followed, and by 1943 the Youth Advisory Council had issued its own report on *Youth Service after the War.* All this involved HMI at the very time when most of them were to be dispersed to other responsibilities. However, progress was now assured and some HMI were able to maintain an interest and play a part in planning for the future.

Day continuation schools

There was general consensus of what general day continuation education for young people – the future County Colleges – should be about, and should be like. The 1918 Fisher Act had legislated for them, HMI had written about them and prepared curricular materials (the then HMI Mr John Dover Wilson had produced an admirable textbook on language work for them), and farsighted employers as well as an exiguous number of LEAs had called prototypes into being. A working group of HMI and Office was set up to write a thoroughly practical pamphlet on Further Education in County Colleges; it was published under the title *Youth's Opportunity* (Ministry Pamphlet No. 3) as early as 1945. Legislators had intended County Colleges as the cornerstone of post-school work; it could not then be foreseen that they would not materialise. However, some of the pamphlet's thinking was later embodied in other structures.

Preparing for the 1944 Education Act and for OFE

We have shown that in most strands of provision there were considerable developments in the years before 1939, while war-time needs themselves stimulated others. Moreover, government had developed a concern for some of the activities which were to become responsibilities of the Ministry of Education after the passing of the 1944 Act. The Board's knowledge of these activities was however variable, mostly limited, and rarely based on much practical inspectoral experience, nor were there other potential sources of knowledge. Major change was foreshadowed by the PT&R Act of 1937 and the subsequent Social and Physical Training Regulations, but they had not yet made much beneficial impact except in relation to the community centres movement and the youth service. However, one decision had already been taken, probably without intending the lasting negative effect it would have on the development of OFE: settlements and educational centres were excluded from eligibility under the PT&R arrangements. Such support as they were going to be able to attract was left to the discretion of the LEAs.

As early as the beginning of 1941 discussion started in the Board about the essential re-building that would have to follow the end of hostilities, and the major improvements which it was hoped might be made as part of that opportunity. Officials learned that cabinet interest was growing, though Herbert Morrison was reported as 'obviously holding social insurance in higher esteem than education'.[3] It was already accepted that reforms must include systematic development of education continuing after school. It was remembered that discussion at the time of the 1918 Fisher Act had recognised a need 'for preventing waste of educational effort by providing ample opportunity for the happy and healthy use of leisure'. It was decided that Board policy should support the universal provision of day continuation schools as well as youth work, and community centres in their own premises.

Office opinion held that LEAs must have a role in financing the work, but that they could not be relied upon to provide the momentum. The idea of regional councils to take over practical implementation was floated. The Deputy Secretary (RS Wood) insisted that the whole system, or lack of system, of evening institutes (EIs) would also have to be reformed to meet the expansion of demand for part-time education which he rightly expected to materialise after the end of hostilities. The day continuation schools, the central pillar of policy thinking, would provide premises for evening use by AE and perhaps youth work.

From outside the Board proposals for this future development of adult education were pressed from many directions. Henry Morris, Chief Education Officer of Cambridgeshire, submitted memoranda in 1941 and 1942 and stressed the case for rural re-development and for adult education and community planning as bearing 'on almost every problem'. Public figures such as Barbara Wooton, Eleanor Rathbone, Sir William Jowett, Sir Ernest Barker and Sir Richard Livingstone argued for the expansion of AE. Livingstone especially propagated the idea of founding copies of the Danish Folk High Schools but was fortunately diverted in the direction of what became the short-term residential colleges. GDH Cole and Harold Laski wanted the Board to develop adult colleges, perhaps based in the day continuation schools, and urged the 'humanisation of technical colleges'.

Much of this pressure was focused in a conference[4] which may have come too late. *The Archbishop's Conference on Adult Education* was convened by Archbishop William Temple on 11 and 12 January, 1944; Sir Richard Livingstone, at Corpus Christi College, Oxford, was its host. Its list of members (all by invitation) was a roll call of 'saints and witnesses', which significantly included RS Wood, now Deputy Secretary of the Board. As a basis for its carefully planned discussions it had before it *Notes on the Provision of a Genuine System of Adult Education*. They were admirably practical and comprehensive, and their principles were embodied in a final resolution addressed to the President of the Board (RA Butler) and signed, on behalf of the Conference, by William Cantuar, Sir William Beveridge, Sir Fred Clarke, Sir Richard Livingstone, Sir George Schuster and Mary Stocks. Two substantial Memoranda, dated January 1943, appear to have formed part of the Conference documents, though they may have originated as the Educational Settlements Association's submissions on the White Paper and continue their emphasis on properly professional staffing and dedicated premises. They dealt, respectively, with *Post-War Residential Adult Education* and *Educational Settlements in Post-War Years*.

A follow-up invitation conference for leading active field personnel under the age of 40 was carefully planned to take advantage of war-time development, especially in Army education. These plans form part of a conference report circulated to members, apparently by William Hazleton of the Educational Settlements Association. So far it is not known whether this follow-up materialised. The text of the Conference Resolution makes it clear that members were fully aware of, and supported the terms of the Bill. It is unfortunate that no-one foresaw the possibility that the comprehensively flexible terms of Section 41 of the Act would very shortly be misinterpreted and eventually used to support philistine arguments against development.

At the time, however, all seemed well, and within the Office Sir Robert Wood (who had been a member of the Archbishop's Conference) minuted Holmes, the Secretary, in support of developing community centres and adult education in its own premises. A minute from HB Jenkins (then a divisional inspector) deserves extended quotation. He supports 'the general principle that public money must be used more extensively to develop facilities for later activity to counter the tendency to rely too greatly upon the numerous forms of amusement which ingenious salesmanship is constantly thrusting upon the public, which call for no effort on the part of the recipient except to sit back and be entertained.'[5]

The Secretary indicated general agreement with these views but had continuing doubts as to whether LEAs could reasonably be entrusted with the leadership in this area of education. They must have a role, but he insisted the Board must continue to share the financing with them. However, he also pointed out that no-one in HMI had direct practical experience of these matters and new staff would have to be brought in. As mentioned earlier there was, however, a great deal of outside pressure towards developing community centres and it was decided that a committee to consider these should be established at once. It included three HMI: a DI, RE Williams, to speak also for the youth interest, T Jack for AE and Miss CLH Cowper for women's concerns. The Office would be represented by F Bray and E Pearson.

On the inspectoral side the T branch was stirred as early as March 1942 to issue a Memo to Inspectors. This considered possible problems in the relationship between evening institutes and the newly popular idea of a youth service. It encouraged the development of evening institutes to provide 'non-vocational subjects of serious study' and recreational classes and hobby activities. It did not envisage them, however, as part of a new AE initiative. Sadly, the educational settlements movement appears never to have pressed the merits of their institutions until the legislation was in draft and moving towards enactment, or possibly did so too late with the 1943 memorandum referred to above. The field was left clear for community centres and the youth service, with county colleges (as the day continuation schools were re-named) as the cornerstones of the newly named Ministry of Education's policies for implementing the duties which the Act was to lay upon LEAs. The evening institutes were hardly mentioned in the discussions and ignored by the Act.

All the various strands of thinking and preparation, some detailed and based on practical experience like those on youth work or day continuation, some vague or less carefully developed like those on adult education, were brought together in an informal document which came to be known as 'the Green Book', issued in 1942, although its thinking on the structure and scope of education after the war continued to be argued about and amended until, and after, the issue of the White Paper which preceded the 1944 Act. When the Green Book was issued those aspects of the education service which had had the advantage of careful preparation and existing structures benefited accordingly. Thus the Youth Service had a great advantage with the Advisory Council's pamphlet on *The Youth Service after the War* already published; the committee of Office and HMI on community centres had completed its work in time for its pamphlet on *Community Centres* (Ministry of Education, 1944), 'the Red Book', to appear as the new Ministry's first publication. True, the Association of Education Committees agreed that AE should be developed in line with paragraphs 6 to 16 of the draft, but the Green Book's proposals regarding schools and the place of denominational agencies absorbed the attention of all concerned to such an extent that little new constructive thinking about the neglected areas of education ensued. The White Paper on Educational Reconstruction followed in December 1943, the Act passed into law, and made it the duty of LEAs to provide adequate facilities 'for leisure time occupation and such organised cultural training and recreative activities as are suited to their requirements for any persons over compulsory school leaving age who are able and willing to profit by the facilities provided'.

However, LEAs were also required to collaborate with other bodies and organisations. Implicit in the conception of OFE was a co-operative partnership of central and local government, of VOs both local and national, of RBs and other institutions and organisations, and of 'individuals themselves as agents in their own continuing education and learning throughout life' (Ministry of Education, 1947). At a more practical level it was also believed (on what evidence?) that education after school and for parents would reduce child neglect: OFE was expected to secure knots in many parts of the social network. HMI was seemingly intended as a – perhaps *the* – crucial nodal point in which the threads of the network came together.

Notes

1. 9.11.38 Ed 136/632 in the Public Record Office. The Committee included HMIs Jack, Grierson and GG Williams together with RS Wood, now Deputy Secretary, who was closely associated with the development of Boys' Clubs, and Antony Part from the Office. Wood, by that time knighted, will be found associated with later as well as earlier pioneering in penal education and liberal studies respectively (*cf* p 139). Cf. also Marriott, S. (1998), 'The Board of Education and policy for adult education up to the Second World War', passim, in *History of Education*, Vol. 27, no. 4, for the whole of this period.
2. Those wishing to follow up these and the remarkable subsequent developments during World War II may wish to consult White (1963), Wilson (1948) and the journal *Army Education* (from 1943).
3. *cf* Public Record Office papers Ed 136/632 for this and the following quotations.
4. *It seems* that all knowledge of the conference and its important papers had been lost until their fortuitous re-discovery in the spring of 2000. We hope to ensure that the documents will be appropriately edited and published.
5. Public Record Office, Ed 136/632.

2 Structure, functions, roles and relationships

Re-organisation of HMI after the Act

Expectations were high of the part HMI would play in the processes of recon-struction and innovation. However, from the earliest stages of policy development the Secretary and Deputy Secretary of the Board had pointed out that the Inspectorate lacked members with practical experience of the new areas of work which were now to be developed. Many school and FE changes had already taken place on the ground, and even more were envisaged in the new Act. A complete re-organisation of HMI was therefore needed. A committee of HMI and officials was set up to advise on this. The structure of HMI was to be re-organised, under its Senior Chief Inspector (SCI), with Chief Inspectors (CI) looking after Primary and Secondary Schools; Teacher Training; Technical, Commercial and Art (Further) Education (TCA); and Other Further Education (OFE). Divisional Inspectors (DIs) would continue to have educational and managerial responsibility across the board in each of the country's administrative regions. The new grade of Staff Inspector (SI) was established to take national responsibility for focusing HMI knowledge and advice in particular subjects (eg, English or electrical engineering) and organi-sational structures or 'phases' of education (eg, primary education, or the Youth Service). Regional Staff Inspectors (RSI) would co-ordinate administra-tive advice on TCA matters such as course approvals and building programmes in each of the inspectorate's territorial divisions. The system of HMI specialist or phase panels (later re-named committees) was revised and extended in support of this structure. Its task was to focus and to make widely available HMI knowledge from around the country.

Structure and functions of the OFE section

The structure of the new OFE section of the Inspectorate was created by its first CI, EJW Jackson, who had transferred from the TCA section. It was outlined in December 1946 by a *Memo to Inspectors (no. Ed S 376 General)*, and lasted remarkably well, with relatively minor modifications, until the eventual abolition of a distinct OFE inspectorate. It was focused on a central Adult and Youth Panel with CI (OFE) in the chair. Working to this there were, eventu-ally, panels for Youth and Community work, for Adult Education (which took almost 20 years to integrate the initially separate Responsible Body (RB) panel and the more dynamic Evening Institute Working Party), and General Studies in FE. All these benefited from the membership of Office representatives.

Panels were intended as permanent and senior bodies. In addition various mostly less permanent or frankly temporary sub-panels, working groups or specialist working parties were formed at various times to undertake more limited tasks, though some became permanent, like that on education in prisons and borstals. Others considered first women's voluntary organisations and later women's interests generally in FE, literacy work (later adult basic education), community schools, the impact of community work generally on education, and other topics. There was useful co-operation and cross-fertilisation with panels mainly concerned with schools and their subject areas, and less widely with TCA panels and their subjects. OFE development benefited particularly at various times from links with panels concerned with drama, art education, broadcast education, libraries, and museums and galleries. Because of the content of much Evening Institute (EI) work there was always a potential link with members of the panel on education in domestic crafts under a bewilderingly changing series of titles. Especially under the guidance of Kay Tobin as SI this blossomed into close co-operation which affected not just standard curricula but supported the development of new movements such as playgroups, new horizons courses and tutor training. At the end of the 1960s all panels were re-named committees.

The system of panels and analogous groups (which was common to the whole of the inspectorate) brought together for day and sometimes longer residential meetings changing groups of HMI with detailed knowledge of practice, and especially of best practice in the field. All of these groupings focused HMI expertise and advice to the Office and to the field on the state of their area of the education service and policy towards it. The basic strength of this inspectoral influence flowed from HMI's detailed day-to-day experience and knowledge of developments in all the educational institutions with which they were concerned. From regular 'pastoral' visiting (which was always recorded in 'notes of visit') they acquired an unrivalled knowledge of what was actually happening on the ground, and of its worth. This was the basis of their influence, but it was supplemented by the formal visits involving a team of HMI, and leading to inspection reports.[1]

Each of the panels and comparable groups became responsible for three special tasks in its area of responsibility: the programme of formal inspections; the production of both informal and published written advice and suggestions for the Office and the field (mostly for the use of, and sometimes distribution by colleagues); and the organisation and conduct of national and other courses of inservice training for professional staff. Finally, OFE committees of most HMI engaged in the work were formed in the Divisions in the early 1960s and continued until the end of the OFE section after 1967.

From the late 1950s until the same time the central Adult and Youth Panel required an annual review of all OFE activity from every district inspector OFE. Taken together, these painted a valuable and up-to-date picture of the field. In addition the Panel sent annual remits to the divisional OFE committees. These required focused inspection and reporting, and thus enabled particular topics or problems to be studied nationally but in depth. Useful policy advice and suggestions to HMI for follow-up in the field resulted. One of the most important of these annual remits addressed co-operation across institutional boundaries between voluntary organisations, RBs and LEAs. This exercise had useful outcomes; in a few instances it encouraged Regional Advisory Councils for FE to create structures for cross-disciplinary co-operation throughout the OFE sector. This had long been an objective of departmental policy; it needed the presence of HMI on the ground, as colleague and critical friend, to create the context and the relationships in which it could materialise. Some of the divisional OFE committees also undertook projects of their own which they reported to the centre, in addition to planning inspection at regional level.

The effectiveness of the divisional OFE committees varied from region to region as well as over time. They depended heavily on the energy and enthusiasm of particular inspectors, and their skill in persuading overworked colleagues to undertake yet more tasks. However, they also relied on the interest in OFE and the sympathy of each DI concerned. A few, over the whole period, did not fully appreciate the purpose of OFE HMI and 'used them as dogsbodies by loading their assignments until they became meaningless'. Some, on the other hand, made it clear that they saw OFE assignments on a par with others, and secured progress by purposeful planning of inspection work and educational development at a local level. Without the managerial support of DIs a range of notable developments, for instance in careers education and in training, which began in particular divisions and spread from these, could not have taken place. The effect may be illustrated graphically: in 1981 the DES circulated to all LEAs, RBs and relevant voluntary organisations a *National Survey of the Follow-up to the Recommendations of the Second Report of the FE Sub-Committee of the Advisory Committee on the Supply and Training of Teachers*. Its distribution maps illustrated fascinatingly the way in which OFE HMI's influence travelled from local or area-based experimental work to encompass successively regional and national patterns, sometimes over many years. A knowledgeable Office colleague described the maps as a plan of X's rat runs. But progress depended not only on particular HMI and those field-based and HMI colleagues they managed to recruit to a project. Major developments of the kind also needed the support of successive DIs. Their quiet but crucial help was needed if ideas and experiments were to flourish, and the information travel through the hierarchy of groups to the Adult and Youth Panel, be received and acted upon on the way down, spread geographically and be maintained over time.

Jackson, as founding CI, also sought to ensure that the new OFE section should be recognised on equal terms with those for schools and TCA, and should have an influence on the inspectorate as a whole as well as the Office. He arranged for the annual residential conferences of HMI in each division to include reports and other items of OFE interest. More importantly, he introduced an annual residential OFE conference of all HMI with relevant district or specialist responsibilities on a par with those of other sections. These conferences also included other CIs and Office personnel; they helped to widen knowledge of and interest in major OFE policy issues. Their main importance, however, was that they created a sense among their participants of belonging to a team, and that they staked the claim of OFE to be an aspect of education no less significant than those which had been longer established. They continued until the end of the OFE Inspectorate.

Local structure

Under the new arrangements every LEA in the country was to have an HMI District Inspector for OFE assigned to it from 1946, in addition to those for schools and for TCA FE. Under strong LEA pressure a short-lived attempt was made to combine the OFE responsibility with either that for schools or TCA. This proved practicable only in smaller Authorities. Separate appointments, usually of main OFE specialists in the division or of other HMI with a substantial interest in OFE, were made elsewhere. OFE District Inspectors were intended to assist and co-operate with their LEAs and act as links between them and the Ministry. In addition they were nominated as general inspectors of every adult education centre, evening institute, community centre, youth club, voluntary organisation, and all general education in post-school FE, careers education and guidance, etc. in that Authority's area. However, in the largest Authorities the burden of general inspection of OFE was shared with other colleagues who were usually drawn from schools HMI, but occasionally also from TCA.

District and general inspection (ie territorial work) thus ranged from liaison with the LEA centrally to each OFE institution or activity within it. Beyond this there was the equally important task of specialist advice: every Division of HMI needed one or more HMI who could provide this, on a foundation of actual inspection as well as personal expertise and up-to-date reading, in each of the separate specialist strands included in the OFE brief. The small national team of specialists inspecting RB classes had been in existence since well before the war, albeit with expertise derived from inspection rather than active personal experience. Now there was to be a specialist RB liaison inspector for every University Extra-mural Department and every WEA District, and each Division needed specialists to advise on AE, Youth Service, General Education in FE, Penal Education, and what was then still called the Juvenile Employment Service. Experienced practitioners in the various fields were therefore appointed HMI from 1945 onwards.

Recruitment of OFE HMI

A first major task facing the Office and more particularly HMI after the passing of the Act was to provide a coherent body of practical advice on how the huge new tasks summarised by the acronym 'OFE' were to be carried out. The Ministry's Pamphlet No 8, *Further Education*, a volume of almost 200 densely printed pages, was issued in May 1947. It was mostly devoted to advice on the development of county colleges and TCA education. The book was largely the work of AE Miles-Davies, a former educational settlement warden who had been brought into the Office from the National Council of Social Service. At a later stage he had the help of Ian McLuckie from Liverpool University Settlement in advising on developing OFE policy. The mere 38 pages of *Further Education* which were concerned with various forms of OFE were very general in their terms. The lack of detailed HMI advice based on practical knowledge contrasts strikingly and sadly with the assistance they were able to provide later, and with that which the pamphlet made available about the conduct of TCA education.

When hostilities ended in 1945 and active preparations for the implementation of the new Education Act were due to start, the inspectorate was seriously depleted, and possessed little real expertise for OFE. The gaps, and the addition of great areas of new responsibility, necessitated rapid recruitment from 1946 to 1948, which continued actively until 1956 and more slowly thereafter, in order to meet shortages especially in secondary education, in TCA and, over a longer period, in the new field of OFE.

Most of the first appointed district inspectors of OFE listed in the 1946 Memo to Inspectors were pre-war HMI, often with relevant experience restricted to RB work (Grierson, Dann, George Allen), and those who had been responsible for art and for 'women's subjects' in the TCA inspectorate (eg, Christine Smale and Miss Bryant). Miss CLH Cowper, a formidable former 'woman inspector' had a major influence as a member of the adult and youth panel when it was established in October 1945, and she also chaired the community centres panel. Bernard de Bunsen, shortly to make a distinguished contribution to the development of university education in East Africa, was also a member of both panels. Percy Wilson (eventually SCI) and Stewart Mason who, as chief education officer, was later to make OFE a central feature of education in Leicestershire, were also on the community centre panel. Lady Helen Asquith and WR Elliot (later SCI) who succeeded Jack as RB staff Inspector were among others brought on to the RB panel.

Other HMI who continued to play central roles in the development of OFE were at this time still drawn from a variety of educational backgrounds. Among the pre-war appointees who later took up senior positions were Blackie and Salter Davies (both subsequently CI for OFE), KJ Ritchie and JA Lefroy as well as several schools HMI who spent important parts of their time in OFE.

However, the first list of OFE district inspectors already included two new appointments, one from the voluntary youth service (Carrie Stimson) and one with experience of education in the services (Miss M MacCullough). They were the forerunners of a substantial group of HMI recruited for their knowledge of and interest in one or more aspects of the whole wide range of OFE. Most or all had played leading or innovatory roles in the field. Early appointments included Winifred Evans from the Girls Clubs and Charles Harvey from the Co-operative Movement youth service, Youth Hostels Association and Young Farmers, Wyn Daniels (later Doubleday) and Ted Sidebottom from progressive county youth services, Margaret Rishworth from an LCC evening institute, Ted Parkinson from Hampshire LEA administration as well as personal experience in RB teaching and other field activity. British Council centres were represented (Mary Bosdet), and RB classes, community and adult education centres (JA Simpson and Harold Marks). Subsequently other aspects of post-school education were covered by recruits from residential AE (eg, David Hopkinson), general and day continuation work in FE colleges (Nora Newton Smith) and the youth employment service (Mrs K Catlin). Several, as has been mentioned, had served in army education and others had been active participants in its delivery.

In the 1940s, 1950s and 1960s (and until the Houghton Report on teachers' salaries in 1972) HMI was able to draw recruits from among successful practitioners who had not only high academic ability but often a wide range of high-level managerial, administrative or comparable experience. This meant that they could be deployed both as specialists and in a broad range of other roles. Against this background a small but important group of schools HMI recruited soon after 1945 came to be almost as substantially involved in OFE inspection as some of the new specialists. A few, who had previous field experience of OFE as well as schools, chose to make the former their main specialism. Others were infected with enthusiasm for the work when they first experienced it during their two year probationary and training period (it was not reduced to one year until the 1960s). To quote one example (JW Barks), an academic geographer, ex-head of a teacher training institution, with experience of high rank and of education in the war-time forces, was no less at home inspecting academic adult education or education in closed institutions such as the army or prisons, or the youth service in a deprived area, than in the secondary schools which were his main area of responsibility. These schools colleagues (and a few from TCA, such as HL Fenn and Kay Tobin) who cultivated their substantial OFE assignments assiduously, played an important part in the development of OFE and its inspection. Not all of them found it easy to come to terms with the inspection of youth work: 'When I visited Youth Clubs', writes a keen supporter of OFE among them, 'I was baffled as to how one could report on them to be of any use to the Ministry! There seemed nothing solid to go on.' Later, as a supportive DI, some youth service reports raised serious doubts in his mind. However, while active schools HMI were part of the OFE section, they formed an important bridge of understanding and a source of inspecting skills between the large established body and the new OFE specialists. The fact that the great majority of the latter held schools (and TCA in the 1960s and after) assignments in addition strengthened the link. This access of commitment and strength from among schools colleagues was crucial in the earlier part of the OFE section's existence. As they retired or were promoted they were hardly ever replaced by new appointments with the same breadth of interests and concern. The eventual loss, after amalgamation, of colleagues whose assignments and capacities spanned the gamut from the nursery to higher education contributed to the isolation of OFE.

By the early 1950s HMI included members with first-class experience of almost every aspect of OFE. They formed the nucleus of a powerful and committed group with wide-ranging responsibilities. Schools HMI (whose assignments tended to be more concentrated, to cover less territory, and to have fewer political overtones) sometimes referred to them as the 'OFE barons'. They were always few in number. When the OFE section reached its maximum in the 1960s it never exceeded a total of 38 inclusive of CI and SIs. This represented at most eight per cent of the whole inspectorate; it was the maximum proportion that was made available to cover an area of education whose participants outnumbered all the rest put together.

These new OFE specialists drawn from the field also represented a large proportion of the very few full-time professionals in AE and YW in partic-ular. Having been well known and leading members of their tiny professions, they were known throughout the field at least by name and reputation and, more often than not, personally. This had advantages but could also cause embarrassment; HMI had to bear in mind the need to maintain their independence and objectivity in a context where informal relationships were the rule.

Assignment structure and the role of OFE HMI

HMI, regardless of the section to which they belonged, generally worked very hard; there were few exceptions. OFE HMIs' work in particular changed over time, especially for the earliest appointees, both because the field itself developed and because more OFE specialists joined. To begin with it seems that senior management in HMI, like the Office and much of the education world, planned on the assumption that post-school education operated quite literally after school, solely in the evenings. There was some truth in this to begin with in most of the country. Until the latter years of our period almost all OFE HMI were therefore given schools assignments in addition to their OFE tasks, and these were not uncommonly equal to those of their schools specialist colleagues. Where the weight of these schools assignments was manageable, they had great advantages: they gave OFE HMI a realistic understanding of the whole range of education, and the opportunity to try and influence its degree of coherence in a given area. Schools HMI holding additional OFE assignments were rarely relieved in recognition of the additional burden. OFE specialists and others with substantial OFE assignments thus carried, almost invariably, bigger assignments than were normal for other HMI. Exceptions were known to occur in the territory of a few DIs at various times. Increasingly as OFE provision developed in the mornings and afternoons, this involved three-session days and weekend work on a regular basis. It has been said that the 'OFE barons' were a powerful and committed group. They needed to be.

The sheer extent of the scope and influence which OFE HMI were intended to develop was first outlined in Jackson's Memo to Inspectors No 516 of 23 May 1950, which was modestly entitled *Ancillary Duties of OFE Inspectors*. It took up the old theme of worries about LEA abilities in this fresh educational field: 'The OFE inspector who knows his ground can give considerable help in LEA planning to develop and stimulate the development of OFE work.' In addition to these and other main functions *vis-à-vis* adult education and youth work, they should co-operate with the TCA inspector in developments for the 15 to 18 year age group, still seen as working through day release and, it was hoped, the County Colleges which had been the 1944 Act's main vehicle for that age group. Inspectors should also, however, familiarise themselves particularly with the youth employment service. The Memorandum also stressed that OFE HMI should concern themselves with a wide variety of social and educational needs, with delinquency problems of young people, the work of all sorts of voluntary organisations, libraries and museums and their needs, helping them, like community centres, village halls and playing fields, with proposals for capital investment. They should also consider the needs of the increasing number of immigrant workers who required help in learning English. All HMI were expected to concern themselves with improvement and innovation on what existed; OFE HMI were intended to assist the field in the *creation* of major new services which embraced most aspects of post-school life. The assumptions made by the Memo seem breathtaking. They also illustrate a degree of diversity between OFE inspection in the 1950s, when both the work and the necessary HMI skills were developing, and the 1960s, when OFE had become a massive and increasingly professional field which was growing rapidly. That OFE HMI 'made their role work' in these altogether more stressed conditions was an achievement of the 1950s pioneers no less than their successors.

The implication of the Memo was that, in OFE, HMI was not only the 'eyes and ears' of the Office, the adviser to the department and ministers, the mediator between the Office and the LEAs, and incidentally and as a by-product, the adviser to the field. All this they had in common with other HMI.

Beyond it, in OFE, HMI was to be a missionary, an activist who would use her or his position to drive forward the intentions of the Act. However, with the rapid waning of Office commitment and varying but generally declining interest of ministers in the Act's intentions on OFE, this active 'missionary' role became a source of friction.

The multiple role came rapidly into play as HMI were required in 1947 to assist LEAs in producing the required Schemes of FE Development by March 1948, including proposals for the development of OFE. In working with LEAs it could sometimes be difficult to discover how far down the hierarchy one had to go to find an officer who would admit to being responsible for OFE. Sometimes chief education officers had to be persuaded to take an interest. 'I'd very much like to see you, but you do know, don't you, that I've delegated the whole of FE to X'. 'Yes, I do', says HMI. 'That's why I'd like to see *you* about it.'

However, LEAs were under a duty, together with the voluntary organisations in their area, to provide a balanced programme which would 'provide men and women with opportunities for developing a maturity of outlook and judgment, for increasing their sense of responsibility and awareness, for helping them to evolve a philosophy of life, and to develop interests which will enrich their leisure' (Ministry of Education, 1947, p 44). Since the Ministry never formally enforced the Schemes which were actually completed, they had little practical influence on LEA action towards OFE at the time. The schemes did, however, provide some LEAs with a basis of ideas helpful in subsequent and often much later development.

Effects of economic stringency on the role

The sense of elation with which renewal, change and innovation were undertaken was soon severely dampened by problems arising from pressures upon a building industry which could not keep pace with demand and, later, by the general shortage of public finance. County college proposals were the first casualty. Some thought that the introduction of universal day release continuing education for all young people offered an even more important potential for British education than the raising of the school leaving age, but it was soon abandoned. Mere encouragement of employer organisations to grant day release voluntarily did not, and could not, have the same effect.

Capital expenditure of every kind to fulfil the intentions of the Act was strictly controlled even for the schools and colleges. For OFE there was to be little or nothing other than grants under the 1937 Act to national VOs and training establishments, and also to local VOs as long as they could raise substantial local funding as well. These small conditional capital grants, sometimes only available for short periods, were made to assist limited, usually hutted, provision for community centres, village halls, youth clubs, and for sporting facilities. They provided a boost in times of growth and a life line at others. HMI had the duty of investigating each application and making recommendations to the Office. For AE there was nothing unless limited funds could be found by LEAs for the conversion of redundant buildings such as unwanted schools or police stations. The use made of the possibility of adding a small wing for adult and youth work to new or re-modelled secondary schools is discussed below (p 56). The Youth Service Building Programme which followed upon the publication of the Albemarle Report in 1958, though exceedingly modest by any non-OFE standards, was the only substantial capital contribution the state ever made to OFE. Only three OFE projects ever found their way into the FE major building programme. Two were immediately diverted to TCA and school use and the third went the same way after a few years.

On the other hand the school building programme eventually freed many old and often inconvenient buildings for other uses. Some LEAs which took an active interest in OFE (eg, Birmingham, East Sussex, Kent, Surrey, West Riding) found means, not without active HMI involvement, of turning some of these apparently unpromising hand-me-downs into excellent accommodation for OFE use. Another major LEA investment was the acquisition and adaptation of buildings for the numerous short-term residential colleges. Most of these were founded in the immediate post-war years, when many large houses which had been requisitioned, adapted and none too gently treated by the Forces, were offered for sale by owners who could no longer afford to 'keep them up'. They became the homes of one of the most successful educational innovations of the time. Sadly, a high proportion was closed during the 1980s, and almost all the rest had their original role greatly reduced.

As early as 1946 the minutes of the Central Panel of HMI and the Office (which controlled publications emanating from HMI) present a picture – endlessly repeated thereafter – of successive OFE CIs struggling to provide OFE with some momentum against Office insistence that nothing must be done to encourage LEA expenditure in this area of their responsibilities. In a paper on the education of adults (it could have stood for the whole of OFE) written for the adult and youth panel in September 1961, RD Salter Davies wrote with masterly understatement 'only rarely in its long history has the Department been able to forward the work of adult education by a show of positive policy'. Progress had been due to 'brilliant and imaginative local experiment; with these experiments HMI have often had a conspicuously unobtrusive association', and he went on to develop specific proposals of 'ways in which we can most profitably continue the association within the terms of current Ministry policy'. In effect, HMI's role was, in part at any rate, the 'subversive' one of encouraging and assisting the field to make whatever progress was practicable within the area in which it had freedom of movement. Thus, with one blind eye, they saw Office policies which were hostile to OFE lifted gently off their feet, while keeping the other loyally on their duty to the Office and its intentions. As a position it had about as much transparency as our mixed metaphors, but AE in particular owed much of its progress to it. Inevitably, not all OFE specialists relished this ambivalent stance equally, nor did they necessarily find themselves assigned to LEAs which were eager for as much development as was practicable.

It would probably be naive to assume that administrators did not realise what was happening. No doubt some, at times, quietly approved. It was their duty no less than HMI's to stand by the spirit and intentions of the Act – something which Government, whatever its colour, conspicuously failed to do in the post-school sector, and especially where AE and community work were concerned. The authors recall just three senior Office colleagues who supported the intentions of the Act on OFE but had their hands tied. Only one of them rose to undersecretary. On the other hand, what contact OFE had with the Architects and Buildings Branch was satisfying and constructive. However, the top of the Office, once Wood had retired, was consistently hostile, especially to AE. HMI had the advantage over the Office, prized by many, of a degree of independence, and of being a long way from Curzon Street or Elizabeth House. There may have been times when they should perhaps have used that independence in a more public fashion. They knew, as one OFE staff inspector said, that 'we are not here to defend the indefensible', and it has been argued that they should have seized more opportunities to expose it. But it is also true that those who tended to do so, however loyally, were sometimes sidelined by their own hierarchy.

Individual loadings

Far from reducing OFE HMI's load, stringency increased it in some ways. Every village hall proposal, every conversion of some semi-derelict Victorian villa into a youth club or community centre, every application for a sports pavilion, had to be scrutinised to ensure it was the best possible among a shoal of deserving candidates, every architect's drawing studied with care, before making recommendations on them to the Office. It was not only essential that a project should hover safely between the Ministry's standards of minimum quality and maximum cost; it had to try for maximum flexibility in order to serve as many purposes as possible in addition to the main one; it had to be sturdy enough to endure three session use seven days a week and not cost more to maintain than the proposers could be expected to afford. Persuading a TCA colleague to have women's toilets included in the plans for a new engineering building could be a lost cause, but it was OFE HMI's approval that was required for a new youth club building. 'You do know, don't you, that Mr X^2 himself is paying for this new boys' club?' 'Yes, indeed, but I can't recommend grant towards it unless there are toilets and a powder room for the girls you propose to let in on two nights a week.' Stringency turned OFE HMI into architectural and planning consultants as well as advocates. All these tasks contributed to the 'attempt to ensure good use was being made of severely limited funds – a very enjoyable job in general.' In working with committed LEAs there was the built-in problem of how and where they might deploy limited human and material resources to best advantage, how and where to train in order to maximise them, how to balance clamant need against clamorous demand with exiguous means. With other authorities, perhaps more often, there was the effort to persuade (and sometimes to shame) them to remember the Act and make what provision they could for OFE.

The same struggle characterised the way in which HMI's own time was deployed. By the later 1950s and earlier in some areas, the total of OFE provision had built up substantially and continued to grow very rapidly. A typical main OFE specialist could thus expect to be the district inspector charged with liaison on all OFE policy matters with a large LEA (sometimes more than one), general inspector of perhaps 300 individual AE centres or EIs of all sizes, perhaps 250 statutory and voluntary youth clubs, varying numbers of community centres, and also be responsible for liaison with libraries, museums, all kinds of voluntary organisations, and the careers service across the city or county concerned. From the 1960s general and Access education in perhaps 20 FE colleges, and education in up to a dozen penal establishments could be added. In addition some would also be RB liaison inspectors to at least one university and one WEA District, and consequently responsible for studying and approving the syllabuses of perhaps 800 or more courses, as well as trying to inspect an adequate sample of them.[3] More than one reader of the draft text gave chapter and verse to prove this list an understatement.

The pace (as far as practicable) and effectiveness of HMI visits in the field gained much in general from an *Inspection Supplement* to their internal handbook. It was first issued in 1955 and gave, for the first time, a systematic account of what was accepted as best practice among HMI. Its impact was no less among OFE HMI than P&S, and wholly beneficial both in training new HMI and helping the experienced to monitor their own performance.

It was in the spirit of the *Supplement* that OFE HMI began to evolve more system and complexity in their own approaches. All their liaison and inspecting could thus be set against a knowledge of the area, its social and economic structure, its configuration, and the practicalities of transport and accessibility as they affected potential students, members or users. Within relatively narrow limits the general content of education in schools and colleges was given, even if they had then more freedom in choosing the mode of its delivery. In OFE the curriculum itself (or its equivalent) needed to vary and adapt itself to kaleidoscopic local needs and conditions. The questions which, ultimately, needed to be asked and answered about it were:

What are the needs of this place, or this area, in terms of its social, economic and physical configuration, and of the particular OFE service concerned?

To what extent are they being met?

How are they being met? What resources exist, and are they being maximised?

What are the potentials for development in people, institutions and services, and how could they be met?

Such systematic approaches to the planning of provision were developed later by HMI as a basis for inspections and area surveys, embodied in training materials for 'Salisbury' (the important annual OFE course and conference held there which is referred to in more detail on pp 37ff) and widely adopted by LEAs and university AE departments subsequently. They made a growing impact while provision was still able to expand.

In addition to all their field tasks main OFE specialists (like other HMI) would also be responsible for advising colleagues, LEAs and institutions throughout the division concerned in their own specialisms – and most major OFE specialists had to acquire other specialisms in addition to their own. Constant visiting, inspection and wide as well as deep reading about education in general, about one's 'phase' of OFE, and about one's personal subject and organisational specialisms, were the means of acquiring the necessary knowledge and keeping it up to date. 'Reading', indeed, requires emphasis: readers may not be altogether aware of the extent, abundance and prolixity of published literature about education, nor the sheer weight of its penumbra of fugitive writing.

The very multifariousness of the task was a daily and salutary reminder of one's relative ignorance, and of the privilege of learning continually together with, and from, colleagues in the field. In both the specialist capacity and as district and general inspector HMI was called in frequently and as a matter of course not just by the LEAs or RBs concerned, but by institutions, and even individuals. The OFE inspectorate had no history and nothing to live down: HMI was a friend, albeit a critical friend, and very often 'one of us'. As a result they enjoyed a relationship of collegiality with the field which meant there was little if any hesitation in calling on HMI to help, or even on occasion to demand to be subjected to the creative discipline of the full reporting inspection. Being trusted was perhaps the greatest privilege. 'You're like a Catholic priest;' said one leading principal to his equally humanist general inspector; 'I have to confess ...'.

Being regarded by professionals and volunteers in the field as 'one of us' could present difficulties. For instance, some national executive members of a voluntary organisation found the difference between an executive member and the Department's assessor hard to understand. 'Why do you keep asking us to consider this, think about that, and wonder what we mean by the other? Why won't you speak out and tell us what *you* think we should do?' In the event of poor practice or worse, it could also make for awkward decisions or interesting ways of intervening. A learned and influential but less than well prepared university professor teaching an RB class was presented after HMI's visit with compliments, but also an up-to-date offprint on the subject of the class meeting. RI Redfern, looking with admiration at the manifestly dishonest class register kept by a hitherto unvisited EI principal who was also the head of the host school, mused gently 'you know, headmaster, the purpose of class registers isn't *just* to make pretty herringbone patterns'.

To sum up: unlike schools and work-related FE, where HMI were dealing with developing but established systems and had the backing of an Office which accepted their existence and need for resources as a matter of course, in OFE they were involved, with duties under the Act, in the creation of a new system postulated by the Act but generally opposed by the Office, and by Government, in the name of economy. Their major impact on the development of OFE was exercised through individual influence on those responsible for the service in the LEAs and the other providing organisations; by private talk with the heads of all sorts of institutions; in discussion with practitioners at every level; through participation in and assistance to innumerable local and regional meetings, conferences and inservice courses even more than the national ones. Meetings with the individuals concerned were almost always informal, one to one, and confidential, and specific influence reinforced, and was reinforced by, the privacy.

Finding, recording and spreading good practice were central to the functions of all HMI. One minor but useful confidential resource available to the whole of the inspectorate for this purpose until the 1960s was the Information Record. This was compiled nationally on the basis of inspectoral visits. It included examples of best practice of every kind to which the field as well as HMI could be referred for information and help. However, HMI were also constantly called upon to advise informally on the problems faced by administrators and those engaged in the generally difficult task of running institutions with resources which, in OFE, were invariably inadequate. As often as not, the problems had no solution, and then HMI's role was to listen and sympathise, to ask questions which might help to open doors through which a problem might be by-passed, to give sensitive support to those who might have to go on living with it.

There was, thus, another aspect to the role which was more concerned with characteristics than duties or activities. OFE and its workers – HMI no less than the field – were, and were perceived by the rest of education and by themselves as *other*, supposedly non-statutory, and therefore less important. In the field, full-time staff always remained a tiny minority. Much of the area of work was frequently under political, administrative or financial pressure, and sometimes under attack. It was no wonder that many OFE staff felt insecure, and this infected those with whom they worked. EI students, too, felt they were engaged in a low status and dispensable activity; boys who felt cast out by the education system had their low self-image reinforced by the conditions in which most youth clubs met. Youth leaders, no less than AE tutors working in long-term residential care institutions or general studies staff with hostile colleagues and students, had to ask themselves continually what learning, what change for the better they achieved.

Whatever their own status and feelings, one of the most important HMI roles in OFE was therefore to reinforce, to build up people's sense of their own worth, of their rights, and of the validity of their chosen pursuit. The systematic development of some HMIs' skills in non-directive group work from the 1960s (and later recruitment of those who had acquired them) enhanced their sensitivity to the needs of others and of their own among the dilemmas endemic to OFE; it enabled them to be more effective in supporting and encouraging those with whom they worked. Yet in essence none of this was new. It was a means of more quickly and generally enhancing attitudes which had long characterised HMI of all kinds at their best, for whom 'inspection, like teaching itself, rested on a foundation of friendly human intercourse; the thread of sympathy which in most cases bound teacher to pupil should also bind the inspector to the teacher, for one part of his duty was to give help, as it had been since 1839.' It was not only OFE to which this applied. Nevertheless, as one DI points out, 'I wonder about impartiality. You were a friendly lot. It has advantages and disadvantages when reporting.' He goes on to remark on some of the peculiar difficulties of appraising standards where these are endogenous to each activity inspected – and the natural consequence that not all judgements were sound or all reports clear.

This critic rightly points out that, although HMI provided and were seen to provide advice and assistance, they had to remain unswayed by personal interest. They were respected as being outside the relevant power structure, but as concerned, widely experienced, and perhaps even wise, individuals. Judgement on this as well as upon whether to accept or reject the views they pressed was entirely at the discretion of the advised. Ann Corbett (in *New Society* on 8 December 1966) quoted the 1949 Report of the Ministry of Education: 'Schools do well to remember that an inspector's advice really is advice and advice that need not be taken.'

Finally, all of OFE HMI's various duties required liaison with the territorial officers of each of the Ministry's branches to which they related. This included not just meetings and the succession of files demanding comment on administrative matters but the urgent ones regarding parliamentary questions and other correspondence with ministers. Because OFE was an emerging and struggling service it was often 'political'. In AE in particular it was often necessary to defend its practice against political obscurantism and materialistic myopia. It was always open season for objections to the teaching of subjects such as economics, politics or even 'current affairs' and the teaching of anything that did not lead directly to making people more efficient employees. 'Albemarle [the great report which established the modern Youth Service] went through overnight because society is afraid of the young', said Salter Davies on one occasion; 'adult education can't expect such support until adults start heaving half bricks through shop windows'.

This chapter has, so far, covered mainly the normal everyday duties of any major OFE specialist. To these would mostly be added a variable but never less than substantial assignment of schools inspection, and work involved in preparing and teaching courses, serving on HMI and Office committees or as the Ministry's assessor on local bodies (eg, every local Youth Advisory Committee, though it was rarely practicable to do more than skim their minutes). A few HMI served as the Department's assessors to national organisations, whose central staffs and committees tended to welcome their contribution and could make considerable demands. OFE HMI (like others) served on relevant committees of international bodies such as the Council of Europe, Commonwealth bodies and UNESCO. Owing to their fund of field experience and their civil service training they commonly found themselves writing their reports for publication. A number of them were, in consequence, in demand for foreign assignments, including training missions.

Coping with the role

It was simply impracticable to cover the whole range of everyday duties. Even over the perhaps seven to ten years of any one posting, no-one could be expected to visit every single institution in such an assignment once, though some would need, or repay, frequent visits. HMI had to select (often needing the help of LEA officers to do so) the most important, the typical, the atypical, the pressure points, and above all those where new potential seemed most likely to lead to development which could carry others along in its slip-stream. They sampled, and tried to seize every opportunity, such as local and regional courses and conferences, of meeting as many as possible of the field-workers, learning from them, helping them to learn from each other and to collaborate. Such meetings did much to make up for the many institutions rarely or never visited, and helped these to realise that they, too, were remembered.

HMI tried to maximise their potential by planning as carefully as the varied demands upon them allowed. Beyond this they had to be ready to drop everything occasionally, in order to stand by an LEA, an institution or an individual in crisis, to welcome and bolster a new centre head or youth leader quailing at the realisation of the sheer size of her lonely task. When large camps were set up at short notice to house Vietnamese and, later, Ugandan refugees, it was OFE HMI who were called in to assist scratch teams in each of them to conjure a system of adaptive, resettlement and language education out of nothing, sometimes in the teeth of opposition from retired army officers with prison camp conceptions serving as camp commandants, and FE college principals whose image of all further education was cast in immutable City & Guilds courses lasting for years.

OFE inspection was never predictable, and rarely less than exciting (if sometimes grimly so); it offered endless variety and the privilege, after all, of being educated in the course of whatever one did. But HMI in this field, more than others, never felt rid of the burden of having to neglect more responsibilities than could be discharged. The privilege of responsibility sometimes carried the penalty of dissatisfaction if not guilt.

It also made for full days. OFE inspection meant covering large distances, and working morning, afternoon and evening, often returning very late at night or having to stay overnight deliberately or because of unexpected obstacles. Even the best prepared reporting inspections were subject to the vagaries of weather. After an evening spent in joint visits with the area youth officer, three HMI, including a notoriously strait-laced woman colleague, were by 10 pm hopelessly marooned by fog, had to find overnight accommodation and reassure their spouses. With their LEA colleague's help a rear window of the divisional education office was forced open, all four climbed in to make their telephone calls and out again to make their way to the one local hostelry for the night. The event was unique in the writer's experience, though not atypical.

Because the vast majority of OFE workers were part-time and often also volunteers, they were only available for courses and conferences at weekends. OFE work meant HMI, too, attending events at many weekends, and still finding time for all the necessary reading and writing. The dictating machine, when it was provided, was a boon. It enabled HMI to record visit notes in the car between perhaps an FE college or a school seen during the day, followed by a short meeting with an LEA officer, a snack and then an evening in an adult centre or perhaps a couple of youth clubs. Whether he dealt with the day's mail when he had driven home or early next morning before the next day's offering, depended on the hour of arrival no less than the priority colour of the Ministry files clamouring for attention.

Most HMI worked from home, which was their 'headquarters'. OFE working rhythms and the numerous individual constituents of these assignments brought about a high frequency of contacts. They made often burdensome demands upon spouses and families; the need to field innumerable telephone calls on his or her behalf, at usual and unusual hours, was a nuisance. Yet most of it was inevitable – even if, in one home, a telephone ringing *after* 11pm meant 'that'll be Patrick again'. OFE HMI needing to contact each other by telephone could often do so only on return from an evening's work far from home, or during weekends. Their families often saw less of them than they had a right to expect, but sometimes had to put up with their presence when it interfered with their children's leisure. A colleague remembers 'a questionnaire we once completed on working hours ... [those of] OFE HMI were well in excess of those worked by junior hospital doctors – no one noticed.' HMI generally worked hard and with great devotion; in OFE the pattern of provision and the size of assignments made it inevitable. No wonder marriages were placed under strain and 'wives had to be understanding, yet know when to put their foot down'.

The picture that has been drawn may seem negative. Yet for anyone who believed in the task and welcomed being stretched, it was both very enjoyable indeed, and fulfilling. Up to the early 1970s, at any rate, there was within the given assignment a high degree of independence, the freedom to choose areas to try to influence, to control one's own work and hours. The work was always varied, and involved contact with literally all kinds and age groups of people. The teaching and other activities inspected covered the range of human interest and experience, not just set subjects of study; OFE HMI could rely on learning how to calculate the cost-benefits of buying (or not buying) a new car, ensure that a skirt would hang straight, understand plate tectonics, practise conversational Spanish, listen to a brass band, or be involved in demandingly academic study. They had the satisfaction of participating actively in a growing movement, sharing the glow of its success and the gloom of constraints; they could almost invariably rely on interesting company and likeable colleagues. It was fun, and utterly satisfying. Hardly any OFE HMI ever left for other work.

Occasional tasks

Full inspections

Full, or reporting, inspections of individual institutions, and surveys, were of course as much part of OFE work as of other inspectorate sections. OFE HMI, like all others, inspected whenever they visited, recorded their findings in 'notes of visit', and accumulated them in the institution's file until enough was known to make a full inspection by a balanced team, followed by a printed report, likely to be beneficial to the institution itself and the education service at large (*cf* comment on general HMI inspection practice in Appendix 1, p 169). It would be hubristic to claim that HMI were never fooled, but overall this approach to the task produced a deep knowledge of what was going on in whatever aspect of education happened to be concerned, and furnished a continuing stream of practical advice and constructive criticism based on it, to teachers, institutions, providers and the Office.

Wide-ranging or national surveys by OFE HMI arose more particularly from some of the annual OFE remits. In addition to others (*cf* pp 20f, 123ff), examples include enquiries into the incidence, methods and effectiveness of training for part-time tutors in AE, or provision for adult basic education, careers work, and so on. These drew upon the regular inspection activity of HMI in their own assignments throughout the country in order to create an overall conspectus. Surveys and inspections conducted to an external agenda and without foundation in prior knowledge of institutions only began during the latter years of HMI and long after the OFE section had ceased to exist.

In the case of small or coherent institutions the standard practice of schools HMI, of concentrating the formal exercise into the shortest possible period of time, worked well. A youth club might attract different clientèles according to the day of the week, and possibly change the balance of its activities with the seasons. Generally, however, the team could cover it for the purposes of a full inspection by visiting on several evenings of one winter week, with a possible follow-up during the summer. The same might be true of a very small evening institute; an area careers service or general studies in an FE college could be covered in a concentrated week or two. Prisons were usually covered in one week. Really large AE institutions required numerous, varied and scholarly teams of specialists to take account of programmes which ranged more widely than those of any other institutions, and the same could be true of full inspections of the work of RBs. Both needed commonly to draw on specialists from other sections of HMI and other divisions. With such large institutions, and when inspecting a territorial service such as an area institute of adult education with, sometimes, as many as a dozen large centres and very many scattered classes, or an area youth service with possibly scores of clubs, the problem of distance was added to the range of expertise required. Such large reporting inspections often had to extend over a whole term or even two. Individual HMI fitted in day, afternoon and evening visits to cover their particular share of the task as and when convenient, and the reporting inspector's managerial task – not to mention that of providing coherent feedback to the institution and a unified report – was the more challenging. The absence of externally imposed curricula, absolute standards, and the prevalence of cross-disciplinary work and activities all added to the complexity of the task even where recognisable 'education' was taking place. The total informality which arose from modern youth work's concentration upon social education posed particularly severe problems both for those who had to inspect and report it and those who had to take delivery of reports (*cf* p 24f, 124).

Courses, training and research

National short courses for teachers had long been a feature of HMI activity. They developed enormously in number, scope and specialisations after the 1944 Act provided so many fresh problems for the schools. OFE had to be content with one national short course annually for much of the period. The initial impetus came from the West Riding LEA, where the OFE district HMI had been concerned with training in war-time army education. The County included 13 members from other Authorities in its pilot course intended for all its adult education, youth service, general studies and community centre staff. KJ Ritchie, since April 1949 the staff inspector for evening institutes, made the second (1954) course a joint Ministry and West Riding one. Ministry national courses were then organised annually at Ashridge and Retford, and from 1959 developed on a much larger scale by Salter Davies (OFE CI since 1958) as the 'Salisbury courses', because they were held in the delectable venue of the (then) Salisbury Teacher Training College, within the cathedral close. The last of them, by that time directed by JA Simpson, was held in 1971.

These courses were of immense importance in defining the character, purpose and methods of OFE and engendering a remarkable corporate spirit within it. They brought together HMI and, over time, a high proportion of the small number of full-time and other professional workers across the whole range of OFE from all over the country, making 'Salisbury' the high point of the OFE year for them. One of its most important aspects was the way it enabled this cross-disciplinary group, whose only organisational commonality was their *otherness*, to have confidence in their right to exist, to acquire a sense of mutuality and professional coherence as they jointly considered problems and methods of post-school education and cultural development overall. In this way 'Salisbury' continued the almost missionary tradition which underlay the provisions of the 1944 Act. National figures were regularly brought in as conference speakers.

'Salisbury' also constituted an important public relations exercise by indicating to the LEAs and other concerned bodies the Department's apparent continuing concern for this area of national educational provision. Indeed, the provision of 'Ministry' or 'DES Courses' as they were known to the profession, seems never to have met with direct opposition from the Office, even if they were devoted to aspects of OFE. This was probably due to the fact that, like all DES courses, they were administratively and financially in the remit of Teachers' Branch, not one of the FE Branches, which would have seen it as its duty to question whether the courses might cause expenditure. In any case their effects within LEA activity and expenditure could not be so clearly traced to the door of FE Branch at Curzon Street or, later, Elizabeth House.

The courses also reflected the development of HMI thinking and that of a broad band of full-time professionals in the field. Small groups met for intensive discussion of problems and policies, methods and ways of overcoming difficulties; this small group work rapidly became more important than lectures. Later, HMI introduced members to the use of various kinds of simulation exercises including case studies and role plays, as well as to methods of creating these. Such teaching materials developed rapidly and spread around the country from about 1960. Some LEAs such as the West Riding re-printed their own illustrated editions of them with accompanying sets of slides.

Following the 1958 Albemarle Report on the Youth Service and the large-scale training efforts it stimulated, it became obvious that only a systematic national effort to create a cadre of really effective trainers using the most intensive methods could ensure the necessary methodological and organisational breakthrough. CI Mr Salter Davies decided that the whole of one year's work in the Youth Service section of the Salisbury course would have to be devoted to training the participating youth officers in the methods of social group work as a training tool. It was typical of his approach that he participated personally with the group of not unapprehensive OFE HMI whom he invited to undergo such training themselves prior to introducing the youth service groups at Salisbury to it. Subsequently the HMI team became responsible for regional trainers' courses which cascaded these developments throughout the country. Having found it effective for the Youth Service, HMI helped to secure a rapid spread of these methods as *one* aspect of training for careers teachers and AE trainers.

In the course of the 1960s the need became apparent for a range of more specialised and professionally advanced courses serving individual disciplines within OFE or meeting particular needs. The development of professional skills and numbers of staff within the field made this practicable. The national scheme of training for careers teachers in secondary schools, directed by HES Marks, provides an elegant example of this systematic approach to in-service training. All divisional specialist HMI were asked to select small teams of the most effective and promising careers teachers and officers from their regions. Their employers were asked to second them, first to one of a series of intensive national trainers' courses, which applied new methods evolved in adult education and youth service training, and subsequently to make them available to staff regional and local in-service courses which used these methods. In this way every territorial division was equipped with a substantial training team which, together with specialist HMI, conducted in their own regions a series of courses for careers teachers and, in some instances, the heads of their schools. The scheme did much to extend and improve the quality of careers education in schools in a relatively short period. In some regions the teams continued operating for some years.

Much of the development of the new training methodologies derived from adult education. HMI who had experience and an interest in them, first from army education and, later, from adult education centres, introduced them into the inspectorate. A variety of curricula and methods were tested out with the help of the field, and development ensued by cascade methods, which spread it rapidly. The evolution of AE training activity started from the ground up rather than the top down, but was formalised rather later there than in the other disciplines. The story will be told in more detail in Chapter 3, pp 49, 57ff, 64–67.

HMI were also intimately involved with the plethora of local and regional courses which were such a necessary element in a field of work whose individual disciplines were developing with great rapidity. All of them were severely understaffed and relied heavily on part-time staff and volunteers. Courses therefore took place almost invariably at weekends, and HMIs' colleagues in the field expected their participation even if they were not leading. Visiting HMI were, more often than not, expected to be participant rather than passive observers. On one YS adventure course, HMI was *instructed* to take the end of the first rope when youngsters were being taught the technique of mantel-shelving up a rock face. After the third time of coming off he could only hug his ribs shamefacedly as the instructor told him in no uncertain terms that he was the wrong shape and shouldn't have tried.

For a few years towards the end of the inspectorate's existence, OFE HMI were also associated with the conduct of an official DES programme of research. Its content was planned by HMI in informal co-operation with leading academics. Contracts were allocated for the creation of an unusually useful series of volumes summarising earlier and current research in all important aspects of the education of adults, and for important original research into a number of methodological, structural and policy-oriented topics, all of which produced useful publications. Some, such as Mee and Wiltshire (1978) and Daines *et al* (1982) played a useful part in arming the Save Adult Education Campaign with hard evidence, as did a number of full inspection reports which detailed the social consequences of steep fee rises. HMI served on all the steering committees, and assisted in the planning and execution of the parallel series of research and other publications which issued from the Advisory Council for Adult and Continuing Education (ACACE) in the wake of the Russell Report. Safeguarding the independence of research and its publication against political interference from both right and left proved to be part of the task. All these activities belong to the period after the dissolution of the separate OFE section, but were the responsibility of its members.

National and other surveys, such as those on the training of part-time tutors in AE, and on the incidence, organisation and methods of adult basic education, or the work of special groups such as the community working party (1964–66), shared important characteristics with research. Some HMI also carried research interests and unsolved questions into their retirement. Major research projects on trainers' courses, didactics, on adult students in FE colleges, on the treatment of ex-offenders, and on various aspects of the work and impact of voluntary organisations resulted from this continuing interest.

The end of the OFE section of the inspectorate

In 1967 the OFE section of HMI was abolished as a distinct arm of HM inspectorate, with its own CI. OFE interests were brought into the general

TCA fold as part of a single FE inspectorate, and the last CI for OFE retired.[4] The immediate causes and particular pressures which led to amalgamation into the larger and always much more powerful and influential TCA inspectorate remain to be established when departmental records are opened for public and scholarly inspection.

As early as 1955, at the height of one of the recurrent financial crises, a paper on OFE had been prepared by the adult and youth panel for the central panel of the ministry, and transmission to ministers. It generally defended the concept of OFE as a proper departmental concern. It included a statement, however, that: 'It has proved neither economically possible nor humanly desirable to employ inspectors exclusively on OFE.' The reasoning behind this statement is unclear; its validity was soon destroyed by the very great development of day-time non-vocational AE activity of various kinds, as well as the new development of liberal and general studies. In spite of the paper HMI continued to be appointed primarily for OFE work.

It seems doubtful whether anxiety for staff welfare was a major reason for amalgamation when it took place. Pressures to economise on staff might constitute a more significant explanation. Again, as early as 1956 there had already been a number of enquiries and working parties looking at the justification for the existence of the inspectorate as such. On the whole it had emerged from these with credit and general appreciation. The need to develop Further and Higher Education in order to improve economic performance was certainly becoming more apparent and widely accepted. Two SCIs were subsequently drawn from the TCA inspectorate for the first time since before 1939. Later a second CI was needed to focus work on the developing provision of higher education, then still in the LEA sector. Moreover, if there were to be economies, there were many both in the Office and the inspectorate who were content to see resources cut from aspects of education which were less influential than others, and to which they accorded very low priority.

When the proposal for discontinuing a separate OFE section was put before HMI concerned it was presented as an amalgamation on equal terms, and on the grounds of educational principle. OFE HMI, in common with anyone else who had knowledge of the field, had always argued that the distinction between what was considered 'vocational' and therefore supposedly useful, and what was 'non-vocational' and therefore considered by some a frivolous luxury, was false. Each of these areas of FE was and remains full of participants some of whose primary motives relate to the other. Each uses and advocates disciplines necessary to both. Each is necessary to a civilised and efficient society. It was suggested that to despise either is, at best, to be shortsighted. This conviction did not mean that within the whole body of FE there were not (and remain) separate disciplines requiring specialist knowledge and consideration.

Acceptance of the unity of FE made it difficult to resist the argument from within HMI itself that it was surely illogical to have separate TCA and OFE inspectorates. They were, after all, serving a single system with a spectrum of objectives, rather than two separate ones. It was accepted that OFE HMI, through their general studies assignments, were already by no means unacquainted with the characteristics and the inspection of TCA institutions. Some TCA colleagues had small OFE assignments already (all in some divisions); all were said to be prepared to take on board the need to learn about OFE. Amalgamating the small and admittedly overworked OFE team with the very much larger TCA contingent would thus lead to a more equitable distribution of the load and consequently a better coverage, in general, of OFE assignments.

OFE HMI were asked to respond individually to the proposal. A minority were impressed by the logic of the case, and convinced by the promises made. Others argued that OFE, still developing, continued to need special care and status. It will take some years yet before all the arguments and the reasoning behind the final decision to amalgamate become known, if ever. The evidence of HMIs' changed assignments shows that there was redistribution indeed. A few OFE specialists lost their schools assignments. The main effect, however, was that formerly specialist OFE HMI had large additional loads as district and general inspectors for TCA colleges added to their responsibilities; most of their TCA colleagues were given OFE assignments, but it was relatively rare for these to receive the kind of attention which had been customary. It was fortunate that some, especially women's subjects specialists such as Kay Tobin and Jean McGinty, continued to play a major constructive part in the development of many aspects of OFE. On the other hand the notable contribution to OFE inspection made a by number of schools HMI was quickly lost. At divisional level the OFE committees were wound up. Nationally the OFE panel or committee structure was much reduced, SI posts from four to three when retirements allowed, and, above all, there was no longer a CI primarily concerned to represent OFE at a high and effective level.

At field level, former OFE HMI continued to hold divisional specialist responsibilities for AE, RB liaison, the YS, community work and voluntary organisations, careers work, penal education, and liberal and general studies. Some and, more rarely, all of these were always combined in a single individual's assignment. Appointments to replace some retiring OFE HMI continued to be made, although few leading exponents, particularly of AE, were prepared to apply. The OFE specialisms as well as the remaining SI posts, especially in AE, came increasingly to be filled by HMI who lacked substantial experience of the fields concerned. HMI influence and effective representation, and information to the Office, were therefore weakened, and support to the field reduced when it was most in need of it.

As always, and in every aspect of HMI activity, there were exceptions. Some former OFE specialists found some of their TCA colleagues generously co-operative. This seems to have been more noticeable in some divisions than in others. The influence of RSI and DI was important in this respect but not all-powerful. The more commonly experienced problem was the unwillingness of a majority of TCA HMI to undertake the kind of work and approach which had been assumed to be their part of the bargain. An important difference between the origins and traditions of the two sections was probably the main cause of this. OFE HMI's attitudes were derived from the mission imposed upon them by the Act and their professional background. Their working methods were derived from the old-established ones of schools HMI. OFE HMI were mostly concerned with identifying and meeting educational potential and needs, and by means of regular visiting in the field improving the ways in which these were being met. The tradition from which the TCA inspectorate had developed was one which concerned itself with the development and control of structures, resources, courses and examination systems, and quality assessment in contexts which differed from those which OFE HMI had developed from those in use among schools colleagues. There were exceptions to, and degrees of, consequences, but the original OFE disciplines certainly suffered from a reduction in HMI attention and support due to the change in the structure of assignments and the lack of central leadership. Conversely, what had been the TCA field benefited from a substantial net gain not just in HMI time, but in the ways in which that time was used. It has been said that there is only one obvious way for a lamb to lie down with a lion. It could be described as a means of economising by staking a claim that the lion was fed 'from existing resources'. Some of the detailed consequences will appear towards the end of the following chapters.

In these we trace the relationships between HMI and the various OFE services through the period from the Act to the introduction of Ofsted and the modified role of its reduced Inspectorate. It can be argued that, in essence, all these relationships partook of the nature of AE because, even in youth work and careers guidance, HMI was engaged in observing and forwarding the education of the adults concerned in delivering them, and communicating to them the teaching and training methodologies and skills which had been developed in social and youth work and AE. In that sense the relationship is a single one, and ideally it should be told thus, integrally, with no more articulation than that offered by chronology. An attempt to do so failed because of its sheer complexity. To produce a clearer picture, we deal with various strands of OFE separately. We chose to begin with AE because here the duty of inspection was longest established, because it is the largest section, and because its tentacles extend into all the others. The various community and voluntary activities follow logically from it. We shall continue by looking at services devoted to younger people, and those which link these activities with those covered by other sections of HMI.

Notes

1. Sir Martin Roseveare, the first SCI after the World War II, used to stress that a formal inspection report should only be attempted when the general (and reporting) inspector knew the institution so well that visiting specialist HMI were really necessary only to fill in the gaps.
2. The head of one of the country's large business empires, subsequently the centre of a corruption scandal.
3. This last task was particularly time-consuming because of a more leisurely generation's agreement with the universities that HMI would stay for the duration of each RB class meeting visited, not to mention extensive subsequent discussion with the tutor. It was often most enjoyable, but it was costly, and unfair to the bulk of assignments, if less absurd than another agreement, not for OFE, that the work of teacher trainers would never be inspected at all.
4. A few years later the head of a remote little evening institute seemed timid about showing visiting HMI an unofficial class under a volunteer tutor. 'It's only costing a bit of electricity, but I'd rather not tell the LEA.' HMI congratulated him on his enterprise – and found Salter Davies teaching a handful of students classical Greek.

3 Adult Education

Introductory

The general or liberal education of adults – that is all those organised educational endeavours which are related to their personal interests and development as compared to those which are instrumentally related to particular vocational aims – was throughout our period a very large and complex undertaking which involved millions of individuals at any one time. A variety of statutory and other providing bodies were active in it and there were certain generic activities or concerns such as training or research which cut across organisational boundaries. HMI were involved both with the organisations and institutions and with these generic concerns; both in turn are the subjects of sections and subsections of this chapter.

We begin with what were probably the best known, because the earliest organised and most vocal, contributors to 'the liberal education of adults'. These were the Extra-mural Departments of Universities (EMDs) and the Districts (ie, the regional organisations) of the Workers' Educational Association (WEA). Together they were designated by the Board and the Ministry as Responsible Bodies for Adult Education (RBs). They (and some other, smaller and temporary RBs) were subject to inspection, to regulations which changed from time to time, and they received direct grant for their class provision. Chapter 1 showed that their creative drive and most of their impetus always came from pioneers within the movement, but the start and continuing development of their work until the eventual cessation of RB status in 1989 owed much to the activities of HMI.

The universities and the Workers' Educational Association (WEA)

Active HMI support had been essential to the start of publicly supported 'liberal adult education' by these, the main 'Responsible Bodies' (RBs), but the creative drive had come from elsewhere. Concerned HMI were not without influence, but this situation continued to characterise the HMI contribution to RB work until its demise as a separate style of provision some years after the end of the present story.

Compared with many LEAs, in 1944 most RBs were already well organised to provide adult education (AE); their direction was generally enthusiastic and often effective. Considerable changes in provision and style sprang from their responses to the developing opportunity, and the rapidly growing student demand. With the help of HMI the regulations under which they were grant-aided had been loosened in 1946 to give them more scope and flexibility in planning their course programmes. Additional universities joined earlier providers and thus reduced the rather excessive territorial responsibilities of some of the pioneers. Both universities and WEA Districts were willing to meet the growing expenditure on teaching and other costs, running to about a quarter of the total. Increasing assistance from the LEAs made this practicable, and was particularly welcome to the WEA. HMI supported the proportionate increases in the central government contribution (70 per cent of total costs including a UGC contribution of 20 per cent), and did their best to resist the pressures for economy which began to check the growth of RB as well as LEA-provided AE very soon after the restoration of peace and the coming into force of the Act which had seemed to foreshadow their growth.

According to Board of Education statistics almost 15,000 students were enrolled in joint University and WEA classes in 1937/38. In spite of periodic checks to growth their number had risen to 249,000 by 1969–70. Growth was particularly threatened in 1952–53 when a 10 per cent cut in RB expenditure was demanded in parallel to steep rises in class fees imposed on what were counted as 'recreational' AE courses by LEAs. A widespread and clamorous outcry was quieted by the personal intervention of Churchill as Prime Minister, which had been secured by the TUC. It removed the particular threat to RB work at the time but, as a sop to critics, the Ashby Committee was established to consider the finance of RB-style education. The SI for RB education served as its Ministry assessor. Far from justifying the attack which had been parried, the Ashby Report (Ministry of Education, 1954) gave RB a generally clean bill of health, substantially greater freedom of action and, eventually, greatly improved funding. Its recommendations introduced a requirement for HMI to consider provision in relation to the needs of relevant areas, while also reducing the burdens of detailed approval of staffing, classes and syllabuses. This loosening of detailed requirements was welcomed by all. It helped the RBs to meet changing student demand more flexibly and gave the profession the prospect of a greatly improved salary structure. The Report had commented (p 41) on the role of HMI 'in whom all the partners have great confidence, [who] play an essential part in advising Responsible Bodies and in helping them to maintain standards in a sphere of teaching where the definition of standards is particularly difficult'. It now created the potential for an even more constructive relationship between them and the RBs.

The report went on to recommend 'a fresh burden upon a senior member of the Ministry staff and upon HMI responsible for adult education' on the grounds that 'the work has an importance out of all proportion to its size and cost and this justifies the special attention given to it.' (pp 44f). It also rejected very firmly the idea of a Ministry 'canon of approved subjects' which would soon become obsolete and whose existence would discourage fresh ideas. It has been suggested (Fieldhouse, 1996, p 62) that HMI played a political role in censoring the provision and teaching of classes on political subjects. HMI experience does not support this view. It can only be argued on the grounds that insistence on the academic presentation of *all* conflicting evidence and views on a topic constitutes such bias. On the other hand HMI frequently found themselves exonerating individual tutors or even whole RBs when they came under charges of political bias, almost always ill informed, from outside individuals or organisations which resented the academic consideration of subjects of which they disapproved, or views with which they disagreed.

Relationships

In practice the cordial relationships between RB administrators and HMI remained little changed though HMI had now acquired a stated duty to discuss policy and priorities in this area of education. Relations generally also remained close and informal in character. Heads of the university departments sought and welcomed the thinking of their liaison HMI on their plans and problems as, not infrequently, did vice chancellors and members of responsible university committees. Advice was sometimes even more eagerly sought by WEA district secretaries, who generally had less professional support at hand. The same informal and collegial relationships tended to subsist with the full-time staff of RBs. The field was small, most of those working in it were often isolated and under pressure; they knew HMI to be supportive, experienced, and willing to listen to and learn with them. It should, perhaps, be stressed that the Board and the Ministry had always treated their relationships with the universities with particular courtesy, and the minor RBs benefited too (see note 3, p 44). When the new team of RB liaison HMI was created in the years following the 1944 Act and the end of the war, it consisted of members whose scholarship and personal experience in RB work and elsewhere continued to command respect. Compared with other branches of the education service, this was an exceedingly small world, where all knew each other.

Inspection

Numbers of HMI 'full inspections' to study various particular aspects, or organisational models, as well as simply geographical coverage by RB work, were carried out up to the end of the OFE inspectorate and, rarely, afterwards. Sometimes they were initiated to throw light on some specific or local problem. Often their findings formed the basis of far-reaching policy discussions, especially in the 1950s and 1960s. Ordinary pastoral visiting and discussion were the basis of close and generally very friendly contacts with all RB heads and their full-time tutors. This was an ideal context for the improvement of individual as well as organisational standards. HMI remained always conscious of the problems involved in inspection even of this aspect of the work of universities. If particular university teachers were rightly defensive of their academic independence, little difficulty was caused in practice. Department heads were glad to be kept informed of HMI's views of work they had seen, and not least so when HMI had visited extra-mural classes conducted by internal academics, whom heads did not like to visit themselves in a critical capacity. HMI thus did much quiet good work in sustaining and sometimes improving teaching standards and, just occasionally, questioning some emperor's dress sense. They also had to devote time, and patience, to the tendency of some power-hungry EMD heads to expend more energy on mosstrooping and territorial disputes at each other's expense than on improvements at home.

Development

From the 1950s on, however, the growth of LEA provision meant that HMI's RB assignments had become a relatively small proportion of their total loading. HMI supported, but could claim little credit on balance for initiating the major changes in RB work which they witnessed, though their influence was generally deployed in aid of development and modernisation. These included a steady growth (if less noticeable in the WEA sector) in the number of full-time tutors. There was movement from the preponderant concentration on the three year tutorial class as the vital centre of good provision towards a growing proportion of one year and shorter courses. Sometimes these were designed as 'modules' (before the term came into use) in a planned and coherent sequence. The curriculum spread enormously into new and interdisciplinary topic areas, with the social sciences receding proportionately. Their later absolute decline was sad in view of the original social purposes of the work. For this, as well as intrinsic reasons, HMI took a strong supportive interest in one- and three-year day release courses for trade unionists, especially but not exclusively for miners and dockers, which were conducted mostly but not exclusively by RBs in the Midlands and the North.

One HMI policy effort of the 1960s, to increase the number of classes in the natural sciences, met with little success, perhaps because most RBs simply lacked enough professional (in both the subject and educational sense) staff who could have carried the initiative. HMI strongly supported the dramatic growth of AE summer schools which marked the period, the expansion of other concentrated forms of provision, and the rapid development of day time classes, which opened the chance of participation especially to younger women with family ties and other new groups of students.

These newer modes of delivery had mostly been pioneered in the adult education centres and by the LEAs, with HMI doing duty as cross-pollinator. However, continuing and laborious efforts to encourage effective direct co-operation locally and regionally, between the various AE agencies had little impact. In retrospect, the opportunity presented to HMI by the Ashby Report to take a more positive role in the development of RB style AE was neglected, or frustrated by the sheer difficulty of the task and the multiplicity of other claims on their attention. Whether any major changes could have been secured by more positive action is open to question.

The most successful HMI innovation lay in pressure towards the provision of more tutor training to improve professional standards. A national full inspection survey by HMI in 1963–64 of training provision by RBs encouraged the few who were active and persuaded a number of others to take a practical interest in raising the standards of their own provision. Several continued to do so after the conclusion of the survey. Above all, some were persuaded that their recognition of the contribution they could make towards the training of teachers and organisers in LEA adult education presented also an opportunity for improving the standard of their own classes. HMI was actively involved in these developments. The growth of AE training generally is discussed in the section on the work of the LEAs. Here one consequence remains to be noted: as the need for the training of teachers for the whole of the post-school sector generally moved high on the DES agenda between 1972 and 1978, professional training for AE at all levels became, belatedly, a much more serious concern of some universities and the ambition of most. The problem now appeared to HMI to be one not so much of encouragement as of concentrating work on those institutions which were most likely to be effective. In this, once again, they had little success.

OFE HMI strongly supported the pioneering experiment carried out by the Nottingham University Department of Adult Education, which tested the methods to be adopted by, and led to the foundation of the Open University (Wiltshire and Bailiss, 1965). They also succeeded in persuading the Office to release RB funding for this crucial experiment. Beyond this, and their generalised support for the principles and practices which the OU adopted and developed, OFE HMI had almost no contact with or influence on this, the major development in the part-time higher education of adults during the period covered by this study. Nor, with its narrow view of its proper sphere of influence, did it press for increased and easier entry by both part- and full-time mature students into university courses. They also took no action to try to prevent upwardly mobile public sector higher education institutions from 'shedding part time students in an effort to achieve status' (Tight, 1982). Surprisingly, HMI did little to draw on their considerable experience of the standard of work which could be attained in the four long-term residential colleges which had the Department's support and enjoyed the help of liaison HMI. They drew no effective conclusion either from the mature state scholarship scheme (*cf* p 71f).

Much was achieved in the whole area of RB work that was more generally helpful. RB influence was crucial at the time of the Ashby enquiry, and the national impact of their most creative leaders such as HC Wiltshire and HA Jones was felt throughout the whole of AE and beyond. Nevertheless the record shows too many missed opportunities. If HMI's contribution to RB work was less creative than in others, it illustrated the effect of the enormous range of responsibilities which rested upon far too few shoulders. Moreover, HMI leadership and representation came to lack their earlier dynamism and never recovered.

LEA adult education

The high claims and substantial reputation of AE as delivered by the universities and the WEA, and the academic's self-confidence and facility with the pen, meant that the term Adult Education (always with upper case initials) became their monopoly. Yet even in the earliest years covered by this study their work in the education of adults was, at least quantitatively, no more than a small fraction of what was on offer to and seized upon by the adult population. RB work had important characteristics which came to influence LEA adult education and, incidentally, the Open University, but it never accounted for more than about a tenth of the total provision. For reasons unknown the Office (though not the statisticians) consistently resisted HMI pressure to produce more accurate statistics of LEA provision generally by the simple expedient of collecting them at the end of the academic year, when they are complete, instead of seriously incomplete in November. Nevertheless, these seriously incomplete records showed some 2½ million adult enrolments in 1969–70, to which the RBs contributed 249,000. Both totals continued to grow for a time but, under the impact of exceedingly steep fee increases combined with cuts in LEA funding, they shrank. What is more, they became so misleading as to be worthless. The multiplication of short segmented courses and reduced course hours produced enrolment counts which ceased to be capable of meaningful comparison with their predecessors. However, these seriously misleading statistics were invariably treated as important arguments by successive Governments in answering the critique of the Save Adult Education Campaign of the late 1970s and 1980s. Two million adult students were still being claimed in 1990, but since their courses were far shorter and the teaching sessions reduced, the actual volume of provision which they represented was probably less than half the 1970 total. This cannot be surprising when it is borne in mind that the average cost of fees per class hour had been forced up by 32 times the rate of inflation between 1954 and 1978–9. Later comparisons are not available, but it is clear that, despite all HMI warnings, in Britain to-day general AE is only available to the reasonably affluent and some of the conspicuously deprived.

During the early part of our period the bulk of LEA adult education consisted mainly of two kinds of activity; to call them structures would be a misnomer. One took place in TCA institutions, where especially textile and catering departments provided courses in relevant domestic crafts which led to City & Guilds qualifications and enabled their alumnae to teach in the evening institutes. Art colleges, on the other hand, provided part-time courses of adult education which reached high standards and led some students on to serious independent artistic endeavour. The rest – and the bulk – was 'night school': a scatter of low-level class provision in a limited range of subjects (mostly arithmetic, technical drawing, typing, shorthand and 'secretarial English') which were, however, the first rungs on the aspiring tradesman's or office worker's occupational ladder. A high proportion of the students were final year school pupils.

Excepting the few pioneer LEAs, such as the LCC and Birmingham, there were two kinds of students in the EIs. For the institutes' purposes the most important (because slightly more lucrative) were youngsters in their last year of school and immediately after, who were trying to supplement their inadequate compulsory schooling in so-called pre-vocational classes. The other group were adults attending mostly classes in domestic crafts and what were dubbed 'men's subjects' – woodwork, metalwork and car maintenance as ownership spread. Few EIs were big enough, or had staff with the flair and energy, to extend their offering to languages or much else, or to provide graded programmes. They mostly met in local primary and secondary school classrooms according to who seized the initiative. They tended to be run by the head of the host school or a deserving teacher who was unlikely to get promotion but was owed recognition and financial reward, which usually ran at the princely rate of at least a farthing per student per attendance. It was rare indeed for a part-time EI head such as the deputy headmaster of Whitcliffe Mount Grammar School (W Pearson) at Cleckheaton to develop an institute with some of its own rooms and its own equipment, a varied programme and a speciality in engineering, which enabled students to rise all the way to the National Certificate.

The status of the LEAs' provision, and of their institutions, was very much lower than the RBs'; it was referred to as evening institute provision, or more often plain 'night school'. It was as late as 1962 when three HMI, in an after dinner conversation at the 'Salisbury Course', came to the conclusion that this nomenclature was not just misleading but positively harmful to educational progress. They decided henceforth to use the term adult education (lower case initials!) consistently for all AE however provided and to persuade the Office to do likewise; the field would follow. So it proved, surprisingly quickly.

Interlude: voluntary AE centres

In a number of important ways the change of terminology foreshadowed a rapprochement, to which some influential signposts had pointed for a generation or more without anyone much taking notice. The first voluntary AE centres (then called non-residential settlements) had been founded in 1908 in

Leeds and York by Quakers who were building on their local Adult Schools. The Quaker network helped the model's rapid spread around the country after World War I; until the early 1950s Rowntree money largely financed its influential national organisation, the Educational Settlements Association (ESA), later the Educational Centres Association (ECA).

Reflecting its origins, the core of the Centre idea was that they were democratic collectives for learning which were housed in their own premises. Rather than concentrating upon the class and its subject as the be-all and end-all of AE, they provided what, in the language of the time, they called 'a hearth and home for adult education'. Each centre belonged to a self-governing membership of learners and teachers who appointed their own professional full-time warden and also provided the substantial input of voluntary labour needed to maintain what were in effect local adult education colleges with their own educational programmes and social life. It was the warden's task not so much to preside over as to facilitate all this activity, and to arrange and supervise a programme of AE which met the needs of current and potential members. This meant that all centres sponsored some of their classes and activities themselves, while a modest amount of provision in some was financed by the ECA during the period when it was recognised and grant-aided as a Responsible Body. The bulk of centre programmes, however, was variously provided by or bought in from the local LEA, the University Extra-mural Department and the WEA district.

There was much talk of 'balanced programmes' in the ECA, whatever that may have meant. What was new and important, however, was that here adults could follow practical, artistic, academic, and physical pursuits on equal terms and under the same roof, both formally in classes and informally; all this happened, moreover, in a self-governing context which enabled everyone to meet in the common room, to influence one another and be part of an exercise which integrated democracy with liberal adult education.

The Centre model was soon applied in the statutory sector, most notably by the Kent LEA which started immediately after the end of World War II to reorganise much of its adult education on that basis, giving the individual centres a realistic form of democratic self-government. HMI pressed the educational value of the model and many more LEAs went part of the way by giving varying measures of internal autonomy to local centres though remaining sole providers of courses. One University RB in particular (Nottingham) created a number of autonomous centres throughout its area, and opened them to a variety of other local activities. One of them, Pilgrim College, Boston, under Alan Champion who had directed a notable Army Formation College, succeeded in developing a very wide range of activity within his centre. Later on, inspection reports revealed strong links between centre members' assumption of voluntary responsibility and serious commitment to study.

Regardless of the sources and types of provision, the idea spread that AE benefited educationally and organisationally from institutional coherence and, where possible, student responsibility. Development was reinforced by two publications (Marks, 1949 and Elsdon, 1962), both by authors who had written them while working in the centre field and who subsequently became OFE specialist HMI.

LEA adult education (resumed)

From 1945, HMI influence on AE became most effective in the EIs provided by the LEAs, which constituted by far the greatest number of institutions and served most people. Inspectors of the old T Branch had seen and supported particularly the pioneering efforts of the LCC adult institutes before and during the disruptions of 1939–45, and a Ministry pamphlet on the subject had been intended, but shelved because of these. The idea was revived at the same time as the OFE inspectorate was established, but again shelved. The enthusiastic drive of KJ Ritchie, when he became SI for evening institutes in 1949, led to a nation-wide series of inspections. Findings from these, together with relevant HMI subject specialist thinking, were incorporated in a draft pamphlet, whose painful history forms part of the sorry tale of AE publications.

Ritchie, the pamphlet's progenitor had angrily handed over the battle for its production and publication to other colleagues. He regarded it as 'emasculated' and some of the more professionally advanced workers in the field thought it banal. The widespread welcome which met its publication in 1956 can only be understood in the context of what LEA AE was largely like at the time. Like the Russell Report of 1973 (but unlike the 1919 Report) the text did not provide enthusiasts with quotations to beat about the heads of unyielding governments, but was full of much needed practicable suggestions which could be picked up without waiting for changes of heart on high. It is not impossible that the cause of AE might have prospered a little better if more of its vocal proponents had been as concerned with the practicalities of the field and of politics as they were with philosophy.

By 1969 the number of full-time organisers and teachers in EIs had grown to 804, plus a full-time equivalent of 141 derived from shared appointments (Education and Science, 1973, p 204), yielding a full-time staff to student ratio of 1:2,656. In 1953 there had been just 212 full-time staff, and the ratio was 1:3,041. At that time there were only a few strong institutes (especially in the LCC) and the adult education centres which had the advantages essential for development of systematic programming including day time classes: full-time principals, an inkling of professional approaches and premises of their own. What the forgotten Archbishop's Conference had made its central plank now became no less important on HMIs' agenda.

Slow progress with staffing

Professionally expert AE staff were very few indeed, compared with school teachers who served the EIs usually in their spare time and whose career interest and professionalism lay elsewhere. This was a major obstacle to development. The appointment of more, and skilled, full-time staff to the service was early recognised as one of the keys to satisfactory progress. OFE HMI also encouraged the appointment of full-time departmental and subject heads in AE institutions as one means of securing the development of programmes and improved standards of teaching. A few LEAs realised, or were persuaded of, the need to appoint professional assistant education officers or even inspectors of non-vocational FE. The growth of technical education institutions made appointments serving both sectors a more commonly achieved objective.

However, progress in creating full-time posts was slow. A memorandum by KJ Ritchie to the Evening Institute Panel's December 1958 meeting includes the statement 'I was strongly opposed by the Office: they thought it was too expensive and plaintively enquired what the full-time heads would do during the day'.

If progress was slow, there was progress, and perhaps most often where energetic and imaginative LEA chief officers were in post, such as Clegg in the West Riding and Russell at Birmingham, and coincided with HMI who were committed to AE. However, by 1961 reforms in work-related FE removed the young students into the colleges. If the EIs were at least to keep going, all had to diversify into a broader, solely adult service, and to attract adults into it. This required more and better publicity and adult accommodation.

Publicity and co-operation

HMI had always pressed the need for properly attractive and informative publicity, and sometimes received help from specialist colleagues in encouraging the production of good examples. The scope and soundness of their advice steadily widened as they gained experience. Towards the end of our period they initiated some modestly successful local co-operation between LEA, RB and voluntary providers in the planning of AE activities and, more often, joint publicity for them. On the rare occasions when they succeeded, the benefit to local communities and potential students was great. However, a considerable expenditure of HMI time was required to secure it, and the practice was insufficiently established to survive after the 1970s, other than exceptionally.

The idea of such co-operative schemes was linked to HMI's desire to develop a better understanding of the potential relationship between a variety of factors, which might lead to more systematic and therefore also more effective planning of provision. The factors which needed to be analysed fell into two groups. Local demographic, social and economic structures, the physical configuration of communities and public transport would be time-consuming to establish but, once known, could be easily kept up to date. Expressed wants and latent needs for the whole gamut of OFE provision, the other group of factors, would demand more difficult and sensitive approaches. Moreover, these had to include the voluntary organisations from playgroups and football clubs to, say, keep fit for the elderly as well as formal provision. During the mid- and late 1960s some HMI carried out a series of local survey inspections, which attempted to investigate the whole range of OFE in this broad context. These contributed substantially to the work, to be described in Chapter 4, of the HMI community working party, but also influenced provision in the field and the content of training courses for professionals throughout OFE (*cf* p 37–40).

Accommodation

The importance of proper adult accommodation had been recognised by an HMI working party as early as 1951 and its uses were illustrated by the voluntary centres in the ECA and, increasingly, those of LEAs and Universities which had followed that example. Encouraged doubtless by their own frequent difficulties in locating EI classes they intended to visit, HMI pressed on authorities the need for attractive notice boards, adequate external and internal lighting, and furniture sized for adult bodies. In one county, HMI, limping after a nocturnal accident, was jocularly informed that it paid to have workmen dig a trench across the school drive if he was expected to visit an EI or a youth club, because external lighting would certainly be installed following real or potential accidents. The tale of the formidable Ritchie's rescue one black night from such a trench reverberated for some years after the event.

HMI also pressed for EI storage space and some accommodation set aside for adult work, especially in daytime, and for properly organised shared use of canteen facilities (often, sadly, defended against adult invasion by the school meals service at all levels including HMI specialists), or at least alternative tea break facilities. HMI was called in by all parties to back them in struggles over the use of specialist rooms and equipment by evening students; even the use of libraries in the good new secondary schools was often denied to the EI. It was often easier to persuade senior officers than the heads of schools and teachers who believed themselves sole owners of 'their' rooms. They saw adults as holding unknown terrors more than as beings like themselves and their spouses, and youth club members as ravening mobs, not as the very people whom they were teaching during the day and whose attitudes to the schools they had themselves played a part in forming. OFE HMI were commonly called in to witness damage invariably said to have been inflicted by them. 'Don't you believe him', hissed one caretaker from his hiding place behind the open front door. 'It's his own kids what's done it, and not the youth club at all.' A particularly importunate head finally drove HMI to ask what he and his school had done to local young people to make them want to smash it up.

The difficulties were all too real but there was progress. The situation was further eased from 1955 onwards when a place was finally found in the Departmental building programme for small allowances which permitted LEAs that wished to do so to add minimal accommodation for adult (and youth service) use to new and re-modelled secondary schools. The 'FE wings' which resulted tended to consist of one or sometimes two rooms with a kitchenette, toilets, and sometimes a small office and store room. The wings also made the new generation of Cambridgeshire village colleges possible, and elsewhere the community colleges or community schools originating from them (*cf* p 98f), but LEAs which ran conventional separate AE services also made use of the facility. The trouble was that new schools were almost always on the periphery of built-up areas and relied on school buses which did not run at night, and that the FE wings were more often than not tacked on to the far end of buildings, away from the specialist accommodation on which the EIs relied. Most schools rapidly filled the wings with desks, denied their use to OFE, especially during the day, and thus added further conflict for HMI to attempt to calm.

A more significant and lasting development was the policy of some LEAs to convert redundant schools and occasionally other local buildings to adult education centres, or occasionally to community centres and village halls which were also available for AE. These centres had the immeasurable advantage of being properly furnished and equipped and, above all, of being available throughout the day as well as in the evening. Wherever such facilities, together with proper staffing, existed, it became more realistic to expect to see AE available to all 'according to their needs and aptitudes'. Throughout the period, as has been stated (*cf* p 28), only three premises were purpose-built for AE under the FE major building programme, and soon lost.

The valuable contribution of the art schools to adult education has been mentioned. Adult education provision overall suffered very severely when, particularly in the 1960s, art colleges were encouraged to upgrade their status and concentrate upon serving full-time professional students aiming at degree level study. In most of them the high quality evening class programmes, which had been so important to many part-time students, disappeared, and with them the challenge of progression and the example of standards which they offered to the local EI centres.

Student responsibility

The desirability of a measure of democratic student participation in policy development, organisation and administration, including a corporate social life, did not yet figure in the 1956 pamphlet. It appears first in HMI policy papers for EIs in 1960. It had been central, as mentioned earlier, to the thinking of the educational centres movement since the first decade of the century, and the inspectorate had drawn both ideas and manpower from that source. It now became a major HMI objective. The development of genuine adult education centres was slow, however, and probably owed more to the experience and the publications of the Educational Centres Association (which was grant-aided as a voluntary organisation when it gave up its RB status in 1961) than to HMI. Its count of member centres grew from about ten before 1939 to about 150 by 1984. Some were the creation of private enterprise, more of universities acting, at times, jointly with LEAs. Most of the new member centres of the ECA were LEA institutions with principals who believed in the advantages of student involvement. Unfortunately few LEAs could be persuaded to follow examples such as Kent or, later, Leicestershire in devolving any real responsibility to adult student members.

Raising standards

The CI paper by RD Salter Davies referred to (cf p 28f) makes the point that 'often teaching does nothing to enlarge [students'] views, to liberate their understanding of their subject or help them to use it to enrich their capacity as citizens.' Referring particularly to art and craft activities, he comments 'Taste is often abominable and out of touch with contemporary standards.' Inspection reports and policy papers from about 1960 onward show that HMI increasingly recognised that the level of LEA AE, though improving, was less satisfactory than the students deserved, and HMIs' activities increasingly focused on raising standards of course planning and teaching.

Yet all the work which went into these developments was based, fundamentally, on the humbling experience of HMI's own ignorance. Whatever their personal expertise, they were inspecting anything from Chinese language to embroidery, economics and industrial relations to harmony and counterpoint, woodwork to psychology. Admittedly, they were schooled in the recognition of what makes for good teaching, but for such ability as they developed to recognise good standards in content and its organisation they had to go to school to those whom they were inspecting even more than to their colleagues in other sections of HMI. Inspecting AE was the privilege of one's own continuing, and endlessly surprising education. 'But how did you know about us?' asked the astonished members of an embroidery class forming the whole programme of a never before visited EI serving a remote Yorkshire moorland village as they unpacked treasured prize-winning pin cushions from their carrier bags for HMI to admire. 'You've missed our cupper, but would you like a bun? Why don't you come back next week and we'll *show* you how to do fine cross stitch.'

The tutor of that class subsequently received visits from others and from county advisers, and helped to train other teachers of embroidery. With the help of such outstanding colleagues in the field, HMI efforts to improve teaching standards and the suitability of course content through their advice became more reliable. These efforts were a central objective of all their regular visits to institutions. The need for this was great. The mass of part-time tutors were untrained. Those who were school teachers tended to rely on their accustomed curricula, techniques and relationships, however little these might be suited to work with adults. The majority of tutors, lacking any beacon by which to steer, relied on memories of their own school education or apprenticeship. Only the exceptional drew on personal and often thoughtful consideration of their task. Most of the old part-time institute heads were no better placed, and rarely saw it as their task to influence class-room practice.

HMI worked hard at the task of developing a more professional under-standing of and approach to effective adult curriculum and teaching in all subjects. They encouraged the planning of proper syllabuses for every class, and the development of progressively graded course schemes which would take raw beginners through to independence and, if they wished, autonomous tutorless working groups. They pressed, with much success, for the range of subjects covered in institute programmes to be enlarged, and to be made more appro-priate to the needs and interests of potential student groups rather than apeing often inappropriate or obsolete subject boundaries. They advocated the devel-opment of short courses to help people develop specific skills or solve particular problems, in addition to the traditional longer courses. They persuaded institutions to find space for daytime classes at a variety of conve-nient hours according to people's roles, and for concentrated as well as shorter courses to serve those who had no regular leisure time, and thus attract new clientèles which had not previously benefited from AE. Weekend and summer courses developed in parallel. Progress in these areas depended largely on LEA activity supported by HMI.

Developing a profession

All this meant that the heads of adult centres of every kind needed to develop a self-concept which had hitherto only been shared by a small minority of, mostly, full-time principals and centre wardens. From small-time operators most of whose time was spent in clerical chores they were challenged to turn themselves into professional adult educators. Their role was re-interpreted for them to involve a knowledge of their environment which helped in the plan-ning of programmes, and went some way towards meeting the enormous range of adult needs and interests, imaginative planning of courses, the training, supervision and support of their part-time tutors, and the skilled observation and evaluation of their own centre's work. Here again progress depended largely on LEA initiatives stimulated and supported by HMI.

In a very real sense such a role challenged evening institute heads, and their senior colleagues in the rare places where they existed, to acquire HMI's own skills and apply them. OFE HMI at this time did much systematic work on the evaluation of teaching and learning and on the organisation of institutions, programmes and courses. The papers and instruments which they developed for their own use were made available to LEAs centrally and to field staff at national and local courses. They gained wide currency, and led to real improvements in standards.

All these and other practical suggestions for the development of evening institutes and their provision were worked out in a series of papers which, in turn, were based on a mass of preceding reports and papers from and memoranda to inspectors, gradually intellectually developed and systematised over a period of years. All were sent to OFE HMI for general circulation in the field, usually with the attached caveat that it must be made clear that their content was not to be taken as representing Ministry policy but only as inspectoral thinking. Indeed, finding new and reasonably elegant ways of exonerating Ministry or Department when speaking at courses and conferences was one of HMI's more innocent amusements.

HMI publications and the Office view of AE

Some of the earlier thinking in the process which has been described is reflected in the first major book devoted to evening institutes and their history (Edwards, 1961). It was the work (during a sabbatical year at Manchester University) of an HMI who had been active in the field and who had taken over the production of the Ministry's evening institute pamphlet when KJ Ritchie had retired in disgust from this particular battle.

Both the impetus for Edwards's book and Ritchie's action were significant. Office desire to restrict development even further may not have been the only reason for the decision – as early as 1948 – not to publish a pamphlet written by the RB staff inspector. Its intention, clearly redolent of the philosophy of war-time army education, was to encourage adult 'political education' with the idea of helping more of the people 'to understand the present in the perspective of the past and the future, and to decide and act as responsible moral beings'. (Jack, then retiring as SI for adult education, continued his efforts in this direction in the more liberal and fertile ground of the Control Commission supervising Germany, occupied by the victorious allied powers after the end of World War II. 'Liberal and fertile' may sound odd in the circumstances, but it was British and British-trained adult educators from the Army Education Corps and other professional sources who laid the foundations of what has become arguably the most impressive provision of AE anywhere.)

The desire of the inspectorate at least to give all LEAs and the general public the benefit of the knowledge they were acquiring in the process of inspection was frustrated. Proposals for pamphlets to stimulate thought and provide advice were constantly rejected by the Office as being liable to encourage expenditure. Reports on inspections, which might have been generally helpful in development, were the only other printed assistance available, but were restricted to the institutions concerned, though some were circulated more widely by their recipients. A draft pamphlet on residential AE was abandoned in 1950, and (Sir) Toby Weaver, representing the FE Branch of the Office, opposed even a reprint of the county college pamphlet, *Youth's Opportunity,* in 1950. A similar fate overtook proposals for a new community centre pamphlet in 1954, when the inspectorate had to be satisfied with a reprint of the now rather outdated 1944 Red Book. In the following year even a publication on *Canteens in OFE* was abandoned as likely to encourage expenditure, and so was a pamphlet on *Education and the Home* in 1957.

The constant efforts of FE Branch of the Office to dampen down any possible appearance of Ministry encouragement led Sir Martin Roseveare as SCI to press Toby Weaver in a letter of March 1952 (ED 176/3 in PRO) to agree that it was right in the spirit of the Act to continue to stimulate the development of OFE even if fresh money was not available. Gilbert Fleming, permanent secretary since 1945, intervened however in June 1953 (ED 176/3) to insist that pamphlet programmes must have Office agreement. He was, of course, under constant ministerial pressure for economy. This resulted in a variety of cuts in capital expenditure on village halls, community centres and sports facilities, and in requirements for raising student contributions. In 1954 it led to the adoption, against HMI advice and despite continuing LEA reluctance to enforce it, of a policy that 'recreational' classes must be self-supporting. Proposals to cut back RB classes and the ensuing Ashby Report have been mentioned. It was pressure from outside education which helped to avert, at the time, economies so drastic that they might have put an end to OFE altogether. The sage comment of EBH Baker, the Assistant Secretary responsible at that time for OFE finances, that economies in this provision could only have a marginal impact on expenditure overall, had little influence. Indeed, OFE always remained such a minimal fraction of education budgets national or local, that cutting it, while severely damaging OFE, could be considered no more than an ineffective publicity exercise.

Opposition to any Ministry policy which might encourage expenditure failed to prevent, though it long held up, proposals for the publication of the Ministry pamphlet on Evening Institutes. Originally accepted as necessary before 1939, and often revived and shelved, the proposal was finally agreed subject to an Office veto on any suggestion which involved expenditure. Its publication followed bitter arguments. The Minister, Sir David Eccles, himself became involved; there was careful verbal filleting of the text to avert accusations of encouraging expenditure, and a wonderfully grudging negative introduction by the Minister. That it became, as mentioned earlier (p 53), a major factor in development was the more surprising. A senior HMI on the Adult and Youth panel, his style redolent of that of John Blackie, the CI for OFE since 1951, produced carefully balanced arguments on the publications issue in a paper of February 1955: 'The extent to which [OFE] is accepted by public opinion as a proper charge on taxpayer and ratepayer is limited and uncertain, and authorities which are trying to cut expenditure look first and often last at OFE ... The voluntary must inevitably suffer before the compulsory. Furthermore, although no educated man' it continues, not without reference to opposition from less enlightened members of the panel, 'would hold that technical and vocational education is more important by absolute standards than OFE, the fact remains that the claims of technical education are more easily understood by the half educated ... the majority may need help.' SCI weighed in in support of OFE and asked if the economic argument was to lead to a change of policy. The Minister (Eccles) took this up with the request that EI development should be based on a change of policy to that of making 'good educational facilities increasingly so enticing to an intelligent democratic people that they should and must become increasingly self-supporting'. Comment on the nature and validity of such arguments and attitudes will appear in the final chapter (p 163f).

Pyrrhic victory or not, the evening institute pamphlet was the only departmental publication in support of AE to see the light since the 1919 Report. Later (in 1963 and 1966) some small comfort could be drawn from two Administrative Memoranda on accommodation and staffing respectively, resulting from long-drawn-out pressure and argument on the part of HMI and the field. Beyond the end of the OFE HMI there was the eventual publication of the Russell Report, though the Department acted grudgingly on just small parts of it, and, later, the Second Report of the FE Sub-Committee of the Advisory Committee on the Supply and Training of Teachers (ACSTT, 1978), of which more below. This it succeeded in delaying for two years before agreeing that it could be published, but only in the name of the Committee. Having thus distanced itself from the Report, the Department duly ignored it.

Other means of dissemination
Given the ban on departmental publications, the dissemination of the wealth of useful knowledge and ideas collected and developed by OFE HMI was generally confined to the confidential papers they produced primarily for circulation among themselves. These developed into what was certainly the most significant writing on adult education practice in its period and in Britain. Later in the 1960s, and into the 1970s, these papers, sometimes also cast into the form of training exercises, were collected and distributed informally as well as being

used consistently on departmental and other training courses. Some of the more innovatory national courses produced 'proceedings' which were widely distributed and reproduced (eg, Department of Education and Science, 1970).

Edward Hutchinson, as secretary of the National Institute of Adult Education throughout this period, always regretted that the knowledge and advisory capacity of the inspectorate were not made more widely available. One at least of the two influential books (Edwards, 1961; Elsdon, 1975) that resulted from OFE HMI being given a year's sabbatical leave was very outspoken, and the Department made no attempt to muzzle it. In retrospect, however, one might ask whether some of the more concerned HMI could and should have followed the example of Matthew Arnold in the 1870s, when he spoke and wrote publicly against the Board's introduction of payment by results.

A new rationale for adult education

AE HMI were thus prevented from carrying out their duty to publish, like the rest of the inspectorate, reasoned advice based on their experience because it was feared such advice would cause demands for expenditure. Such writing on evening institutes and other aspects of AE as they were able to contribute was directed to improving and extending practice. However, it also made a unique contribution to developing thinking about adult education, its social basis and its variety of purpose and impact. This was largely the work of KJ Ritchie's successor as staff inspector, JA Simpson, who took over in 1958 and held the post until 1971. He elaborated a theoretical background and a philosophy for the evening institute as a basis for an adult education movement which would subsume the arguments for 'liberal adult education' provision that had supported the university extension movement and later the WEA. A first article entitled 'A Philosophy for the Evening Institute' appeared in the HMI house journal, the *Inspector's Bulletin* in March 1961.

Simpson's essay linked 'the educational clarion calls of heightened awareness and graceful living' with 'the compelling socially useful blast sounded by adult education' and staked the claims of the evening institute to help in meeting them as 'a well designed focal point for that sociability which so many people want' and which 'emerges as a by-product of a common interest'. It referred to the evening institute as becoming 'by the habitual exercise of control over the content of circumstances of [people's] congregation ... a valuable school of democracy for people who have no interest in the academic study of politics'. He defined the role of the evening institute also as meeting the need for 'satisfying pursuits among a people which had come to regard work as realising the only dignity'; he referred to the therapeutic value of creative activity of different sorts made possible in evening institute activities by developing the resources people have in themselves, and argued the moral significance of this channelling of their desire for power. Characteristically of the writer, the paper argued that such a philosophy 'would not be entirely a fiction anywhere' and 'would be matched by reality in increasing measures'.

These ideas were developed in detail and refined with the benefit of HMI panel discussion in a number of papers subsequently circulated to interested individuals from the middle 1960s onwards. They drew upon thinking about community and adult education centres which had been elaborated and later published by KT Elsdon, who had joined the inspectorate in 1960. They were further refined by Simpson and contributed particularly to a long paper on permanent education and community development which he wrote into a Council of Europe volume (Council of Europe, 1971) and Simpson's own research study written for the Council (Simpson, 1972). Of special importance for both philosophical and organisational thinking about adult education was Simpson's re-casting of the idea of 'liberal adult education' as not restricted to a range of particular subject content but as 'general, personal and social education' *delivered through whatever subject it happened to use as its vehicle*. These ideas, in turn, contributed to the foundation for the methodology of AE training in philosophical thinking and learning theory, on which Elsdon was working (*cf* pp 64–67). Following his retirement Simpson worked further with the Council of Europe's Council for Cultural Co-operation in Strasbourg which had, for a time, considerable influence on European thinking on what came, in Britain, to be called 'continuing' rather than 'permanent' or 'lifelong' education.

More directly, Simpson's thinking both as an assessor and later as a committee member, together with that of other OFE HMI, was of considerable significance for the view of AE and its needs and possibilities which emerged fully from the report (DES/Russell, 1973) of the committee of enquiry into adult education (the Russell Committee). Its task was defined as looking into '… the appropriateness of existing educational, administrative and financial policies' and 'make recommendations with a view to obtaining the most effective and economical deployment of available resources to enable adult education to make its proper contribution to the national system of education conceived of as a process continuing through life'. The Russell Committee was appointed in February 1969 by a Labour Government. It seemed to represent a finally successful outcome of the pressures over a long period from a host of outside forces as well as from the inspectorate. However, its careful investigations and drafting were so prolonged that when its report finally emerged in 1973 on the day the oil crisis broke, the political climate had already changed totally. Publication, in practice, marked the end of a period of hope and expansion for adult education, and not the dawn of a new and happier era which its initiation had seemed to inaugurate.

Two trends of thought affected some AE through organisational patterns, especially in the 1970s. They were school-based AE under various names and 'community education' especially where it signified an amalgamation of AE with YS provision. More often the term was used as a fashionable flag to wave over anything educators did or wanted to do. These matters will be discussed in Chapter 4 (pp 98–100).

HMI and training

From the early 1960s and increasingly through this and most of the next decade OFE HMI made a major contribution to the development of professional training for youth and adult education workers, and others in the post-school sector of education. As indicated earlier, much of the development of the new training methodologies which spread across all OFE and beyond derived from adult education. HMI who had a particular interest in new practice brought it into the Inspectorate from army education earlier on and later from adult education centres. With willing help from LEA colleagues in two West Riding Centres, which provided the original test beds, they tested a variety of curricula, methods and course durations. Development cascaded rapidly from these within that LEA, across Yorkshire, and then into neighbouring regions before spreading, as a result of DES courses and HMI publications, nationally and internationally. The evolution of modern training activity in AE thus started from the ground up rather than the top down. As a result it was formalised later than in the other disciplines to which its practice had spread immediately. The early history of this interesting co-operative exercise in educational development is told in greater detail in Part 1 of Elsdon (1975). There were important parallel developments of training methodology which took their inception from some youth and social work practice which had been influenced by the work of the Tavistock Institute. They were energetically developed by the National College of Youth Leader Training (with HMI seconded as principal and two future HMI on its staff) following the publication of the Albemarle Report, and by the Salisbury course after the Second Report on the Training of Part-time Youth Leaders (cf pp 39, 111).

Almost contemporary with these developments, a national full inspection survey of adult education training by RBs was carried out in 1963–64. The report created something of a stir, and one of the universities printed its own edition of it for wider distribution than the Department had vouchsafed. The exercise caused a number of university RBs to start training their part-time tutors, and to evolve advanced courses of study. The findings from the Yorkshire LEA experiments and the RB report formed much of the staple material for a Council of Europe Course on Training for Adult Education, which HMI had been asked to organise and direct in 1965. Its three group reports greatly influenced practice in Britain and several other European countries.

With the resources of expertise which were thus being created, regional and local training courses spread rapidly and HMI became involved both in these and in assisting with the conduct of trainers' courses to improve their standard, and the setting up of training schemes for adult education in a growing number of regions. It was clear that all this activity needed to be grounded in much more systematic scholarship. This led to the creation of what was essentially a research conference held at Cambridge in January 1970.[1] Given the lack of other sources of finance it was prepared and organised as part of the DES Teachers' Short Course Programme. In preparation, HMI commissioned and supervised the production of a series of research papers by leading scholars and practitioners covering the specified field. These were circulated to some 40 leading 'scholarly practitioners' and researchers for study and comment before the whole group came together with an HMI team in January 1970 to study the implications of the papers and produce conclusions on the rationale, the content, methods and organisation of training for adult education. The whole of this material was collated, edited, and distributed as a volume of 'course' proceedings to all LEAs and RBs. Thus it became available for use as the fundamental text on relevant courses throughout the country and in a number of Council of Europe (Pflüger, 1978) and other countries for many years, under the title *Explorations in Adult Learning and Training for Adult Education*. In addition to several printings by the Department, some LEAs and universities made reprints of their own. When OFE HMI was absorbed into a single FE section the future of these developments seemed secure and was to remain so for some years.

The Cambridge research conference on adult learning and training, and the almost immediate publication (albeit unofficial), of its proceedings, marked the end of professional development activity by OFE HMI as such. However, the momentum which had been created now seemed unstoppable. Having facilitated the creation of the research base and a text, adult education HMI were able, in their turn, to progress to setting up a series of national and regional trainers' courses. These used the methods and organisation which had, by then, proved themselves with the Youth Service and Careers education. They also applied the system of research conferences followed by unofficial but nationally distributed publications to two further special areas involving major new development and related policy issues. Some of these were linked to personal research activities by HMI, who was given a sabbatical year and research funding to complete what became an influential book on the history, rationale and practical methods of AE training. It was followed, after some years, by a further volume on the organisation, methods and effects of intensive courses for trainers (Elsdon, 1975, 1984).

A national scheme of professional development?

By 1972 articulated modern field-based AE training schemes for part-time tutors were in place in three regions and starting elsewhere; six UK universities were offering full time or part-time courses leading to advanced diplomas or master's degrees. It was in this respect, and in the research that has been mentioned, that co-operation between the RBs and the LEAs, so long unsuccessfully pressed by OFE HMI, finally had a major effect. Some University AE Departments (especially Leicester, Manchester and Nottingham, followed by Bristol, Southampton and Surrey) were collaborating closely with LEA part-time tutor training in their areas; most of the participants in and the graduates of their advanced courses had been released from, and returned to LEA service. Later some of the polytechnics joined in these developments.

The new type of three-stage part-time tutor training, increasingly delivered by 'scholarly practitioners' who had themselves been through demanding trainers' courses, spread rapidly. By the time of the 1981 survey referred to (p 21) regional schemes were in place except in the West Midlands, Wales and Scotland. At least the first stage of good modern training specifically for the education of adults was thus available to the great majority of the 70,000 part-time tutors who were known and the 100,000 who were thought to be involved in AE. A growing proportion of the more advanced LEAs were insisting on new tutors successfully undertaking a Stage 1 training course during their first year of service, and encouraged them to continue to Stage 2. Some also made such training compulsory for tutors already in post. Secondment to part-time courses leading to Stage 3 for newly appointed or would-be full-time and some part-time subject specialists and new centre heads was becoming customary wherever the course was available. The schemes were at different stages of maturity, but in the North West, the East Midlands, part of the South West, and London and the South East it was now possible for adult education students to qualify part-time in their teaching subjects and, if they were appointed as part-time tutors, to progress by a part-time route through three staged levels of training to full professional qualification as teachers in the post-school sector.

HMI and the Regional Advisory Councils had no difficulty in securing the acceptance of this original and remarkable scheme of training for AE as it was nationally formalised by the FE Sub-Committee of the Advisory Committee on the Supply and Training of Teachers (ACSTT); it was demonstrably more effective, and cheaper, than any alternative. The Sub-Committee took on board what was probably the most obvious and at the same time the most central and original aspect of all the development of training courses since Salter Davies's initiative for Youth Service training (*cf* p 39). This was the insistence that training needs to do more than equip teachers with knowledge; it needs to initiate permanent changes in their attitudes and their behaviour. This meant that training had to be exemplary, and it could not be exemplary if the trainers were not themselves capable of exemplifying the skills and attitudes, as well as the knowledge concerned, from personal experience of the field, and were themselves trained in modern training methodology. HMI was asked to draft the revolutionary paragraph 34 of the report to express this (ACSTT 2, 1978).

The text of the Report was finalised as early as 1976, and used extensively on DES short courses for FE teachers. It was welcomed by LEAs and the field, who saw in it a great advance on inflexible and expensive course provision, often delivered by personnel who lacked the kind of characteristics defined in para 34 of the Report. The Department finally gave in to demands to the extent of arranging for the report's publication in the name of the Committee, in 1978. It refused, eventually, to contemplate the cost of setting up the very limited national machinery required to moderate the regional schemes. As a result of this and the severe cuts in provision which followed, much of the progress that had already been made was undone and – incidentally – the costs of training rose very considerably above those of the collapsed regional schemes.[2]

These events not only post-date the end of the OFE inspectorate as such, but they approach the time of wholesale cuts and destruction in AE, and the eventual substitution of the present arrangements for the original HMI. About the time of the end of OFE HMI itself it was still possible to look forward with considerable optimism. Thus, by 1971 there had come into existence 'a recognisable and recognised group of professional people engaged in AE (about 1,500 strong), two thirds of them LEA-based, engaged in gaining an appropriate body of professional knowledge and experience, beginning to test and support it with research and proving a claim to a career structure' – which was in fact emerging. It was no unworthy memorial to OFE HMI. So was the fact that the developments in methods and organisation of AE training had affected the training of the whole range of people working with adults, including the technical, managerial, social work and even medical and nursing areas, leaving only the schools relatively untouched.

Moreover, the Advisory (not 'Development' as recommended) Council on Adult and Continuing Education (ACACE), one of the few positive responses of the government to the Russell Report, was eventually set up in 1977 and ran for two three year terms. Serving and former HMI supported it and its various working groups as assessors and in other capacities, and contributed much to its useful stream of publications. On the other hand AE specialist HMI with substantial experience were retiring; not all were replaced and leading professionals in the field openly declared their unwillingness to apply for vacancies. Following the retirement of HES Marks the SI leadership of AE was further reduced to a single post and subsequently replacements were appointed from backgrounds other than AE; consequently the group soon ceased to represent the profession's expertise.

Access education

The minutes of the now much rarer meetings of the adult education committee of HMI record, in March 1972, the comment that 'in some respects the field is overtaking us'. The influence of HMI concerned with OFE provision on the major developments of the 1970s (other than training, professional development and research) was in fact relatively less marked. This is hardly surprising since, by this time, AE specialist HMI were beginning to be reduced in number and had assumed very great additional responsibilities for work-related FE.

One major development of the time was Access Education. It was by no means new, since the opportunity for adults to take courses leading to qualifying examinations for university entry had long existed and was well provided for in colleges of FE in particular. In its new form of bridging courses to prepare adults for such studies it stemmed from the concern of Enid Hutchinson, wife of the secretary of the NIAE, to help more mature women to enter higher and further education by acquiring the necessary skills and self-confidence to enter courses leading to examined qualifications. Her first course with this aim had been established in 1966, but by the late 1970s the drive had expanded nationally to press for and provide general preparatory Access courses which might help anybody to examination qualifications. As the impetus grew and resources in the AE institutions which had pioneered the work shrank, courses tended to be increasingly provided in the primarily vocational FE colleges. By this time the OFE section had disappeared; surviving AE specialists had played little part in the initiation of this area of work, though they acknowledged and fostered it in all forms of adult centres and FE colleges. However, they advised against its early tendency to block potential career paths by concentrating on arts and social science content to the exclusion of either applied or pure sciences. Much later Access became a major concern of Government, as did literacy education and general preliminary education for the disadvantaged. HMI became strongly involved in these developments.

Adult basic education

The second major initiative, beginning only towards the end of the OFE inspectorate but using its remaining members subsequently, was in literacy work, later developed into adult basic education (ABE). The large-scale mobilisation of manpower from 1939 on had revealed the need to provide literacy and numeracy education on a large scale in the Forces. When the newly formed Adult and Youth Panel was planning for civilian needs in April 1947 it was well aware of the underlying need. It therefore considered an enquiry into needs and possibilities in literacy education, but nothing was done. It was probably thought that with the planned improvements in schools the general need for such work which had shown up in the army would disappear. The inspectorate made a considerable impact on the continuing provision of remedial literacy education in penal institutions, particularly under the influence of Tom Cradock and later John Fish, who were primarily concerned with general remedial education.

Elsewhere it made no more than scattered individual efforts to address the problem.

The initiative which led to the literacy campaign in the early 1970s came from the British Association of Settlements. Its remarkably rapid success owed much to the enthusiastic participation of BBC adult education officers and especially John Robinson, and to their understanding of continuing education. Following FE amalgamation OFE HMIs' ability to respond was reduced, and some at least were uneasy about what they regarded as the haste and inadequate preparation with which the campaign was launched. Their contribution was made mainly through their usual practices. They drew attention to the substantial and successful experience which was available, and their careful inspection and national comparisons contributed to a better understanding of the kinds of teaching methods and organisation which were most effective. They stressed the need for training all literacy tutors, including the many school teachers who volunteered, in specifically adult teaching methods, and assisted with training trainers. Their national survey of literacy provision which followed shortly threw much light on the causes of the problem.

Following the publication of the Russell Report, the Department established a national agency (ALRA, later ALBSU) in 1975 to fund adult basic education with government money. Significantly, the agency was linked with the National Institute of Adult Continuing Education, though the link later broke down. HMI continued their association with the work and with the agency.

Broadcasting and adult education

The impact of broadcasting on the literacy campaign was an impressive, but by no means entirely new feature. The importance of broadcasting as a factor in AE provision had greatly increased since the appointment of the first BBC further education officers in 1962. HMI had kept in touch with them and with others responsible for radio and television education, and involved them in some of the training schemes. OFE HMI had always been associated as observers and assessors on the committees and groups which forwarded this new development in adult education. These continuing links contrasted with the absence of direct HMI involvement with the Open University, which was mentioned earlier (*cf* p 49).

Education for the disadvantaged

A third major trend in AE in the 1970s was for education of the disadvantaged in general, over and above the specific area of literacy and numeracy work. One aspect of this was language education for the growing communities in Britain whose first language was not English. OFE HMI had been given a brief for this as early as CI's Memo to Inspectors of May 1950 (see p 26). Surprisingly, systematic and large scale action on this was not initiated until 1974, when an industrial language training programme was financed by the Department of Employment through the Manpower Services Commission. OFE HMI were only brought in to advise at a late stage. The situation was rather different with some of the earliest discovery of the language and social and educational needs especially of women immigrants in East London and elsewhere. This was first exposed by the researches of HMI Jean McGinty in 1970–71.

The Russell Committee's report had voiced its concerns and recommendations for more AE provision for disadvantaged groups, including those affected by the whole range of disabilities. Significantly, though, the recommendations they made were based largely on a study commissioned for the Committee from Peter Klein of the ILEA. OFE HMI had investigated both the needs and the provision, but had been generally rather cautious about pressing for more of it. The impetus for it came from elsewhere – mainly health and social services, which sought resources from AE for responsibilities which had been traditionally their own. An explanation for HMIs' caution is found partly in their traditional concern for educational standards, reinforced by a tendency to doubt the rightness of devoting much of the limited, and shrinking, AE resources to expensive experiments in activities which, it was argued, would be more properly financed by the social services than by AE. HMI attitudes were coloured also by the historic concern to defend AE work as properly education and against the charge that public money could, through it, be wasted on activities which, while worthy in themselves, could not be described as meeting educational criteria. If some adult educators proved cautious in the face of new challenges it was also true that occasional excesses needed to be questioned. In fact, charges of frivolity, together with others of providing solely for the middle classes, were only too successfully pressed against AE in the 1970s and 1980s by pricing it beyond the reach of anybody else, while the demand for immediate short-term economic benefit from educational expenditure changed the whole pattern of AE activity, organisation and staffing.

Residential adult education

The long-term colleges

The history of the long-term residential colleges[3] goes back to the early years of the century, when Ruskin College had been established at Oxford. Over the next few years it was followed in England by Fircroft, a Quaker foundation in Birmingham. Hillcroft in suburban London, a first residential establishment for working women, came next in 1920, and then the Catholic Workers' College in Oxford in 1921. Wales acquired its quickly established Coleg Harlech in 1927 and Scotland a less successful college at Newbattle Abbey in 1937. Following a specific recommendation of the Russell Report (very unusually followed by action) and enthusiastic support from surrounding LEAs, the Northern College near Barnsley was added to the English list to serve a part of the country which had so far been neglected. Ruskin began to admit women and broaden its curriculum only during the period which we cover. Fircroft, surprisingly for a Quaker foundation, admitted men only, until very recently. Hillcroft's single-sex status has been deliberately maintained to assist women, who so often need to build or regain a measure of confidence to enable them to sustain the stresses of personal and career change. The Northern College created important precedents by admitting women from the start and providing child care.

All these colleges owed their origins largely to the efforts of concerned individuals. They secured grant aid from the Education Department as part of its AE(RB) provision, and thus fell into the purview of HMI throughout the period. Woodbrooke, another residential college and also a Quaker foundation, was not grant-aided. A college established for the Cooperative Movement in 1919, with splendid premises of its own after 1945, was largely devoted to studies relevant to the Movement's principles and organisation. It received less help and then only towards its varying contribution towards general adult education. HMI had little contact with these two.

Adult education, like the role of HMI, is in great measure about discovering potential and assisting it to become reality. The chance, for mature individuals, of going beyond the possibilities offered by part-time classes in order to pursue academic interests as far as practicable and, possibly, make this the occasion of a career change, had always been a desirable goal for some students. Historically however the quest for personal development, cultural understanding and social effectiveness were the primary aims. Either or both were close to the heart of HMI, and reflected the previous personal field experience of some. Their support and general acceptance of such aims for AE students were given added impetus by the large scale and often highly successful work initiated by the armed services in residential settings, to meet some of the problems of demobilisation and the needs of the economy in the immediate post-war period. Of these experiments the Army Formation Colleges (p 87) were the most developed examples.

The Ministry had given the idea of residential AE a further considerable boost in the post-war period by the establishment of its Mature State Scholarship scheme. From 1944 until the 1960s 30 scholarships to the universities had been made available annually to adults. They were awarded to them on the strength of their experience as adult students and their performance in an essay followed by an interview: candidates were not expected to go through the hoops of an examination system designed for adolescents leaving school. One of OFE HMIs' most interesting and rewarding jobs was their association with open-minded distinguished academics in helping to identify the most suitable among applicants and sometimes also following their most interesting progress. Later grant regulations *seemed* to make the scheme redundant, but the principle of replacing inappropriate hurdles with appropriate ones was lost in the process. However, the residential colleges gave many more adults an intense experience of full-time higher education. They also often led them on to take degree courses at universities. These were now open to adults on the strength of the diploma qualifications many of them gained in the colleges.

Each residential college had an HMI as its 'liaison general inspector' who kept in touch with it and its problems. In the half century after 1945 these were both varied and considerable, reflecting change in social conditions as well as economic problems. They mirrored and, in some instances, exaggerated student movements of the time. Some colleges were the subject of formal inspections; all enjoyed normal informal visiting, with HMI endeavouring to help and advise them towards the maintenance of good academic standards. The style of college work and the nature of the student clientèle sparked off criticisms which were often politically motivated. It usually fell to HMI to defend them against these. More regularly they supported, if with varying success, an unending search for increased LEA as well as central government grant aid, and help from other sources. HMI particularly helped in efforts to meet serious problems in adapting and usually shortening courses to meet varying circumstances. Securing better provision for women was seen as specially important. Hillcroft College had been among the first institutions where the need for improved access for women into further and higher education became clear in the 1960s. The developments there and at Northern College were part of the attempt to find answers.

Generally with the long-term residential colleges HMI did their best to help, but they were not the main proactive element in bringing about change. They also tended to distance themselves from 'student revolt' problems which troubled Ruskin and led to the closure of Fircroft for a five year period. It re-opened in 1980 with a mixture of short and long courses designed to meet local needs more effectively, and admitted women.

The Northern College developed in part from the three-year day release courses provided by the University of Sheffield for Derbyshire and Yorkshire Miners' Union members. These had, from their start, received considerable HMI support, as valuable and imaginative experiments in extra-mural provision which achieved very high standards. They also foreshadowed progress towards paid leave for purposes of general as well as vocational education; this attracted growing interest particularly after the mid-1970. The College was enthusiastically promoted by its first principal, who came from the Sheffield University Extra-mural Department, and it opened in 1978 with aid from surrounding LEAs as well as central government, and further HMI encouragement.

The college developed an imaginative variety of course patterns. These were carefully designed to meet the needs of adult students with more limited educational experience and outlook than had been historically demanded of students in the long-term colleges. The courses varied from five weeks to two years in length. The experimental stance of the college and the close relations which, like Ruskin, it had with the Labour Movement and which were central to its purposes, created problems for supporting LEAs as well as over DES funding. They exercised HMI after the OFE section had ceased to exist.

The mix of study for vocational purposes with more purely 'liberal' educational objectives and changing 'community' and social concerns had always raised problems for the long-term colleges. With changes of political climate in the late 1970s and early 1980s, and in educational funding, they moved out of the HMI sphere of concern. In 1980 there were rather fewer than 600 students in all the colleges together, and half their finance was coming from central government sources. They had had the consistent support of OFE HMI while these continued to exist; insofar as they found themselves assigned to individuals who could bring sound experience to the task, they benefited from the relationship.

The short-term colleges

Short-term residential adult education was of much more recent origin. Holly Royde, the imaginative creation of Ross Waller of Manchester University, started as a voluntary body, then called the Lamb Guildhouse, in 1938. At that time it was also intended to serve its local community and its constitution had much in common with those of educational settlements. Requisitioned during the war and finally wound up because of the demands of the Inland Revenue, which would not recognise it as an educational institution, it ceased to operate. However, in 1945 Waller became the first Professor of the newly created Department of Adult Education and set up Holly Royde as the first permanent centre of its kind. He remained, throughout, a powerful advocate of the idea.

Waller's advocacy was, however, overshadowed by the enthusiasm of Sir Richard Livingstone, whose rather muddled account of Danish Folk High Schools – the model for *long-term* colleges – was not tempered by direct knowledge; he assumed that the short-term institutions he advocated were their equivalent. It seems that his presidential address to the Education Section of the British Association in 1936 was his first public utterance on the subject. His immensely influential war-time publications followed, and by 1943 both the White Paper on *Educational Reconstruction* and the briefing papers for the Archbishop's Conference (*cf* p 16) had taken the idea on board.

The pioneering developments initiated by the armed services during and immediately after World War II were, if anything, more influential. Their experience had suggested, and somewhat exaggerated, the existence of an enormous pent-up demand for AE. Residential courses for all sorts of military purposes had become a central and accepted feature of life for millions. During the demobilisation period the army's 'Formation Colleges' and smaller local centres were designed to help slow the release of manpower and ease re-absorption into civilian employment. They provided a very extensive programme of residential short courses, mainly of 'pre-vocational training' but sometimes also 'liberal' in their coverage and purpose. The short courses on discussion group methods of the 'ABCA' College at Harlech had trained considerable numbers of junior officers as leaders and encouraged some interest and understanding about AE. They also demonstrated the professional possibilities of training for AE generally. The college drew upon some experienced adult educators among others, who were later to be among the earliest OFE HMI, and it trained some other future HMI. (see also p 11)

Waller and Livingstone dreamed of cultural and intellectual adult studies being housed in attractive surroundings contrasting with the general use of makeshift and often sordid premises. The dream coincided with the end of the forces' use of country houses which were now no longer viable as family residences. The Ministry's *Pamphlet No 8* encouraged all LEAs, either alone or in partnership with voluntary bodies and universities, to acquire such buildings for their AE work. A number did so, though it proved difficult to get building permits for the necessary adaptations.

Various bodies concerned with AE, other than the LEAs, also opened colleges. The Oxford Extramural Delegacy and the local WEA District worked together with the LEAs to establish Wedgwood Memorial College, one of the first, in 1945. The YMCA and the National Federation of Women's Institutes (which had started experimenting in 1942 and came under Livingstone's direct influence) opened more specialised institutions. Some private individuals and trusts opened colleges in their own houses. By 1950–51, 24 short-term colleges catered for nearly 21,000 students, and numbers continued to grow to 'something over 35' colleges reported to the Russell Committee as catering for at least 100,000 students annually. Further foundations followed.

HMI supported the colleges strongly from their beginnings, encouraged LEAs to provide them, to set fitting standards of staffing and amenity, and to consider grant-aid to students where this was appropriate. They encouraged both local LEA centres and RBs to co-operate with the colleges, and the colleges to co-operate with each other. Thus AE tutors were urged to devise concentrated residential courses in which either a class with its tutor or several together might address aspects of their subject or craft which benefited from intensive and continuous application. For new students, who soon became the majority, the colleges could offer concentrated glimpses of what local centres offered over the long term and at a more leisurely pace. Colleges were also encouraged sometimes to provide series of coherent and consecutive short courses to take the place of normal weekly courses for 'the surprising proportion of the population which is not free to attend a class for the next 24 Wednesday nights'. In all the work of the short-term colleges the essential element was joint residence, the element of community-in-remoteness from ordinary life and its routines, which enabled intensive learning and sometimes change to take place.

HMI were not the creators of this development. Their most important role was only a supportive one. Mainly, perhaps, it meant acting as confidential advisers to somewhat isolated wardens working with a wide range of other institutions, often struggling with LEAs' own financial problems when the relatively high cost of such provision became more obvious to them as circumstances became straitened. HMI did what they could individually in their usual style to help with such problems as they could, to keep public financial and student support, and to encourage both curricular development and good academic standards. A number of colleges were the subject of full inspection reports.

The possibility of running intensive courses occupying the waking hours of a long weekend (or even as much as a whole week) and utilising the potential for personal change brought about by being in residence, came to appeal increasingly to LEAs. It also appeared to them as a partial solution to financial problems. Earlier it commended itself to HMI concerned with local and regional training courses for AE teachers and youth workers. For these such courses became an essential aspect of inservice training. Numbers tended to be limited and could therefore be easily accommodated in most colleges where this seemed desirable. HMI also made use of the experience and the facilities of some of the colleges for their national short-course programmes.

As industry and administration followed AE in realising the benefits of residence for staff training, the LEAs themselves took up a growing proportion of space for their own staff training in the colleges they controlled. As financial support shrank further, many colleges were forced to accept ever more commercial lettings in addition to LEA training. These activities largely squeezed out most of the original purpose of residential adult education. In some colleges it disappeared. From the 1970s and especially in the 1980s a number of colleges closed altogether. Thirty remained in operation in 1997; most of these provided programmes in which only some courses still reflected the purpose of the movement's founders.

Of all the practices and structures of English AE which influenced other countries or were taken up in their entirety during the 20 or so years when it could be confidently claimed that England led the world in AE matters, the short-term residential college was one of the most influential. By the 1950s the model had been seized upon and was flourishing in places as far apart as the USA and Germany (where Army adult educators had moved into the Control Commission), and even in Denmark where the original long-term institutions were glad to introduce short courses as demand for long ones shrank. With the development of AE summer schools and indeed AE practice generally the model greatly influenced the pattern of work adopted by the Open University.

Penal education

Without question the most affecting and too often heartrending but also often encouraging visits paid by OFE HMI were those to penal establishments. Their reception would generally reflect the ethos not just of the version of education the institution held but of its whole philosophy and style. Sometimes it was suspicious and grudging, the more so as one moved from governor down to talk with individual officers. Even education could be affected. Often it was heartening to see what was achieved in appallingly difficult circumstances by hardworking and devoted educators, backed by sympathetic governors. After watching a poor inadequate young woman scribbling apathetically in what purported to be an art class because 'it helps to pass the time' one left near to tears. Even among all the suspicion, harshness and key rattling of some dispersal prison, the education wing could prove an oasis of recreation in the full sense of the word, where men or women who had been savage were becoming gentle, thoughtful, creative – and even unselfish. These were gripping assignments.

A slow start

We noted in Chapter 1 that individual HMI as well as the Board had informally interested themselves in educational provision in penal institutions before 1939 and the 1944 Act, though it is not surprising that the Act made no mention of it. Nevertheless Sir Lionel Fox, the progressive Secretary of the Prison Commission from 1924 to 1934, and its Chairman until 1960, resolved to make a fresh start (Fox, 1952) when peace and the new Education Act created the opportunity. He wanted this to be established on a properly professional basis and revived the 1938 proposal for co-operation with what was now the Ministry, and with HMI in particular. In 1946 the Commission set up a Prisoners' Education Advisory Committee, which included Margery Fry, Graham Savage (ex-HMI and now Director of Education with the LCC), WE Williams of the British Institute of Adult Education and now running the Bureau of Current Affairs which was continuing in civil life the work of ABCA, and Miss Mellanby (then a Prison Commissioner), together with HMI Mr EJW Jackson.

It produced just one report, in October 1947, which was thoughtful and farseeing if rather generalised. This argued that LEA assistance was essential to any satisfactory scheme, stressed the need for adult teaching methods to be adopted, and gave priority to the development of physical education and vocational training. However, influenced by war-time experience, it saw a place for developing discussion and interest in current affairs, the teaching of English, the arts including music and drama, and for craft activities. It advocated day education in all Borstal institutions, and the development there of self-organised activities in a 'club' atmosphere.

As early as February 1946 the Treasury agreed to the appointment of an HMI as a full-time Chief Education Officer and Assistant Prison Commissioner. Grierson, one of the four specialist RB inspectors, was suggested for the post 'since he has been in on prison education in the past' (SCI minute of 16.2.46 in ED86/55 Box in PRO). Roseveare as SCI soon made it clear, however, that nobody could be spared with all the work to be done by his diminished team. It was agreed that enquiries should be made for a candidate among senior retiring HMI, and DI Mr Jenkin was appointed to the post in 1946. He had at one time had specialist concern for approved schools.

As Director he had initially an annual budget of £4,000, two thirds of which was being spent on correspondence courses which had been offered at a cut rate by one particular firm. Much of his time was spent in fostering further voluntary class provision, but he also encouraged LEAs to follow the example of Durham. This LEA had been using, immediately after the war, what they believed to be their powers under the 1944 Act to provide FE in Prisons. Buckinghamshire followed suit, and by the end of 1946 LEAs were providing classes in 18 penal institutions, while one enjoyed classes provided by the Oxford University Tutorial Classes Committee.

Progress was now checked by the discovery that, contrary to SCI advice, LEAs were prevented by clauses in the Act (which were concerned with the exclusion of boys in Borstals from compulsory county college attendance) from using central Government grant for work in penal establishments. There were also problems connected with LEA payments for students normally resident outside the areas where they were held in penal institutions. Jenkin was thus hampered in his efforts to forward Fox's hopes of better educational provision: he was having to press LEAs to provide penal education without any Ministry grant aid. The Treasury also starved him of funds; the Prison Commission had no separate education budget, and education activity in the prisons was hampered by a mass of petty regulations.

In spite of the problems a growing number of LEAs gave notable support to penal work, and the papers in the PRO include HMI comment on their helpful attitudes. By 1948 one Borstal already had a full-time teacher in post. The Prison Commissioners also took action on the priority recommendations of the 1946 Advisory Committee regarding vocational training and physical education. Unfortunately, however, these were developed separately from what was recognised as 'Education'. Instead, vocational training was narrowly restricted to certain craft level occupations and closely linked to internal building and maintenance works and industrial production. The scope and style of physical education still tended to reflect old-fashioned army 'PT';

efforts were made to improve on it by the appointment of an organiser in 1952. He is recorded at the time as receiving some help from specialist HMI, but physical education was not considered part of the education programme and HMI were not encouraged to report on it. The major financial problem was resolved in 1952, when the Prison Commission agreed to reimburse LEAs for their expenditure. This solution was very heavily criticised by KJ Ritchie HMI, but it may well have helped in the earlier stages at least towards the spectacular subsequent development of penal education.

A new impetus

Jenkin died following a breakdown on the job in 1951. He was replaced in the Commission by an able serving governor, Charles Cape, who was given responsibility half-time for overseeing education, with welfare as the remainder of his brief. He still lacked even adequate clerical support as well as finance, and had to work by persuading individual governors. Moreover, he lacked Jenkin's status in dealing with LEAs. In a 1956 report he gave a characteristically modest description of his task as being 'to interpret the wishes of the Commissioners to the Ministry and to interpret the policy of the Ministry to those concerned in prisons and Borstals' (Banks, 1958). In reality educational progress at this time was in considerable measure due to the devotion, hard work and persuasive gifts Cape brought to the difficult ask. He sat on the HMI panel, and joined in inspections.

At the Ministry KJ Ritchie as staff inspector took over responsibility for penal education in 1952. He was a remarkable, driving and formidable though physically handicapped character, with a background in the Colonial Service and academic interests in history. For a variety of reasons he determined to make an impact on penal educational practice as well as on EIs. In this he was remarkably successful. In his own words he 'established [him]self as the sole contact between the Prison Commission and the Department'. As early as 1951 he formed a carefully selected sub-panel of able colleagues to develop expertise in this area of education. Active early members who made considerable contributions to development included Ken Ashurst, Elizabeth Hess, JA Lefroy, HES Marks, W Ray, RI Redfern, and ES and WL Roberts among others and, from 1953, Tom Cradock who also took over Ray's task of advising on literacy education.

Following the example of inspection of public schools, Ritchie restricted participation in inspection to selected specialist HMI in each division. A centrally organised programme of full inspections was agreed by SCI and the Prison Commission, and Ritchie covered 37 of these in his first three years as SI. The total had risen to 62 by his retirement in 1958, when he had personally accompanied his specialist team members on visits to every penal institution in the country, leaving a trail of shattered nerves and car seats but, above all, transformed education services.

The remarkable improvement of educational activity in penal institutions during this time was certainly due in great measure to the equally remarkable close working association which Ritchie formed with Charles Cape, and to the stimulation of the inspections. Expenditure on class provision grew from about £1,000 when Jenkin had started work, to £200,000 overall in 1958 in the 75 establishments now in existence, compared to 48 in Jenkin's early days. By 1964–65 the annual education budget stood at a half million pounds, though the effects of inflation have to be borne in mind.

Central to the policies HMI urged on the Commission (who were long resistant) was the universal appointment to institutions of full-time or at least half-time organising tutors, with better salaries and conditions. Twenty-two full-time and 30 half-time tutor-organisers were in post by January 1957. Some of the most significant early developments in the institutions resulted from these tutor-organisers' single-minded devotion to this particular area of education. However, there were built-in disadvantages to a career solely in penal education. HMI increasingly, and successfully, advocated secondment of staff for a period from LEA FE service to penal establishments, and back again.

The tutor–organisers (and subsequently other education staff) were encouraged to join others engaged in all forms of OFE on the Ministry's short courses from 1956 onwards. Much HMI assistance was also given to the Commission's own 'Education Conferences' which were organised regularly from 1952.

HMIs' observations on regular pastoral visits, and conclusions from full inspections, were regularly focused in discussions at meetings of the Prisons and Borstals sub-panel. On that basis HMI constantly pressed the need for better accommodation for penal education, for more classes to meet the constantly discovered unsatisfied demand, for changes in the restrictive regulations about repayment of material costs which inhibited the development of craft education, for the encouragement of 'homework' in cells, for better provision of books in classrooms, for improved library provision as a skilled function of the institutions' education departments, rather than under the well-meaning historic control of chaplains.

The need for better teaching is a recurrent theme of reports, and improvement was aided by the agreement of the Commissioners in 1956 that subject specialist HMI could follow up full inspection reports with pastoral visits. In later years many tutors and some full-time education staff participated in general adult education training as this developed. Development of more varied programmes was frequently urged and, particularly, more provision for the improvement of literacy at all levels. Later on pre-release classes were suggested to help inmates' re-settlement in the community after release. It was argued that classes held during the day would be justified for both purposes.

Ritchie retired in 1958. He strongly opposed a suggestion that at this point responsibility for the inspection of penal education should be passed to a

Prison Commission inspector. He was succeeded by Ted Parkinson, who retained an active interest in this among other OFE preoccupations. However, the leading HMI influence on penal education had passed by 1960 to Tom Cradock, who had been influential in the area since joining HMI in 1953. He was particularly involved with assistance on literacy problems, which linked with his background in special schools.

Organisation reinforced

In 1962 Cape retired but Duncan Fairn, who had previous experience of AE as warden of the York Educational Settlement, was appointed as Chief Director of a now re-titled and re-organised 'Home Office Prison Department'. His influence was important in fostering a new mood of experiment in penal treatment generally. Educational innovations were developed by governors in a number of institutions, particularly Borstals. One of the most imaginative was at Dover, where the governor, with the strong support of HMI, developed for selected trainees a regime based primarily on day time classes, often with examination objectives. At his suggestion, too, physical education and vocational training provision were for the first time included in an HMI full inspection. The practice soon became normal.

Probably HMI were helped by Fairn's influence when, from 1962 onwards, they pressed for educational provision to be looked at in the context of the whole regime. Sometimes this created problems for them as 'outsiders' but it became increasingly accepted. It helped especially where education officers, too long in post, had slipped from an educational into a custodial ethos. Generally their enthusiasm was remarkably well maintained in difficult and wearing circumstances. HMI, however, remembers the end of an inspection, when the education officer resisted his suggestions one by one as being impracticable 'because of security'. It was the governor who remarked, somewhat acidly, that education should seize its opportunities and leave security to him! Inspection was also concentrated year by year on particular kinds of institutions in order to focus HMI impact on educational provision, whose value seemed to be increasingly recognised by the Commission.

The absence, since Cape's retirement, of a senior figure primarily concerned with education in penal establishments, and able to give detailed attention to all the administrative and other problems arising in them, became an increasing worry to HMI. Cape was, in fact, brought back from retirement for a period to help. Nevertheless between 1963 and 1967 the development of penal education slowed generally, though in some individual establishments provision still improved. General progress was also impeded by disciplinary problems as the prison population grew, and by concentration on security following the spectacular escapes of 1966 and the ensuing Mountbatten Report.

The composition of the HMI panel changed as a number of HMI with particularly detailed knowledge and great interest in penal education retired, but others, no less committed, took their place. Cradock continued to make his major contribution as successor to Ritchie, though not as SI, until his retirement in 1974. One of his last major contributions was to lead a survey of day education in 21 penal institutions.

Chief Education Officer appointed

In the middle 1960s the HMI sub-panel's major policy preoccupation lay in continuing pressure for the appointment of a powerful director within a specific education branch of the Prison Department. Such a branch would be able itself to forward all aspects of educational provision, and not have to rely on other branches for goodwill and finance. Such an appointment, as Ritchie had argued in his retirement memorandum, would enable the Prison Department 'to stand much more on its own' and the Commission would no longer have 'to lean far too heavily on HM Inspectorate'. The post was advertised in 1965 and, after considerable delays, filled in 1967 by Alan Baxendale who had experience in the administration of FE in Britain and abroad. He was given responsibility for penal education, but vocational training was not included in his remit until 1972. He held the post until his retirement in 1985.

By 1967 educational activity had become a significant and major element of life in penal institutions, though there were still great variations in the quality and extent of what was available. Its helpfulness in the satisfactory running of institutions had become clearer. Its potential in preparing for release and helping reabsorption into the community, and possibly even in reducing recidivism for some, was recognised. To these ends vocational education and training were being developed, and eventually became integral parts of the new Chief Education Officer's responsibilities. Education directed towards preparation for release was increasingly undertaken. It had therefore also been more widely accepted as a valuable daytime activity in institutions other than those serving young people still of compulsory school age, where half day schooling had been the rule since the war. Differences in styles of provision to suit the needs of different types of institutions had become more widespread. Overall, much more education had become available, though it was still very unevenly distributed. Improvements in accommodation had been secured, staffing in institutions increased, and more fruitful links with outside FE developed.

In 1947 the prescient Prison Commission Chairman, Sir Lionel Fox, whose steady support had been so essential to educational development in difficult times, had seen its purpose as 'not to improve the general standard of education but to counteract mental deterioration, to provide interesting activities for leisure hours, to stimulate thought, to provide material for reflexion'. HMI had, especially in the two decades up to 1967, exerted a notable influence in developing such education further both in purpose and in practice.

After 1967 the newly appointed Chief Education Officer in the Prison Department of the Home Office began to establish an effective central service. OFE specialists were now much more heavily preoccupied with vocational provision in FE colleges, but continued to influence the development of penal education, if less signally. Prison education did not stand high in the new scale of priorities within which the increasingly directive central administration of HMI organised the work of individuals. Inevitably, their involvement diminished.

The Prisons and Borstals sub-panel of OFE HMI, which had been central to development, only met annually after 1968 and ceased in 1973. Its concerns rarely surfaced on the crowded agenda of the (also annual) main AE Committee, whose occasional sub-groups never included penal education. Until early in 1973, AE HMI were much preoccupied with preparation of the Russell Report. When this finally emerged it had very little to say about what it seemed to regard as a minor aspect of AE, to the disappointment of the Prison Department. Very close co-operation developed however between the new Home Office Chief Officer for Penal Education and Tom Cradock, and with the responsible SIs, Ted Parkinson and HES Marks when he took over in 1972.

Effects of HMI reorganisation

Following amalgamation of the two FE sections of HMI, and again later in the 1970s and 1980s, some efforts were made to spread knowledge and interest in the problems of penal education among current and newly appointed FE inspectors, whose expertise and concerns lay with major subjects taught in, and the organisation of, FE colleges. Some of the in-service training meetings held for them at the time dealt with penal education, but the success of such internal HMI missionary activities was variable.

However, the new HMI organisation meshed with the developing Prison Department policy of linking education in its establishments with neighbouring FE colleges. This led to some helpful HMI assistance to the vocational training programmes in penal institutions. With help from the Manpower Services Commission and related agencies this branch of prison education received growing attention after 1972.

A few of the old and some more recently appointed HMI with a 'TCA' background developed a new area of concern for penal education (Hastings, 1998). So did some new HMI from an OFE background, especially John Steel who joined in 1972 and David Hibbert (1985). With Marks's retirement and the reduction of SI posts in AE from two to one, John Steel was given special responsibility for this area of work and for liaison with the Prison Department. Close co-operation continued.

From the 1970s onwards the programme of full inspections by HMI had to be reduced in view of the diminished manpower. However, it continued for some time to be organised on the basis of, every year, taking the essential close look at work in five or six institutions of a similar type and clientèle, to assist the Home Office with policy development as well as establishments individually. Such exercises dealt in turn with the problems of most types of penal establishments. The Home Office pleaded for more help, but pressures on HMI to devote more time to what their senior colleagues regarded as their 'main duties' increased.

Work expands

From its inception the new Prison Education Branch of the Home Office had grown steadily in effectiveness and influence. It developed a proper administrative base; by 1972 it was able to develop and finance provision in the establishments on its own responsibility. Policy documents covering all aspects of its remit were prepared following discussion with HMI, and published. Page 1 of Policy Statement No. 1 of the Home Office Prison Department includes the statement:

> The Prison Department wishes to place on record their debt to HM Inspectorate for the part they have played over the years in fostering the cause of education in penal establishments, and to express their satisfaction in the continuance of the relationship.

The Chief Education Officer acquired two deputies and later four regional organisers. Library provision was greatly improved with the help of the Department of Education Library Adviser and the Library Association (Forster, 1981, ch 5). Better integration of all educational provision, including vocational training, was encouraged (*ibid*, ch 4). Relations with associated LEAs were regularised and strengthened.

By 1985 every establishment had an education officer, though some were part-time. Daytime basic education classes had multiplied to absorb 40 per cent of teaching resources by 1987, and full-time teachers were appointed to run them. Between 1967 and 1982 full-time staff numbers rose from 129 to 403, and a career structure parallel to that of the FE colleges' provision was developing.

The number of classes held had grown by more than 50 per cent over the same period, more than half of them during the day. Over the same period vocational training instructors doubled in number and dealt with two and a half times the number of trainees. Overall education expenditure, which had risen eleven-fold between 1964–65 and 1970, doubled again (at constant prices) by 1980. The expansion was genuine, but must be seen against the background of a rapid rise in the numbers incarcerated. Between 1952 and 1962 average daily population had increased slowly but remained below 25,000. By 1972 it was 38,000.

The period from 1967 to 1985 was one of genuine development and optimism. A 1991 survey showed that at its end 47 per cent of the prison population were attending classes; half the remainder wanted to do so but provision for them was not available for various reasons. Unevenness was still a hallmark of the service as it was throughout adult education. Long-term prisons and youth establishments did best; local prisons and remand centres were served relatively poorly.

Expansion began to be halted by financial cuts in the middle 1980s and provision did not keep pace with a still more rapidly rising prison population, which approached 50,000 at a time in the 1990s. Penal policies and institutional atmospheres became less and less favourable to education as a major element in regimes. At the same time diversion of resources to full-time teaching caused a reduction in the valued educational services provided by 'outside' part-time teachers. This, and the overcrowding of accommodation, led to a deterioration in quality in some places.

The Prison Inspectorate

With less HMI time available it was no longer practicable to provide the wide knowledge derived from visiting which had been central to its influence; consequently influence over developments in penal education thinking and organisation declined. At the same time the staff of the Home Office Prison Department grew. This now allowed it to draw directly on a more detailed if less independent familiarity with what was happening in establishments. From 1972 the Home Office also had its own Prison Inspectorate, which was sometimes drawn into co-operation with HMI. In 1979 this was replaced by an independent Prison Inspectorate which gained greatly in status and published its own reports. Especially under the chairmanship of Judge Tumin, it included education as an increasingly important area of its concern, and sometimes brought in independent education experts, including John Steel as HMI and after his retirement.

New influences on policy were also developing. A Home Office Advisory Committee was established in 1980 and brought together all interested parties including HMI. The National Association for the Care and Resettlement of Offenders (NACRO), under the imaginative guidance of Vivien Stern, became for a time a major contributor to thinking about the place of education in enlightened penal practice. It did so through an educational advisory committee from 1978 to 1981, whose powerful membership included two interested MPs, one a shadow minister, Lord Peston, leading LEA officers, prison education officers, and former and serving HMI. A widely read paper (NACRO, 1980) commissioned by the committee pressed the case for developing penal education and linking it with continuing further education provision available in the community after release. The working group was chaired and the paper largely written by Marks after his retirement from HMI in 1976; John Steel later became an active member. Subsequently, interest shifted to the place of education in contributing to community-based supervision and punishment, and to the necessary development of co-operation with the probation service. A DES–Home Office conference on the subject was organised in 1989–90.

Resurgence of HMI participation

Pressure for progress in educational provision as central to good penal practice grew also from the recommendations of the Enquiry into the Prison System chaired by Lord May. Other agencies developed an interest in forwarding penal education; they included the FE Staff College (which took over some prison staff training), ALBSU (on whose governing body the Chief Education Officer served), the Youth Service, and also the Arts Council. Further powerful political influence also sprang from two reports of the House of Commons Select Committee on Education and the Arts (Select Committee 1990, 1991/2).

Penal education also became a topic of international interest. As the main concerned HMI, John Steel participated in two government-sponsored international conferences, and another in 1984 organised by the Prison Department and the Open University. These led to the establishment of the International Forum for Penal Education, with a permanent UK element as part of its network.

In spite of the low priority given to penal work by HMI management, and widening alternative expertise, the Home Office still valued and asked for HMI help. In the earlier 1980s a few surveys of provision in different types of institution continued to be organised, but after 1987 penal education figured in formal inspection programmes only as part of the inspection of particular FE Colleges or of LEA FE services generally. A modest amount of pastoral visiting continued; in 1990 HMI help to penal education was estimated for the Commons Select Committee to occupy 100 HMI days overall and to involve visits to just 20 establishments. Against a background of increasing uncertainty about the future of the Inspectorate as a whole, Home Office pressure led to David Hibbert being nominated to help Steel in organising more inspection, and on Steel's retirement in 1990 he took on the 'special responsibility' until his untimely death in 1992.

In the last years of HMI's existence further pressures from the House of Commons Select Committee on Education and the role of HMI led to recognition that HMI credibility in the area must rest on improved knowledge and detailed familiarity acquired through visiting and inspection. The dilemma posed for future policy by this and the lack of HMI time was solved by the impending change of the whole basis of penal education provision from that of co-operation with local LEAs, which had been developed by the Home Office on HMI advice over the years. LEA provision of FE was about to disappear with the Further and Higher Education Act of 1992, which made the FE Colleges independent institutions financed by a Further Education Funding Council and other sources. The new Council also assumed responsibility for 'quality control' of their activities. Penal education was then the first area to suffer untried ideologically inspired privatisation into a service provided by contractors to individual penal establishments, while their governors assumed full (including financial) responsibility for educational services under the guidance of a reduced Prison Department Education branch.

The Home Office Prison department report for 1993 claims that 'the changeover to the new contractors is providing better quality education with better controls and at a lower cost, and has helped standardisation of provision and easier accreditation.' The volume of educational and vocational activity appeared for some time to remain relatively unchanged. Some still improving provision for vocational work is linked with NVQ arrangements. It remains to be seen whether the new system is likely to match the kind of imaginative stimulus to education or the evaluative expertise in penal institutions with which OFE HMI, following an older tradition, assisted so signally during the preceding half century.

However, HMI have not yet entirely disappeared from the penal education scene. When the FE Funding Council took over the FE colleges from the LEAs, the responsibilities they inherited and developed in their own ways included some concern for penal education. Theoretical OFSTED responsibilities seem in 1998 to have been largely neglected, though new HMI represent OFSTED on NACRO advisory groups concerned with crime prevention and the part schools can play therein. More importantly, a retired HMI, JB Stevenson, served with the Prison Inspectorate from 1993 to 1998. Like Cradock, he had previous experience of and a particular concern for provision in 'secure' schools.

It is difficult, however, to see where independent professional educational assistance, based in the sort of detailed knowledge which the old HMI teams brought to the job, can be found. Who, outside the Prison Department itself, and the Independent Prison Inspectorate, will be in a position to advise on the development of the role of education in regimes generally? Who will be able effectively to forward the now needed development of education and training in penal treatment in the community, paralleling the impact of HMI on penal education in the past?

'And yet,' one commentator adds, 'education continues to have a more substantial role, even an accepted presence, in the penal system than it did in 1945. Whether or not this would have happened without HMI, it did in practice *because* of HMI: possibly one of HMI's outstanding performances.'

Education in HM forces

The remarkable development in 1939–45 of education in the armed services has been noted in the present chapter and previously in Chapter 1. It had its most dramatic extension as hostilities were seen to be coming to an end.[4] Problems of demobilisation and the re-building of a post-war economy now became major concerns. There were useful, if variously effective precedents, including the development of education in the reconstruction plans after the earlier convulsion, in 1918–19.

As early as the beginning of 1944 a new Director of Adult Education in the Army, Philip Morris (later Chief Education Officer of Kent when the AE centres were created there, and to be knighted as the Vice Chancellor of Bristol University) succeeded BJ Bickersteth, and a scheme of education for the release period was formulated. The Army Education Corps was greatly enlarged; the army was scoured for educational talent and interest to provide the necessary manpower. In 1947–48 alone, 1,700 sergeant instructors were recruited and trained for the Corps and these new recruits helped to disseminate interest in and some knowledge of AE as well as providing much of the continuing staffing for the 'release educational and vocational training scheme' which ran from 1945 to 1948. Its scale was remarkable: five Army Formation Colleges were set up in the UK and another six abroad, to provide mainly hastily improvised pre-vocational training courses but also some general education. Some indication of the scale of the operation is provided by the figure of 20,000 students who passed through the Rhine Army College alone, mainly on month-long courses, in the four years of its existence. The Mount Carmel College in Haifa had been active since July 1944. In January 1946 the month's 'Modern Studies' course was led by Major Alan Champion (later of Pilgrim College, Boston), his assistant, Major Huw Wheldon (later of the BBC), and six others. It attracted 83 students to groups on Modern History, Law, English Literature, French, German, Geography and Political Theory. In the same month they had 175 students for 'Instructor Training', 21 in a 'Unit Education Officers' Course, 5 in an 'AEC Transfer Course', undefined numbers in an Arts course where the distinguished painter Leslie Marr, then an engineer, discovered his talent. In addition the College was running all the resettlement and vocational courses and provided everyone with two hours of ABCA discussion a week. 'Mr Gibbon HMI visited' and, not surprisingly, 'stayed for several days'.[5] By 1947 the work of residential colleges such as this was supplemented by the activities of 105 local education centres which were movingly described by Sir Ronald Adam (see note 4) and affectionately remembered by some future HMI who taught there.

National service was continuing, though only until 1957, and the scheme also recognised the national servicemen's need for further general education as adult citizens; it was also intended to ease their transition back into civilian life no less than that of wartime servicemen. From 1945, under this scheme, all servicemen were to receive six hours a week of education, comprising citizenship education (which included the ABCA discussion period), general education, and education in military procedures and traditions. A 'Forces Preliminary Examination' equivalent to the then School Leaving Certificate was devised to be of use to those demobilised from post-war service and, later, national service. An effort was also made to offset the wartime decline in general educational standards by the establishment of preliminary education centres. These endeavoured, in six weeks, to raise the educational level of those who needed it to that of the School Leaving Certificate courses, or remedied literacy deficiencies in those who needed such help. HMI were represented on a post-war Army Education Advisory Board chaired by the new Director and subsequently by Sir John Wolfenden. Comparable arrangements were also made for the continuing education needs on demobilisation of airmen, who were more stringently selected. The extra-mural departments' 'Regional Committees' were reorganised to continue providing effective help from the RBs and LEA colleges.

With the re-establishment of an active inspectorate after the war, HMI began to play a growing part in the work. Looking at the future of army education, Major General Cyril Lloyd (later to be Director of the City and Guilds of London Institute), the Director of Army Education (1946–49) who succeeded Philip Morris and who now also had ABCA in his remit, wrote 'Arrangements have been made with the Ministry of Education for the release scheme to be inspected by HMI from its inception. The army will welcome the continued cooperation of these experts in its educational work, and remembers with gratitude their assistance in the planning and execution of the release period scheme.'[6]

From 1943 on, one HMI gave much help to the growing 'illiteracy work' and many of those who were later to form the nucleus of the OFE inspectorate travelled widely in the UK and abroad to look at the work of the Army Education Corps (AEC) training schools for instructors, and also at the formation colleges, the local centres, and work in units.

A regular annual programme of inspections of army work was then agreed with the AEC inspectors. This activity was popular with OFE HMI as it provided opportunities, generally rare except for SIs, of foreign travel. One recalls a visit to Hong Kong, and inspecting special classes for Gurkhas 'highly motivated and producing spectacular results'. HMI were almost always accompanied by members of the newly constituted AEC inspectorate, who, of course, also inspected army education on their own.

The army valued HMI's contribution principally as a validation of the work they were doing, and also for its contribution as a source of 'practical advice', including assistance given to a 'general education handbook'. An HMI Services Education sub-panel under the chairmanship of successive SIs for RB work met regularly to consider policy and educational issues – from 1950 in the pleasant surroundings of Eltham Palace, which became home to the Institute of Army Education. It is clear, however, that the inspectorate had relatively little influence on the development of the army's education policy.

The services asked from time to time for more definite guidance on standards, but HMI continued to hold to their usual cautious approach in publicising judgments. Indeed, they went further than usual in this respect because in services education matters these judgments had to be based on one-off 'spot check' visits and not on the thorough, long-term-based knowledge which generally informed their conclusions on other institutions. They were conscious, too, that an authoritarian organisation such as any of the services might give undue weight to their advice.

Unlike the prison service, the army in particular and, to varying extent, the other services had their own well developed hierarchical structure for educational administration and policy making. In 1949 the first of a line of senior AEC officers, almost all of whom had experience of the corps before the war, took over direction. Education certificates, linked to promotion, were re-introduced as a central feature of the provision for army education. The Bureau of Current Affairs, which had briefly succeeded ABCA, was wound up in 1951 and the provision of current affairs material passed to the new Institute of Army Education. There was much discussion within the AEC about methods and purposes, including the value of and appropriate styles of work in current affairs. Indeed, the value of army education was questioned altogether, and a Major General Duff opined that it 'is mainly a waste of time' (*Army Education*, vol XXIV, no 4, December 1950). Some proposed that 'its work should be more closely [directed] to training requirements and social control' and that it should help to create in the army 'a vigorous community structure characterised by high morale'. Such views had implications for the liberal values which had so exercised education opinion before and during the war. Some members of the AEC, as well as the regional committees generally, stressed the need for education of soldiers as citizens, particularly up to the end of national service. The more restricted view, however, prevailed. The AEC became the Royal Army Education Corps (RAEC) in 1956, and in 1959 achieved its long-term ambition to become an all officer corps.

Links between services education and HMI continued. They included TCA inspections of technical education facilities which grew in importance, as well as help with more general educational work for promotion examinations at all levels. These included relatively advanced academic current affairs, defence studies, and foreign languages. With the end of national service in 1957 the army was faced with a serious shortage of junior non-commissioned ranks and 'junior leader' and similar young soldiers' units were established. HMI gave these substantial help through large-scale full inspections which were sometimes backed up by some informal visiting.

HMI had relatively little contact with education in the other two services, which tended to be mainly concerned with their technical requirements, although the RAF's concern for AE for its families was reinforced by HMI advice. The Navy, seemingly unaware of the achievements of the Seafarers' Education Service, thought educational provision for seagoing personnel impracticable until 1944 when, as one OFE colleague recalls with naval under-statement, a 'destroyer idling its way around the Russian convoys' received a collection of useful material and a guide to running an education unit and its activities. Since he was the most junior, he became education officer, and the collection enabled him to run 'a sort of evening centre with almost as many subjects as students'. Years later he met the author (John Blackie), by then a former CI for OFE, when interviewed for the Inspectorate.

It is also the case that, like the RAF, the navy was, and remains, in a posi-tion to select its recruits more stringently than the army, including higher educational standards. It assumed that its provision of the necessary science and mathematics was sufficient for the needs of sailors ('there was strong resistance to anything outside') until pressure forced a response, at any rate West of Suez. Is it possible that proverbially long naval memories thought citizenship educa-tion as provided by ABCA might not be conducive to good discipline? It certainly preferred to demobilise its wartime manpower with helter-skelter speed rather than experiment with Formation Colleges. On the other hand the navy's assistance to its cadet force was always generous and enabled it to contribute substantially to this modest segment of the Youth Service.

Notes

1. The choice of location was purely political. Cambridge was convenient, and the seat of an RB and an LEA neither of which could be accused of having influenced or contributed to the findings.
2. The principle, if not the proven methods, of compulsory three-stage training throughout FE was finally accepted by Government late in 2000 for implementation in 2001.
3. Fieldhouse (1996) summarises it in its ch 9.
4. 'Adult Education in the Forces', a masterly brief summary by General Sir Ronald Adam who had just been elected President of the British Institute of Adult Education, was delivered in his 1945 Conference Address. It is re-printed in *Aims and Action in Adult Education, 1921–1971*, London, NIAE, 1971. Interestingly it refers to the important contributions made, here as elsewhere in AE, by the ubiquitous Sir Robert Wood.
5. Information drawn from College reports in Alan Champion's papers, courtesy of Mr Huw Champion
6. In *Army Education*, vol XXI, No. 1, March 1947.

4 Community centres, other adult voluntary organisations, community development and the arts

This chapter traces HMI's relationship to a great variety of activities which share the one common denominator of not being part of the statutory sector. The voluntary youth organisations have always been an important part of the voluntary sector, but it will be more convenient to discuss the whole of youth work together in Chapter 5.

The 1944 Act acknowledged the existence of the voluntary organisations (VOs) and such institutional expressions of them as village halls and community centres as parts of OFE; moreover, it laid a duty upon LEAs to frame their plans for the post-school sector in conjunction with them, and this was re-emphasised in subsequent regulations and the guidance on the framing of FE schemes. The intention implied a degree of co-operation which was by no means always achieved. It could flourish as intended only where sympathetic LEA policies and officers, co-operative VOs and uncovenanted resources came together. Thus LEA interest in fulfilling some of their new obligations towards adult and community provision varied widely; it was often affected by social and other concerns which related to both earlier and war-time conditions and problems.

In general, though, co-operation on equal terms was rare and many LEAs (whether more or, usually, less active providers) saw themselves as sufficient if not omnicompetent. However, OFE HMI had been firmly encouraged (see p 26) to see village halls, community centres, the VOs and even museums and libraries as part of their brief, and as contributors to the quality of life to be encouraged and assisted. With the benefit of hindsight it is clear that HMI were never particularly well informed about *the whole* of this range, and their influence, in general, was patchy and limited (see pp 92–94).

Community centres

However, there was one kind of VO on which the Board and the new Ministry had developed a policy, and involved HMI. They looked first and particularly in 1944 to community centres to provide the foundation for the social and adult educational developments which they envisaged (see p 17). Practical proposals for their provision were detailed in the *Red Book* (Ministry of Education, 1944), one of the very few major statements about OFE interests which Board, Ministry or Department published.[1] It reflected the views and experience of the National Council of Social Service (NCSS) and existing community centres rather than any special knowledge on the part of HMI or

Ministry staff. For urban areas it recommended universal provision of centres by LEAs, which would also pay wardens. Centre management would be in the hands of the users who would also give much voluntary service. Village halls would be the most suitable centres for the countryside. Provision should be made for use of the facilities by young people, and for co-operation with interested local social and educational bodies. Plans for all this provision were to be inserted in the FE development schemes, to be submitted to the Ministry.

Hopes were thus raised for a widespread development of new community centres. They did not survive the bottlenecks caused in the building industry by reconstruction and innovation of all kinds, and the Ministry's restrictions on expenditure. Only a small minority of LEAs, including some which had encouraged developments before and during the war, now devoted further relatively large resources to this particular form of provision.

Inspectorate commitment outlasted the Ministry's enthusiasm. The new OFE section's Community Centres Sub-panel encouraged HMI interest and developed knowledge and policy initiatives, while the Architects and Buildings branch of the Office evolved administrative arrangements for building grants and constitutions. In the light of much later developments and insights the, then, current insistence on the inclusive neighbourhood principle proved to be unrealistic. The Sub-panel welcomed the decision to establish and finance short courses to train professional neighbourhood workers, followed by two six-month full-time courses at Fircroft College. Shorter course provision followed later. By 1947 there were 60 full-time wardens in post in the movement, and this had increased to 221 by 1956. In spite of all the obstacles the number of associations with centres of their own grew from 300 in 1947 to around 1,000 by 1960. The promotion of new associations and centres was largely the work of the movement's own enthusiastic travelling officers.

Inspectorate thinking about community centre provision and, sadly, its weaknesses, was developed through a number of reporting inspections of individual centres, based as usual upon rather more informal visiting. This helped the movement as well as the LEAs in developing policies, and standards. The National Federation of Community Associations (NFCA) was grant-aided for its work with centres by the Ministry, as was the NCSS itself for its parallel work in developing village hall provision. The NFCA was good at development, but there was much feeling that the relative failure of many centres to fulfil their potential resulted from their unhelpful model constitution, which tended to cause conflict and restrict the establishment of centres.

Approach to the task

Various factors influenced development. The interest of senior LEA officers, as in Hampshire, or of statutory authorities such as some New Towns, could be crucial. Many HMI were not sufficiently informed to take action, nor did all display similar interest in the movement, or have the same opportunities to influence it. For these among other reasons the rate varied at which different kinds of VOs sprung up in assignment territories. If community centres grew in the wake of some individuals, village halls thrived in that of others, just as later co-operative and community development schemes seemed more likely to materialise where yet other HMI had operated. Such differences were minor and in no way the result of policy; they simply grew from the ways in which HMIs' earlier backgrounds and immediate preoccupations caused them to react to the opportunities and pressures in different contexts. Those serving in great cities were unlikely, after all, to be associated with village hall development and had their hands more than full with large institutions.

Given the size of OFE assignments and the way of life they generated, anything resembling an attempt to know, assist and encourage the whole of the voluntary sector in any OFE HMI's assignment would have been impracticable even if the LEAs, the RBs and the schools had not existed. Those with a specialist concern for this area of work could attempt it in a small LEA's area, and be aware of virtually all those groups which might be to some extent affected by the statutory services to which HMI related. Conversely, a non-specialist would only be likely to know organisations where problems had arisen, and this may have affected their perspectives. Generally knowledge in this field tended to be patchy and uneven; however, wherever detailed knowledge existed it was often possible to extrapolate from it.

For much of the time most HMI reacted to events in this area rather than inspecting systematically. A surprising variety of stimuli might trigger reactions on HMI's part, if nothing else. Thus, an MP's letter to the Charity Commission about alleged misuse of a local 'institute' – a late eighteenth century village reading room now stranded in a large conurbation – turned out to arise from a minor local squabble. However, it revealed the existence of a rarely used building ideally suited for day time AE classes, which the committee were happy to let to the LEA. A market town wanted a swimming pool and needed advice on how to set up an organisation, a steering committee to plan a voluntary and co-operative scheme, and find out about funding. A choir had lost its volunteer conductor and wanted to know how to fill the gap. A young mother, claiming support from her friends, wanted to set up a children's playground. The possible range of demands was very wide, resources were exceedingly scarce, but HMI could and did help surprisingly often.

The most common stimulus was an application for capital grant under the Social and Physical Training Regulations, to assist in constructing a village hall, a community centre or improved sports facilities. HMI's role was to investigate the viability of the project, the strength of its support and its potential uses; if it was viable in principle, then advice on further support (and users and funds) might be given, and help with planning. At a practical level, OFE HMI made a valuable contribution over the years simply by persuading applicants to think fundamentally, in terms of well-equipped and flexible multi-use buildings rather than the traditional reach-me-down of long narrow tunnel-shaped huts with a permanently fixed but inadequate platform stage, and the unergonomic tubular stacking chairs which had long been the heritage of VOs.

There were relatively few individual exceptions where HMI could be said to be proactive in the manner suggested by CI's 1950 Memo to Inspectors (see p 26). Indeed, it proved impracticable to construct a reliable picture of just how large was the universe of adult VOs in any locality, and the experience of some New Towns in this field was ignored. Even the attempts made by some HMI in the 1960s to make really complete trawls of the needs and resources of partic- ular areas, by surveying all forms of leisure provision and activity, only succeeded fully in one small and isolated community. Elsewhere HMI conducting the surveys came up with tallies in the range of three or four VOs per 1,000 in the population, which were comparable to those of very recent well-known studies such as those on which Deakin (1996) relied. They had no inkling of the real density (averaging 20 to 25 VOs per 1,000) of voluntary endeavour in local communities – knowledge which was left for the researches of former OFE HMI to uncover many years later.

During our period neither the knowledge nor the means of discovering it were available. There was invariably goodwill, a readiness to help energetically when approached and an intelligent perception of how this might be done most effectively. But, by and large, HMI's relationship to the adult voluntary sector was mostly willing but limited. Their position was much as it had been on one occasion, when HMI, on loan to the Indian Government, arrived with his Indian colleague in a remote Rajasthani village at nightfall. They were invited to sit down and everyone assembled in respectful silence. Then the crowd parted. Two men escorting a very ancient blind woman came forward and she asked who the visitors were. Told that one was Her Majesty's Inspector from the Vilayat, she cried out for all to hear that he had 'come to us from the Protectress of the Poor' and proceeded to give him her blessing, as he embraced her feet. If not quite the way HMI were received at English village halls or community centres, it reflected the same assumption that they came as friends and potential helpers who would listen to problems and woes, sympa- thise with difficulties, do their best to think of practical ways of overcoming them, or help to loosen purse-strings a little – but represented remote powers.

Co-operative relationships

However, various forces were at work throughout the period which were to make for change in this relationship. One was internal to OFE HMI. It sprang from their consistent advocacy of ways to introduce student responsibility, autonomy and as much by way of democratic structures as practicable throughout AE (and Youth Work), which has been mentioned in its own context (see p 52f). HMI gave their support, wherever possible, to self-governing VOs where they existed, and especially where they had a recognised AE element in their work, as with the relatively well developed women's organisations. They encouraged LEA and RB institutions to assist them, for instance by means of affiliation schemes which provided them with such tuition, meeting rooms, equipment as might be required. Thus a physical education specialist tutor might be found to act as coach and to conduct circuit training in a school gymnasium for an amateur football club, or a dramatic society would have the use of rehearsal space and receive tuition in the form of a qualified person to act as its producer. The rehearsals, or training sessions, would be recorded under class regulations, but the autonomy of the VO was not infringed. Another increasingly common outcome of HMI's attempt to encourage higher standards in AE institutions was the creation of graded courses wherever possible, to enable students to progress in the subject or activity of their choice. They were encouraged to hive off groups of students who had progressed through such schemes into autonomous VOs. These continued practising on their own while using the facilities of the AE centre and were able to call upon specialist assistance when they felt in need of it. In these and similar ways support for and the extension of the voluntary sector were a natural outcome of HMI's support for AE in general.

In addition to help at the local level, nominated OFE HMI were able to assist some of the wide variety of national VOs through their role as assessors to their central committees. They helped mostly through their direct contacts with senior staff of these organisations, but also attended some meetings of central bodies and visited locally. Links with the NFCA have been mentioned in this connection; those with the national headquarters of the women's voluntary organisations were often particularly fruitful as, for example, in Kay Tobin's work with the National Federation of Women's Institutes and its Denman College on the content and standards of their work.

The impact of community development

The community development movement was changing the emphasis of public perceptions affecting informal community and social education; it became a major force for change in the relationship between HMI and the voluntary sector. Community development was pioneered by British colonial officers working in, especially, West Africa. Returning to the UK, their ideas and their teaching were rapidly taken up by the British Council and propagated worldwide in the 1950s. They made an especially powerful impact in the USA. In Britain teaching (pre-eminently by TR Batten at the London University Institute of Education) and practice (eg, Peter Kuenstler's in the East End of London, Muriel Smith's with the London Council of Social Service, John Spencer's Bristol Social Project and the work of some New Town social development officers) were slower to develop but benefited from the supportive interest of the Gulbenkian Foundation. Surprisingly little was known more generally until English professionals returning from visits to the US began to reinforce the quiet work of the pioneers. Batten's (1957) seminal work, a development of his British Council handbook which was never publicly available in the UK, was the first substantial publication to explain and support the practice of community development.

The 'colonial' model largely overlaid, or – as some would maintain – submerged a more individual and flexible indigenous pattern of work which developed from pre-1939 voluntary sector trends in the UK and found its culmination in the work of some social development officers in the post-war New Towns. By the late 1950s the attitudes and working practices of some serving OFE HMI and some who were to join in 1960 and soon after, had been strongly influenced by both patterns of work. HMI were hardly in the habit of rushing into new practices, but a first survey to take a whole coherent community, study its social and economic structure, resources and educational and leisure needs, and *then* set the findings of a reporting inspection of OFE provision against this before making recommendations, was conducted in 1964–65. Before it was completed the decision had been taken at the top of the inspectorate that, politically speaking, there was now a chance to pick up from the *Red Book* of 1944 and develop a modern community policy for the DES. Meanwhile, however, the Department and HMI continued to support the community association movement and to help, advise and also grant-aid new centres as well as sports provision through the Physical Training and Recreation mechanism, until this duty was transferred to LEAs in 1975.

HMI became somewhat disenchanted with the community centre movement, at any rate as the main institutional basis for AE and related social development as envisaged in 1944. In the early 1960s the responsible CI noted that the movement seemed to have 'lost its way'. The reasons were complex, partly due to the rigidity of a constitutional and organisational pattern based on subsequently overtaken notions of 'community'. The pattern had been adopted long ago, while now neighbourhood had come to be seen as not the only or even the best basis for community organisation. Still, the number of centres continued to grow, if slowly, and some were outstandingly successful in affluent areas like Lymington in Hampshire, and also in solid old working class housing estates (Clarke, 1990). They failed, however, to attract the support particularly of the relatively deprived in the urban population.

Another element suggesting the timeliness of a review of DES policy in this area may have been increased interest in the place of the community school or community college in educational provision, and concern for its effect on adult and youth work. The most substantial development came as early as 1964. A Community Working Party of OFE HMI was set up by CI Salter Davies, very typically with a set of radically searching 'Questions for Discussion' as well as a formal brief. Its composition must have been devised with care. Its chairman, SI Ted Parkinson, a man of fierce energy and driving analytical intelligence and an early pioneer in his time in the field, is certain to have been closely concerned. It included two members with deep knowledge of old-established HMI expertise and the range of work in the field, one of the original post-war OFE HMI with close links to major national VOs, two joint secretaries who combined field expertise and organising ability with a nose for politics, and two driving proactive 'young Turks' with recent practical and research experience. Using his team's range of skills, the chairman secured what could almost be described as a cornucopia of, eventually, some 30 papers during the three years of the working party's official existence. They ranged from surveys and evaluations of relevant current policy and field practice in the UK and abroad, to intensive studies of particular areas, organisations, institutions or practices, reporting inspections of work of particular interest, philosophical, economic and political aspects of the topic, a search of all the relevant literature and even the creation of the first ever international bibliography of community studies. The latter was deposited in the DES Library with a view to being kept up to date and made publicly available, but quickly forgotten.

In 1966, when the working party had completed its draft report, 'English Educational Policy and the Community', all the conditions – educational, political and economic – seemed favourable for it to make an impact comparable to HMI influence on evening institutes. Even so, problems appeared in making the final text acceptable to the Office. Draft upon draft was hammered out among a certain amount of wailing and gnashing of teeth. Before agreement could be reached on this, the financial crises of the later 1960s supervened; then the not altogether unsympathetic Minister fell victim to Labour's election defeat, and was replaced by the young Mrs Thatcher. It became clear that the effort to persuade the Office to adopt a community policy, however anodyne, must be abandoned.

On the surface this might appear to be an instance of expensive wasted time. Yet there can be no doubt that the working party's influence was considerable. Its enquiries had affected the thought and practice of the many institutions and organisations which had been studied by it. Its papers and draft reports had been read by a large number of people, and continued to be borrowed from its members for many years. Its findings made their way through DES and other courses into the common stock of thinking on the subject.

The ideas inherent in community development and its aims, such as interdependence, co-operation, autonomy, the common pursuit of 'quality of life', the mutuality between the voluntary and statutory sectors, spread rapidly and surfaced again in a variety of forms and activities. They affected a number of early developments which were stimulated by the Youth Service Development Council, the Home Office's Community Development Projects, the Urban Programme and the Department's own Educational Priority Areas policy. It should not be imagined that OFE HMI were the sole or even the main proponents of community development thinking. What is certain, however, is that the working party's exercise had caught the attention of audiences which might not have been brought to listen by other means.

One immediate practical and substantial local outcome survives. Early in the working party's life one of its members was asked by the local community council at Ingleton (Yorkshire) to visit and discuss a problem. As a result, the meeting asked HMI to survey and conduct a reporting inspection of all provision in the area. This intention was converted into a joint exercise by local people and HMI to lay the foundations for a community development project. The local community took this on board, constructed their own organisational base, and began a process of creating facilities and transforming opportunities which, after more than 30 years, still continues. However, outcomes such as this, the comprehensive locality studies and reports, and some of the Working Party's cross-disciplinary and cross-departmental papers found no echoes in either HMI or departmental thinking. The problem was, and remains, that community development takes its point of departure from people, their needs, intentions and resources, while both education and government in general continue to think in terms of given subjects and structures.

OFE, the school, and 'community'

Since this aspect of educational community policy touches upon both AE and the YS, as well as the VOs, it may be more economically considered in the present context. In its institutional form the attempt to integrate services originated between the two world wars in the Cambridgeshire village colleges of Henry Morris. By the early 1960s a number of other LEAs had initiated comparable developments. The most active of these was Leicestershire which opened its first 'community college' in 1954. It and several other LEAs were developing their overall educational provision, including AE, the YS and use by VOs on this basis.

The original version of the concept was based (among other notions) upon a geographical understanding of the nature of community. In that original rural context it had a dual function: to counteract rural depopulation and ensure the availability of a wide range of opportunities for the whole of an isolated and largely immobile local population. It was achieved by placing the, then, modest range of out-of school or post-school activities under the school's organisational roof and making modest additions to school buildings and staff to enable non-school activities to take place during the day as well as the evening, when the whole of the buildings would be available.

The model worked well in the conditions and times for which it was designed, and where the full pattern of wide provision was respected. However, in the 1950s and 1960s the need for expanding, and professionally delivered, AE and YS provision, as well as for other necessary socio-economic developments, was becoming increasingly clear. The school-based pattern of meeting all these needs often raised many problems of use, access and curriculum. Because of the manner in which these institutions usually organised staffing for their post-school work they came, increasingly, to differ from ordinary schools with FE wings (see below) used by professional AE or YS. The main reason was that in village or community colleges post-school work was usually controlled and staffed by individuals whose professional expertise and career commitment belonged to school teaching.

The 'community school movement' had many very vocal advocates, including some HMI with only schools experience. Its value to school pupils was undoubted, and considerable pressure was brought to bear upon OFE HMI, mainly from outside the inspectorate, to advocate the model as generally desirable and as the most advantageous and effective way of delivering support for AE, youth work and the voluntary sector. In the light of the field evidence, OFE HMI remained generally unconvinced. After the demise of the OFE section, pressures on behalf of the 'community school' became so strong that individual HMI and finally the adult education committee felt the need for a substantial test of the evidence. Reporting inspections of all individual types of such institutions were carried out, and a substantial sample made the subject of a national survey in the mid-1970s. This enabled comparisons of standards and efficiency of their AE and Youth provision to be made with the work of more conventional models. The outcomes confirmed that more effective work and use of physical resources could be expected from those who were committed to, organised and trained for the work they were doing, than from placing provision and resources under the control of individuals whose major interest and expertise lay elsewhere. The survey also provided evidence of the weakness of whatever influence remained to HMI concerned with non-vocational and non-school activities: it was suppressed within the hierarchy, as were a number of papers on related topics.

However, a different arm of the Department sponsored an important national research project to compare the effectiveness of free-standing, FE college-based and community school provision of AE (Mee and Wiltshire, 1978). The National Institute of Adult Education also commissioned a more limited study (Jennings, ND/1980), to which HES Marks, now retired, contributed. Both projects had the support of OFE HMI. Those caring to read the research reports had access to the evidence.

The old geographical concept of community, misapplied in the Milson and Fairbairn reports to the Youth Service Development Council (see p 118, 119, 120f), also surfaced in the concept of 'community education', which was usually applied as a fusion of AE and youth work. It was first given respectability by the Scottish Alexander Report, which hoped to reinforce an exceedingly weak AE provision by drawing on much stronger youth work resources. Persuaded by the publicity created as a result of the combined Milson–Fairbairn report, and an apparently total absence of any policy steer or other interest on the part of the Department, a number of English LEAs rushed into similar arrangements. The need for savings in the light of renewed stringency may also have played a part. Educational services provided by AE to youth work may well have become more easily obtainable, but educational standards in AE and the appropriateness of youth provision could both suffer (see p 121).

In general the Department left LEAs free during the late 1960s and early 1970s, without central advice on whether or not to develop a community schools policy. However, it gave capital assistance and help with experimental design problems to some, and inspections by schools and OFE HMI together helped some individual institutions. Other LEAs did what they could within normally available limits; most did not experiment with this form of provision.

Broader initiatives

OFE HMI were little called upon to help local or central efforts to follow up (mainly through primary schools) the *Plowden Report*, to meet the needs of designated Educational Priority Areas, or to develop adult contributions to the amelioration of their problems. Together with the Youth Service Development Council, they had rather more involvement with projects initiated by the Department of the Environment under the Urban Aid programme, wherever these had some educational content. Centrally they gave some advisory assistance also to the Home Office when, in 1969, its newly established Voluntary Service Unit initiated a series of large-scale community development projects with unprecedentedly generous funding. A further large-scale experiment, launched in 1973 under the joint aegis of the Departments of the Environment and Education, was intended to provide a model for the improvement of leisure facilities and enhance the 'quality of life'. It involved four sites (two in England) selected according to criteria whose choice was said at the time not even to raise doubts, generously funded but only for three years. As far as has been discovered, OFE HMI were only consulted when some of the results were to be assessed. One of those concerned commented with inspectorial restraint: 'The outcomes were, as usual, a curates's egg.'

The arts and OFE

As OFE developed, the practice and appreciation of the arts had been growing substantially in formally provided AE and, both with AE help and independently, in very many VOs, and in statutory and voluntary youth clubs. There it was indirectly fostered by the National Youth Theatre and Youth Orchestra movements and their Local Authority links and offspring. National youth organisations modestly encouraged the performing arts, and both schools and OFE HMI were involved at all levels. A number of Government initiatives added to the momentum of developments in which non-educational services,

AE, the YS and VOs were so interwoven that it seems best to discuss them as part of this chapter rather than attempt to disentangle developments which benefited from not being based in a single organisational framework.

The 1965 White Paper *A Policy for the Arts – the First Steps* was followed by a Joint Circular of the DES (8/65) and the Ministry of Housing and Local Government (53/65). It summarised the substantial powers and opportunities open to Local Authorities at all levels, including the raising of a rate for the arts. It encouraged action and co-operation between Local Authorities, Local Education Authorities, all phases of the education service, and both amateur and professional organisations in the arts, in creating active local and regional policies. The use of 'Housing the Arts' grants was encouraged, and local government was urged to lead in setting up local arts centres as well as local and regional arts associations and committees. In 1969 the DES followed this up with an Administrative Memorandum (9/69) which gave guidance on the creation of arts facilities 'in educational and other establishments'.

HMI generally, and certainly OFE HMI, had very little if any connection with the framing of these policies, which seemed to pay relatively little attention to the large and enthusiastic public commitment to voluntary amateur participation or to study, appreciation and practice of the arts in AE and some YW. The main concern, as the policies were interpreted, appeared to be with providing more facilities for professional performance including new art forms, and encouraging the formation of more and bigger audiences for them. 'Community Arts' provided some local exceptions to this. However, for OFE HMI in the field there was the challenge of trying to encourage a fuller and if possible more democratic exploitation of the opportunities. Several of them were much involved with local AE professionals in helping to persuade local government to use its powers to raise an arts rate and to set up representative local committees to spend it. In this way some local adult education centres and some community centres became the arts centres for their areas. HMI were also instrumental in encouraging the creation of some of the Regional Arts Associations and ensuring that the interests of amateur practitioners in the voluntary, AE and YW sectors were given a voice in them.

A remarkable and widespread development of arts centres followed upon these government initiatives. By 1976 there were 113 arts centres in England, a few of them linked with AE centres. A number of the community development projects and some special youth projects had also been arts-based, and their support had come from Local Authorities and private sources as well as the Arts Council. HMI connections at policy levels remained restricted. In the mid-1970s, when an OFE staff inspector was invited in a personal capacity to join an Arts Council working group concerned with these developments, professional arts practitioners generally were expressing hostility to ideas of developing closer connections with arts provision in AE agencies, fearing that this would 'put off' participants.

Arts Council policies continued to be preoccupied with funding professional activity and encouraging subsidised passive participation. Interested HMI, however, sought by their activities in the field to build bridges; they tended, rather, to see opportunities to raise the standards of amateur participation and provide professionals with more sensitive and knowledgeable audiences. Some slight echoes of this were to be found in the 1976 Redcliffe-Maud Report to the Gulbenkian Foundation on *Support for the Arts in England and Wales*. The remarkable development of education in the appreciation of the arts which followed was largely due to the concern and work of Sir Roy Shaw, a distinguished adult educator before he became Secretary General of the Arts Council. Adkins (1981), in describing the situation and making proposals for the future, shows no HMI impact at this policy level.

There was some nationally inspired and focused activity by OFE specialist HMI. Led by the SI for AE and in co-operation with Robert Hutchison of the Arts Council, they carried out a short series of full inspections of AE establishments specialising in the practice and study of the arts and one voluntary arts centre closely linked with an AE centre. The resulting reports were of great interest and may have helped to shape Arts Council policy as well as encouraging further development in the field.

The end of professional involvement

HMI's direct and particular relationship to the voluntary sector was necessarily diminished with amalgamation into a single FE inspectorate, simply because they had less time than ever, and fewer tentacles in the community. A single HMI retained a role as assessor to the major national women's voluntary organisations, and probably devoted more time to it than intended. In 1978 the Home Office Voluntary Service Unit took over from the DES the task of aiding the now re-titled National Council for Voluntary Organisations and the growing number of voluntary service agencies. Also included was the National Association of Voluntary Organisations (later 'Community Matters'), which developed more comprehensively work previously confined to the community associations and centres. For the DES as well as for HMI an era of attention to voluntary organisations had come to an end, presaging changes in concern for adult culturally oriented education, which were soon to follow.

Some former OFE HMI carried their interest in VOs into retirement and devoted to it expertise they had gathered earlier. Sometimes this led to active participation, but also to teaching, research and publications.

Note

1. See Clarke, R. (ed.) (1990) *Enterprising Neighbours*, London, NFCO and CPF for details of the origin and subsequent development of the community centre and association movement.

5 The Youth Service

We noted in Chapter 1 that active Departmental interest in youth work was stronger than in AE (other than that of the RBs), for a variety of reasons, both before and during the 1939–45 war years. War-time conditions had led to efforts to improve its organisation and coverage. Concern for young people linked always with school purposes; to this was added particular worry about the effects of social disruption and blackout on their well-being; powerful and very well connected individuals and groups were interested in youth welfare; well established voluntary organisations could and did exert pressure. By the end of hostilities there was, however, still no volume of HMI expertise in this area of OFE.

The 1944 Act made no specific mention of the Youth Service, a matter of disappointment to many but probably due to oversight rather than deliberate policy. As with other OFE developments the service relied for legislative approval, and the willingness of LEAs to fund, on the generalisations of Sections 41 and 43.

Circular 133 of 1947 required Local Education Authorities to produce plans for the development of the Youth Service as for other FE areas. The schemes which materialised varied widely in intention and scope. Some, like those of the LCC with its considerable existing provision for young people, and other large cities such as Liverpool and Nottingham, were far-reaching and carefully thought out. London's recreational evening institutes were quickly supplemented with LEA-provided youth clubs. Services developed rapidly in other Authorities, especially Essex, Middlesex, Derbyshire, Hampshire and New Towns such as Stevenage, which were in the van. On the other hand there were otherwise outstanding LEAs which had no statutory youth provision at all prior to the Albemarle Report.

Circular 133 had offered HMI help to LEAs in their planning. The relatively uninformed advice of pre-war HMI including Salter Davies, RE Williams and women inspectors like Miss Cowper and Miss Power, was early supplemented by new recruits. Winifred Evans came from the Girls' Clubs; Carrie Stimson had had relevant research as well as practical experience; Charles Harvey came from the Cooperative Youth Movement; Margaret Rishworth from an LCC institute; Wyn Daniel (later Doubleday) and later (1949) Ted Sidebottom from well established county services; and Ted Parkinson had been already in charge of a county FE provision. A panel was established by 1949 with RE Williams as its chair. In 1948 a full inspection of Manchester youth provision had provided a training opportunity for HMI as well as being a first attempt to take a comprehensive look at a youth service.

With expert guidance now available, HMI over the whole country began the novel and fascinating experience, always central to their effective contribution, of looking at and later reporting on a type of social institution often very different from school, and indeed any other provision with which they were familiar.

The new area of concern presented many HMI with difficult problems of understanding purposes as well as of assessing success and value. Generally, their interest was heartily welcomed, though on occasion one was turned away from the door even of a grant aided voluntary club; a rather tall pair of HMI had difficulty in persuading a Bradford club that they were not police officers. Progress in developing the service was very variable. If the LCC by 1953 had enormously increased the scope of its work, Kent still relied some years later on grant aided voluntary clubs and had no responsible County Youth Officer. Other authorities were reluctant to cooperate fully with voluntary youth organisations, a central requirement of the DES policy. They may also have found the task difficult in view of the diversity and usually national structure of the voluntary sector, and their ignorance of its extent.

Building restrictions hampered the development of youth work as of other OFE; the Youth Service in general was marked by improvisation and make-do, with clearly inadequate resources. HMI helped as they could with thoughtful and increasingly professional advice and with a show of interest and concern. They supported an overwhelmingly untrained group of voluntary enthusiasts.

More formal Ministry help came at first in relation to the training of full-time leaders. The MacNair Report of 1944 had already looked at the relation-ship between the training and status of youth leaders in relation to school teaching. Departmental committees in 1949 (under the chairmanship of the OFE CI) and 1951 looked further at the problem. HMI were constructively involved in the creation of national voluntary youth organisations' training schemes from 1948. The impact of these national courses was soon felt and led to local development. It was closely followed by the inception of courses at Westhill College, Birmingham, and at Swansea University College. A Central Advisory Council pamphlet, *Out of School,* of 1948 helped to feed interest in the role of the Youth Service and led to continued growth and development.

So in the same year did a big Jubilee Trust conference held at Ashridge, in which HMI participated. So did young people themselves. The 1950s saw the emergence of what became recognised as a youth culture, with the growth of adolescent groups roaming the streets and with occasional violence involved, even of a racist character. The groups sometimes coalesced into informal movements first of the teddy boys, then mods and rockers, later skinheads and hippies. Some were mobile and able to travel beyond local areas. The change was paralleled in other countries.

With increasing affluence as the economy improved, young people for the first time became recognised as a relatively independent and autonomous group in society. Their 'youth culture' was fostered by commercial interests which quickly recognised the emergence of an important new market.[1] There was much criticism of the alleged stereotyped poverty of the culture as well as apprehension about its effects on the fabric of social control.

A memorandum of 1951 from one of the OFE SIs (WR Elliott who later became SCI) closely concerned with the Youth Service in its early days, summarised views being pressed by HMI at this time. He commented:

> The following paragraphs set out the main difficulties encountered in Youth Service, and suggest some possible ways of meeting them.
>
> 1. Ignorance of the purpose and aims of Youth Service on the part of the general public, and lack of understanding of the club technique, and lack of sympathy with young people, constitute the greatest number of problems. There is a good deal of opposition to Youth Service in the teaching profession, many members of which do not recognise youth work as a part of the educational system: where it is accepted as such it has to meet similar opposition and criticism to the 'activity' methods in schools. The low standard of work in some civic youth clubs, where everything is provided, stimulates such criticism.
> 2. The establishment of LEA clubs and centres which are generously staffed by untrained and in some cases inexperienced leaders, all of whom are paid, is threatening to kill voluntary effort. It is also resulting in poor standards.
> 3. There is an acute shortage of voluntary helpers and leaders due to 1 and 2: another difficulty is that people with time and money to devote to worthy causes no longer exist.[2] Voluntary helpers will have to be recruited from fresh fields in future.

Elliott and other HMI in their reports pinpointed other problems, notably failure to cope effectively with behavioural problems, lack of leadership skills in extending the range of interests and activities, especially of an educational character, failure to provide for the needs of girls, failure on the part of Authorities to provide adequate accommodation which would allow the work to develop.

These seemingly negative internal comments were based on close HMI contacts especially with the voluntary youth organisations which, at that time, were responsible for the bulk of youth work, and especially with their national and local training schemes. Elliot's memorandum was therefore able to propose a number of helpful measures. They included concentration on the training of leaders through conferences and courses, taking full account of the voluntary organisation methods which needed to be studied, and the issue of a pamphlet elaborating and supporting the aims of the Youth Service as part of education, or a more general publication dealing with all aspects of the education of young workers.

The pace and effectiveness of HMI visiting and inspection of OFE was stepped up by the circulation in 1955 of a fairly comprehensive *Inspection Supplement* to the standard HMI handbook of procedures (see p 30f). The Youth Service benefited considerably, at least by more systematic and knowledgeable observation and evaluation of its work, and consequently a clearer account of its problems as they were seen by HMI. Moreover, visits of inspection helped individual clubs and leaders, and HMI effort was devoted with varying success to informing LEAs and pressing them to provide better facilities and more support to the work. It may be a mistake to assume that the more limited distribution of franker full inspection reports made these less effective than later published ones. Reports were in the hands of the clubs and services concerned, of leaders, management committees, LEA officers and elected members, and they were discussed with them. It is hard to believe that exposure in the press would have made them an even more effective means of educating the providers.

All this amounted to a substantial inspection effort. It was strategically important in preparing opinion and furnishing expertise for the launch of the Albemarle Committee, for its choice of areas and clubs to visit, and of witnesses to invite. Later, and in tune with Albemarle themes, the ubiquitous influence of the Salisbury courses in supporting and encouraging workers and related administrators in national VOs, the LEAs and the Office should also be noted.

HMI was not the only source of pressure. Whether or not this followed Elliott's pamphlet suggestion, also in 1955 the King George V Jubilee Trust issued a report, *Citizens of Tomorrow.* It looked at four aspects in the development of young people: school; the influence of employment after school; the influence of leisure time post school; and the influence of a period in the armed services, which the report saw as particularly important in view of the unexpectedly early termination of National Service. However there had been considerable development of cadet forces of the three services during 1939–45 and of outward bound adventure courses together with Kurt Hahn's County Badge scheme afterwards. All these were seen as part of the Youth Service, and many regarded military service as a 'good thing' though others questioned the educative effects which were claimed for it and for the more extreme interpretations of the Outward Bound philosophy. HMI, particularly physical education and some other schools specialists, had substantial influence on the schemes and tended to emphasise more humane and educative aims and methods. Somewhat later, the Duke of Edinburgh's Award Scheme bore some relation to these developments, but was closer to contemporary educational thinking, though its effect was gradual. By the 1960s and 1970s it was helping to meet some of the needs which had been identified in Elliott's memorandum of 1951. It brought large numbers of adults and young people into fruitful contact, sometimes through the agency of AE provision, and developed a number of useful common practices throughout the youth service. All HMI YS specialists had at least some contact with the Scheme, and some influenced it more substantially at regional and national levels.

Both HMI and the Ministry gave evidence to the Jubilee Report, through its four working parties (all of distinguished membership and diverse approach). These unanimously saw the contribution of parents and home as the most profound in childhood and adolescence. Adults with whom young people came into contact in their daily life, teachers in school and FE, employers or youth leaders were seen as important adult role models. 'The evidence before us', the Report said, 'suggests that in recent years there has been some weakening of the sense of parental and personal responsibility ...' It also stated 'the road back to responsibility is the road back to Christian principles'.[3] The detailed arguments and recommendations for the Youth Service included an increased provision of leisure time facilities; additional funding; a policy for the recruitment, training and conditions of service of professional leaders; the establishment of a 'National Youth Advisory Council for Education ... to deal with questions relative to every aspect, including leisure, of the welfare of all young people whether at school, at work or in the services'. This report was used by the voluntary youth organisations (and particularly the large number with religious links) as evidence to apply pressure on the Ministry to act in the vacuum created by the lack of aims and resources in the YS.

Albemarle Committee set up

The various pressures were enhanced by many individual reports from educationalists and sociologists, as well as from HMI on clubs and on ILEA and other LEA services. They combined with the 'menacing' statistic that the 14–20 population was expected to rise from just over 4 million to just under 5 million between 1957 and 1964 and to fall only slightly until well into the 1970s. All these pressures helped to decide the Ministry of Education to appoint a Committee under the chairmanship of the Countess of Albemarle:

> To review the contribution which the Youth Service of England and Wales can make in assisting young people to play their part in the life of the community, in the light of changing social and industrial conditions and of current trends in other branches of the education service: and to advise according to what priorities best value can be obtained for the money spent.

The Committee worked from November 1958 to February 1960 and presented its report in 1960. This (with modifications and developments) laid the foundations of the modern Youth Service, and these have generally remained in place. Because of the short time-scale the Committee set itself, it limited its parameters primarily to the Education Service (closely linked to school): it has been criticised by some for not looking more widely at other important social, economic and administrative influences on the Youth Service, including that of other Government departments.

HMI influence in the deliberations was significant. Great efforts were made to ensure that the Committee would receive evidence from every known source of expertise. An HMI specialising in Youth Service matters (EJ Side-bottom) was seconded as Secretary; the CI for OFE (Salter Davies) attended all meetings and serviced the Committee with information and ideas available from HMI inspection reports. The fact that OFE specialists were so few, but were known to form a high and respected proportion of the relatively small YS profession (see p 152f), made it possible for the Committee to know and make use of most of them, and of their field as well as their current experience. Members of HMI have happy memories of taking Lady Albemarle and her colleagues to clubs they knew. Office personnel also serviced the Committee.

The Committee's Report commented upon HMI at unusual length (paras. 177–78). It described their roles and methods of keeping in touch with the Ministry, the voluntary sector organisations, the LEAs, and the work in the field, in linking all these with each other, and in informing and advising them. It stressed the importance of the reliable local knowledge HMI were able to supply, and relied upon them to continue their work of raising standards. They were to remain a major source of information and policy advice to the new Youth Service Development Council and the Ministry. The Committee asked for a 'sufficient number' of HMI with youth work assignments and 'sufficient priority' to be given to them. With sensitive appreciation of HMI's confidential relationships to the Office, the field, and their duties under the Act, the Committee wisely did not comment formally on the way HMI had been pressing LEAs to do better by their Youth Services.

Albemarle recommendations

The Report's main recommendations were for a ten year development plan (five for catching up, a second five for the establishment of a secure permanent structure for the Youth Service); this should be overseen by an advisory committee to be called the Youth Service Development Council (YSDC); opportunities for 'association, training and challenge' should be offered by the Youth Service – an important development from the previous Maud Report's vague call to meet the needs of young people in 'mind, body and spirit'. Albemarle called also for a 'generous and imaginative building programme' for Youth Service with specific attention given to the design, decoration, and furnishing of buildings by the Architects and Buildings Branch of the Ministry; the needs of the Youth Service should be taken into account in the planning of new secondary schools and improvements to existing ones (eg, with wings or club facilities); residential provision for a variety of activities, indoor and outdoor, should be expanded; the Ministry of Education should establish a programme for long-term training of full-time leaders with easy transfer possibilities (never achieved) to other professions from which full-time leaders should also be recruited. Full-time training done by Youth Service voluntary organisations should be recognised when appropriate; grants to students in Youth Service training should be increased in range and number with a target of 600 new youth leaders by 1966 (with 90 in the first and 140 in subsequent years). These would come from an emergency training college offering one year courses. The committee asked also that scales of salary, superannuation arrangements etc. should be negotiated by the Ministry of Education with representatives of employers and youth leaders from both statutory and voluntary Youth Service; basic grants for headquarters administration and training purposes of national voluntary bodies should be radically increased and special grants for experimental or pioneering work established; local authorities should review their areas' needs for the Youth Service and, in addition to new developments in local authority provision in line with relaxed but consistent financial regulation, greater support should go to local voluntary bodies and Youth Service units where it was merited. The 'new developments' for which the Committee called included a wider range of provision, including detached work with the 'unclubbable'.

Acceptance and implementation

Uniquely, the report was accepted overnight and in total by the Ministry of Education, and its recommendations for emergency action put into operation immediately. Preparations within the Office and HMI had been put in hand before the Committee finished sitting. The YSDC was established forthwith with 12 members, chaired by the Minister, and with HMI support as necessary from chief and staff inspectors.

Within six months of the report's issue, the Ministry of Education had put out Circular 11/60 listing developments which had taken place and asking for LEA cooperation. Preparations for a National College for the Training of Youth Leaders (NCTYL) were already well in hand. The HMI who had been secretary of the Albemarle Committee was seconded to the post of principal and held it until 1964. Ninety students were to start on 1 January 1961. Their average age was 28, mostly younger but mature adults. Their exploitation of the kind of learning opportunity which the college created illustrated the fact that good adult personal and good adult professional learning are one and the same experience.

The output of full-time leaders from the existing courses at Swansea University and Westhill Colleges was to have greater support, and additionally optional Youth Service courses were to be introduced into teacher training college programmes. Courses organised by the YMCA and National

Association of Boys' Clubs as well as other voluntary organisation courses were being considered for recognition (which was later granted). Particularly important was the £3m now available for building programme starts in 1960/62; £4m would be available in 1962/63.

HMI involvement

HMI in the field continued to help with comment and advice on building proposals and, through its panel, HMI offered corporate views and suggestions to help the Ministry's architects, especially in the preparation of a Building Bulletin offering detailed advice nationally on building for the Youth Service. A revolution ensued in thinking and practice regarding buildings that would make a positive contribution to the social education of young people.

To propagate information, discussion, ideas and developments about the Youth Service, a national Youth Service broadsheet, distributed widely by the Central Office of Information, was inaugurated in late 1960.[4] HMI helped on a small editorial group. They also assisted the YSDC in assessment of special grants for experiments and in provision and training for the part-time youth leader in the field.

In its statement about distribution to local authorities of the general grant for 1961/2 and 1962/3 the Ministry of Housing and Local Government emphasised that following Albemarle 'the provision made in the general grant takes full account of the need for further development of the [Youth] Service and substantial developments are being made in this small but important field. Higher expenditure is expected on the employment of youth leaders and maintenance of youth clubs and on grants to voluntary bodies participating in the Service.'

An inter-departmental committee was set up and in another joint circular of 1964 (DES 11/64) to Local Authorities it was noted that the government intended increased expenditure on developing general sporting facilities and pressed for direct help in this respect for the Youth Service in particular as well as general encouragement of use by the public of educational facilities.[5]

HMI influence on educational development had rarely if ever been so obvious or so successful. HMI were now able to encourage improvements in the Youth Service generally and in the geographical areas for which they were responsible, with unusual confidence if still with varying success. It is certainly true, however, that the run-up to Albemarle, the process itself and its follow-up were a prime example of the constructive potential of interaction between the field, politics, administration and HMI. Unquestionably the recruitment of highly expert YS specialists who were much respected by the field was crucial. They brought with them the particular professionalism, including the political skills and the controlled activism of the OFE specialist. However, they learned to deploy these with the age-old evaluative, interpretive and diplomatic skills of the traditional schools HMI, just as some of these were to assume the OFE mantle with no less passion and aplomb. The welding together and the overall steer of the whole development from its earliest preparatory steps and over nearly two decades owed most of all first to Elliott, and then, pre-eminently to Salter Davies – both of them classic schools trained HMI of the pre-war generation. After Salter Davies's retirement the role was assumed by Edwin Sims on the HMI side, with greatly increased support from the Office. A field worker at that time, later HMI, adds 'The impact of Albemarle on the field was immense. Morale surged, and this was accompanied by the recognition among the small core of professionals that this achievement owed much to HMI. It raised their status in the field and their influence on it in the 1960s. This rather wore off in the 1970s!'

Some further developments

The Youth Service Development Council with a Minister in the chair and HMI assessors started work promptly alongside local development which the Committee had advocated and which was now bolstered by Central Government support and consequently improved morale, together with some changes of approach by voluntary providers.

One of the Council's early concerns was to encourage training for the mass of part-time paid and voluntary leaders on which the service so heavily relied. A working party under Gordon Bessey, assisted as usual by HMI assessors, reported in 1962 and proposed the establishment of local training agencies bringing statutory and voluntary bodies together to establish basic and more advanced 'training the trainers' courses, and suggested content.

By 1964, 110 of 146 LEA areas were covered by some sort of a joint training agency. Some comprised voluntary and statutory agencies alike; some were LEA only; some excluded uniformed organisations. A number of training officers were appointed by LEAs and some of these were full-time. However, there was much HMI concern about the content, methods and standards of many courses. A second report on the training of part-time workers was chaired by Lady Albemarle in 1966, surveyed the development, and pinpointed weaknesses. It required better statutory/voluntary collaboration providing common training as well as training specific to the work of voluntary organisations, and especially better methods. The DES was urged to take the initiative in stimulating regional training courses for the further training of trainers and to increase the staffing of the Youth Service Information Centre to enable its work in the training field to develop. Co-operation was not easy to secure. In 1964/5 the DES consulted widely to try to get progress. HMI locally were of great importance in gathering information and suggesting ways forward. They also participated widely in organising, teaching or directing the trainers' courses which ensued (see pp 64f).

In years which followed, most Regional Advisory Councils (established by the Department to enable LEAs to collaborate in planning provision of HE/FE training) set up committees to develop training for youth, community and adult workers, sometimes separate and sometimes combined, and comprising representation from local authorities, voluntary youth organisations, other associated bodies and professional workers, with HMI as assessors.

Other developments stemming from Albemarle succeeded more rapidly than such collaboration. HMI pressure was important in ensuring the existence and continued support of a number of central institutions and organisations serving youth work. These became responsible for a degree of structure, accepted status and widespread professional development to which adult education could never so much as aspire. Albemarle's 'intelligence unit' was prepared for by OFE HMI, Edwin Sims, eventually set up by the DES in 1964 as a Youth Service Information Centre (YSIC), and called into dynamic life by its first (and single-handed) head, Alan Gibson, who had experience in both AE and youth work, most recently on the staff of the National College for the Training of Youth Leaders. Until 1970 it was based in the College at Leicester, and then became independent, with DES grant. Its tasks were to collect and disseminate information about developments in work with young people at home and abroad; about full-time and part-time leader training developments and materials and similar developments in the training of trainers; to survey the research available and identify areas for future research. The first director, Gibson, left in 1969 to join the Inspectorate. By that time YSIC had issued comprehensive annotated lists of books, projects, training films and other aids, summaries of research work, lists of courses, conferences and much statistical and other information as well as contributing to the editorial board of the DES periodical *Youth Service*. HMI and DES officers as assessors influenced the direction the Centre took. Other organisations which largely owed their initiation and existence to HMI were those which were variously concerned with professional training, its methods, content and standards, for both full-time and part-time youth workers of all kinds. Sims and Gibson in particular were responsible for devising and helping these developments. Eventually regulation or accreditation of all the various voluntary and statutory schemes came under the aegis of acronymic bodies such as INSTEP (In-Service Training and Education Panel) and later CETYCW (Council for Education and Training in Youth and Community Work), and these were linked, increasingly, with participant HE institutions.

In 1963 the YSDC also set up a committee, chaired by the CI for OFE, to consider the specific problems of rural youth work. Its report and recommendations for LEA action were issued in 1965. OFE HMI were heavily involved with other national projects in addition to their now more onerous normal local inspectoral duties in connection with the Youth Service. Together with teacher training specialists many helped with the assessment and final acceptance via the DES of other university and voluntary organisation sponsored training courses for youth leaders, and with the new youth service options in the teacher training colleges. Trained youth leaders now qualified for rates of pay secured by a new negotiating committee. HMI was also assigned to keep in touch with the growing number of nationally grant aided experimental projects as well as with others sometimes initiated by LEAs. There were 102 such developments listed by the YSIC in the mid-1960s, rising to 379 in 1971. They ranged through coffee bar projects, special activities in the arts, adventure provision, community services, street based work, counselling, drugs related projects, and efforts at forwarding better community relations. Many of the projects were characteristic of the growing realisation that 'clubwork' (ie, youth work based on *membership* of clubs or units) was not the only or indeed the main answer to the needs of youth, and one which was increasingly less attractive to older young people.

Following Albemarle a separate youth section primarily concerned with the service and grant aid to it had been created in the Office, and was working closely with HMI. It spent £32m on new buildings by 1969 and a further £9.5m was planned for 1970–71, a quarter of this now on sports projects. Many more projects were submitted to the Department than could be accepted and HMI spent much thought and effort on advising on priorities. Another £1m was spent on developing work with youth in specified 'disadvantaged' areas. Grants to the headquarters of voluntary organisations were more than doubled. Numbers of full-time and now mainly professionally trained workers increased from 700 in 1960 to slightly exceed the Albemarle target of 1,300 in 1966 and reached over 2,000 by the end of the decade. Some progress had also been made towards more training for part-time staff. Above all the morale of what was becoming a well informed professional leadership had become high, and popular awareness of the Youth Service and its purposes had been greatly increased.

The implementation of the Albemarle proposals was projected to last ten years. The record of success was impressive compared with the past history of the Youth Service and with DES support for other aspects of OFE.

HMI organisation and the structure of the field

Part of the interest in HMI's relationship to the YS lies in the fact there were two kinds of universal providers, the statutory and the voluntary sectors. HMI worked with both, but in necessarily different ways which reflected their different structures and ambience. The statutory relationship was much tied up with what reports said should be done, how far financial provision could be made to implement recommendations, with DES attitudes and influence on the one hand and the attitudes of LEAs and their CEOs and other officers on the other. Regardless of local variables, the statutory sector was unitary, and

HMI's relationship with it was the usual one of nurturing, challenging and influencing the core and scaffolding of provision in each locality, often in its less favoured parts, much as they might in other areas of education.

The voluntary sector, on the other hand, was multifarious. The staffing, scopes, aspirations, financial muscle and fields of action of its many member organisations differed widely. Some found all the reports, circulars and sources of advice relevant to their work, others few. They had far more freedom in local decision making and more control of finance, if much less of it. They might or might not be open to HMI influence, but also to the pull of the grants system, which HMI affected strongly, though only at the centre. It was the voluntary end of the spectrum which was expected most strongly to develop new and often original initiatives, and very often did so: sail training, handicapped/ablebodied work, and many other kinds of specialised activity took their origins from here. They could all be linked to its badge schemes, the Duke of Edinburgh's Awards, and adventure training whatever its source.

The voluntary sector was thus an alternative to the statutory work in the drive to achieve desirable development, and the very large national VOs had their own staffing structures in parallel to those of the LEAs. Sometimes these worked in partnership with HMI, and no less demandingly than the LEA service. Elsewhere there could be little or no voluntary structure. HMI had to be ready to play both systems, to integrate, encourage experiment, help find ways of developing a successful line of work, or see developments hived off as new separate bodies which would need grant-aid in their own right. And they had to realise that some of these developments needed nurturing over many years.

There was further recruitment for OFE HMI in the 1960s and into the 1970s to match so much expansion, especially of the Youth Service, and compensate for retirements. New OFE HMI came from a variety of backgrounds, including voluntary youth organisations, the YSIC, social work and community development. More schools specialists with experience in out-of-school activities including adventure courses were also appointed.

With the growing numbers and emphasis on the Youth Service an additional staff inspector was appointed to the OFE team in 1960. As well as leading and helping HMI in their local duties the staff inspectors shared responsibility for liaison with the national voluntary organisations. They chaired the Youth Service national sub-panels and working parties and participated in the work of similar groups in the divisions.

From 1964 onwards district and general HMI interest in helping Youth Service continued steadily before reducing, in the long run substantially, after 1967 with the new overall further education organisation (cf Chapter 2). Specialist SIs continued to chair what central structures remained, but most of the new combined divisional FE committees rarely found time for the youth service. The panel, or committee, system and inspection modes were adjusted to fit the bringing together of Youth Service work and more general community provision.

Other developments

Beyond concern for the quality and extent of provision, especially within clubs, which were relatively easy to visit and assess, HMI interested themselves in the growing number of detached and outreach youth workers who attempted to provide help and counselling to those who were not interested in coming to clubs. The need for such an extension of effort was often pointed by examples in the pages of *Youth Service*; it chimed in with growing DES and other interest in educational counselling. The number of such youth workers grew from 10 in the mid-1960s to 42 in the 1970s and many more by the end of that decade. Their work connected with growing concern about drugs and violence often associated with the poorest in society, and with racial prejudice. There were 18 youth drug addiction schemes known to exist by 1970 and 26 community relations projects. These latter had been more widely established after publication of the report of a committee established by the DES under the chairmanship of Lord Hunt in 1967. While recognising that what the Youth Service could do to help was limited, the committee advocated its taking a multi-racial and integrationist approach and advised that specific steps should be taken to improve the capabilities of youth workers in this area. Little in fact resulted, possibly because the policy was misinterpreted, but the range of specialised kinds of YW aimed at particular types and areas of real need continued to grow.

The development of Youth Councils was another area of particular action for some HMI following YSDC concern. Councils had been active in various forms for many years. Traditionally they were involved in organising inter-club competitions, social events and charity fundraising, but were sometimes seen as an opportunity for a youth voice to be heard and for the personal development of the members. Known Councils numbered some 250 by 1949 in England and Wales, but they fell out of fashion in the 1950s, recovering somewhat in the late 1960s to about 100 in number. They took on different forms in some cases to allow young people to express their views on the problems of youth generally, sometimes critically.

Community service by young people through the medium of specialised organisations was another strand of youth work to see a considerable development. Starting as a result of field pressures, it was of interest to HMI and others centrally rather more than locally. It may have been one expression of a general tendency, much encouraged by Albemarle, towards diversification and, consequently, a degree of specialisation. The new approaches were publicised by YSIC. They tended to be less concerned with membership, as of clubs or uniformed organisations, and led to the multiplication of outreach workers, workers with unattached youth, unattached workers, and subsequently counselling agencies and centres, voluntary service centres and projects.

Policy development based on experience, as well as publicity, may have been reasons for this concentration on some of the new specialist organisations. By some, however, it was seen as divisive compared to support for existing community service by the young, which had developed well during the 1960s especially in voluntary organisations. Its origins went back to the 1920s and 1930s; they included particularly work in refugee camps and the promotion of international understanding and peace, such as that of Service Civil International, founded in 1920. Its UK branch, International Voluntary Service, was sending young volunteers aged 18 and over to work camps and placements in both developing and developed countries. In the late 1950s Alec Dickson founded Voluntary Service Overseas (VSO), designed originally for young people to undertake before university study, but later increasingly recruiting new graduates and also mature individuals. This movement triggered the development of many local community service schemes in grammar and public schools, sometimes as an alternative to compulsory games or cadet forces. In the 1960s, stimulated by educational thinking, very many more schools established community service schemes; Alec Dickson founded a new community service organisation, Community Service Volunteers, in 1962. The conclusion of their first pamphlet said: 'This endeavour is concerned not just to place candidates in projects – but to explore new patterns of service, to expand the role of the volunteer in society, and to discover what contribution the young can make to the care of the community.'

CSV grew rapidly, offering helpful services and advice. Such ideas had already characterised the programmes of some YS organisations for very many years, and had been manifest in the youth or cadet elements of the Red Cross, St John's Ambulance Service, the Salvation Army and various church activities and uniformed organisations such as the Guides. CSV and the London 'Task Force', later established in other parts of the country, claimed to be providing these services in the mid-1960s.

A working party of the YSDC, set up to consider the development of community service by young people, reported in December 1965. It stressed the need for a co-ordinating body. The DES commended it in Circular 15/66 and subsequently issued a further joint Circular 8/68 with the Ministry of Health (Circular 15/68) together with those of Housing and Local Government (Circular 20/68) and the Home Office (Circular 94/68) announcing the establishment of an independent trust, the Young Volunteer Force Foundation. The Foundation was to be partly financed by the DES for three years initially but it would depend for additional income on voluntary and LA sources. The Director of Task Force became the Director of the Young Volunteer Force Foundation. The Trust's three officers were senior politicians.

With this explosion in community service activity during the 1960s, HMI was once more closely involved. An OFE SI (Edwin Sims) had been an assessor to the YSDC Community Service Working Party, and Adult Education and Youth Service as well as Schools HMI were now again asked to evaluate current practice. Thereafter they were much involved in discussion with DES, especially since politically (for all three parties) community service was appealing as an appropriate vehicle for harnessing the nation's young to good causes. The parallels to the US Peace Corps on the one hand and to national service on the other seemed plain. As far as some in the education service were concerned, however, this was primarily another part of the overall curriculum for young people, providing for personal development and social education. Sadly in many schemes, though compassion and concern for the plight of others were properly developed, social learning was not. Some local tensions developed, and political worries grew.

A report on the YVFF was expressly requested by an incoming Secretary of State for Education (Mrs Thatcher), and in view of political sensitivities a special team of HMI was set up to inspect its work. Apart from various matters of structure and administration, their report concentrated on ways in which what had been intended as clearing houses for the development of community service on one hand and, integrally linked, social education on the other, had often developed into community work mainly by the Foundation's field staff. This raised questions about the distinctions between community work, community development, straightforward service activities, and the YVFF teams' intended basic work with young volunteers in co-operation with the schools. The report's analysis resulted in some clarification of policy thinking as well as practical changes. Political concern was allayed, only to be revived by various aspects of the Home Office Community Development Programme and some features of Urban Aid. By the end of the 1980s further clarification was needed, and YVFF was transmuted into what is now the Community Development Foundation, with a precise research and development brief.

From about 1964 when the Schools Council was established and particularly with the move towards developing comprehensive secondary education as part of an educational route to more equality, Educational Priority Areas were established from 1967 and Urban Aid programmes started in 1969. Thinking about the purposes and possible practice of secondary schools and of the Youth Service was beginning to coalesce. Steps being taken towards raising further the minimum school leaving age helped the movement on.

Voluntary service was only one area of common interest. New thinking and even practice in relating schools to their communities provided another. The village college idea was being extended to other Authorities (see Chapter 4), particularly Leicestershire, and other experimental community schools were built. Thinking about what may be loosely styled community development led to other action described elsewhere, in relation to adult education as well as to changes in attitudes to and modes of provision for general community welfare and education. HMI, including OFE HMI, were deeply involved in research enquiries and surveys of what was going on in the field. As far as the Youth Service was concerned some practitioners wished to base youth work more firmly in schools. Their case was countered by others who saw a need for it to move in the opposite direction towards independence from formal educational institutions. This tension was very evident in the reports of the Milson and Fairbairn Committees.

A paper had been prepared by HMI in 1966 on 'The Youth Service and the Schools'. It surveyed developments in the field and took account of recent discussions that officers of the Schools Council and the DES had had with NAYSO (the professional association of full-time Youth Service officers) and the Standing Conference of National Voluntary Youth Organisations (SCNVYO) or its successor. It noted the schools development described above as well as innovations in social and community education. The growth of dual use of schools and in the number of joint appointments to teacher/youth leader or youth tutor posts within schools also demanded attention. There were some 500 to 600 appointments to such posts at the end of the decade and many more were approved.

In view of all these developments the Youth Service Development Council in 1967 established two main working committees, one on the Youth Service in schools and further education (with Mr Fairbairn, then Deputy Education Officer of Leicestershire, as chairman) and another on Youth Service and community, under Dr Milson of Westhill College. In the event, the character of the resulting documents, their reception by the Office and in the field, as well as political and social developments, may have caused these enquiries to produce very different effects from the realistic and authoritative synthesis which had been hoped for.

Changes in HMI personnel also played a part in subsequent developments, and the disappearance of a separate OFE section with its own CI was crucial. Although it did not appear so at the time, the first dynamic phase of HMI involvement with the traditional YS, statutory and voluntary, gradually declined during the late 1960s and early 1970s, as new concerns came to need and receive a greater share of their attention. The OFE specialists, together with a small number of enthusiasts from the P&S and former TCA sections of HMI, continued to know and care for what went on in clubs and units which formed the core of youth work provision. Much specialist OFE attention and effort shifted, however, to new YS developments. HMI, as noted, were involved with an enquiry into the Young Volunteer Force Foundation, with the emergence of the National Youth Bureau from the original YS Information Centre, with the creation of new training courses in higher education institutions and, towards the end of the 1970s, with the substantial efforts of the statutory and voluntary sectors to help the young unemployed. However, the new inspectorate organisation also placed limits on their contribution as OFE specialists. Some of their writing became increasingly cautious. The atmosphere changed – and with differential effect on the various sectors of the YS. One specialist colleague writes of

> growing suspicion in some quarters of the newer creations (ie, non–club work), and I think HMI support was chiefly significant as a defensive element. LEA provision suffered the greatest stagnation without really seeming to do so. The raising of the school leaving age, the rapidly growing number of teacher/leaders, who were in practice seen and used mainly as teachers, and a greater variety of school and community activity, masked some falling off in specific YW, and a considerable decay of LEA influence as a co–ordinator and support of community action for young people ... I believe the voluntary sector survived best and indeed expanded, partly because it had a real element of independence, partly because government thought it approved of self–help but did not greatly care what direction it took.

Not all specialist HMI took quite such a bleak view. Nevertheless the raising of the school leaving age, and the acknowledgment by schools of the need for personal and social education, led (among other trends) to the appointment of many more teacher–leaders mostly in secondary schools. They were mostly qualified teachers, appointed as members of the school staff, and worked on the school premises. There was always a risk of their incorporation into the teaching and curriculum activities of the school. OFE HMI's efforts often had to be deployed to preserve or claw back such staff time for out-of-school work and for service among young people no longer attending school. Staff time and budgets of the traditional YS, too, had to be often defended against competing demands from other, sometimes powerful, trends. With some exceptions, the role of LEAs as the main co–ordinator and support of their communities' provision for young people tended to decline. Conversely, the voluntary sector grew stronger, partly because of its independence and partly because it could take advantage of the entrepreneurial climate which was being fostered. Maybe the alternative view differs more in degree of caution than in substance.

There was thus some continuity of traditional YS patterns, though leavened by experiment. New organisations were formed and an increasing number were supported through headquarters grants rather than locally. Environmental concerns, work with those with disabilities, sail training and the arts were among the expanding activities. In some areas LEA free-standing out-of-school provision may well have shrunk while their school-based resources and efforts accumulated. Even so, and especially if in-school personnel, resources and social education are included, the early 1980s saw a service far larger and better staffed than that of the early 1960s. With all the school-based, unattached, counselling, community action and unemployment provisions being made, its scope was broader than in the early 1970s. At this period, when specialist – or any – HMI attention to OFE at large was eroded, the YS suffered less severely than the rest of OFE. Indeed, the expanding scope of the YS had drawn the time and talents, and perhaps some admiration, of many non-specialist as well as YS HMI to the wider application of youth work skills and insights. This particularly applied to those HMI concerned with personal development in schools, and others with vocational education and training responsibilities who saw work with the unemployed.

The last phase

Unlike other sectors of OFE, the 1980s saw a newly heightened profile for YW within the Inspectorate, owing to increased interest in the YS within the Department and pressure for more published reporting by HMI overall. The former reflected a number of public concerns about what was happening to young people. Such concerns ebbed and flowed often in a series of moral panics. In the early 1980s they were stimulated by disturbances in Bristol, Liverpool and elsewhere, and by the sharp increase in youth unemployment. From the 1970s, even before these crises, youth unemployment had stimulated various government initiatives, notably the Youth Training Scheme and the Youth Opportunities Programme. These were orchestrated by the Manpower Services Commission, which was seen by many in the education service as a powerful predator. Others welcomed these schemes as a source of much-needed new funding for social and informal education, albeit conducted in a work-oriented context.

Specialist YS HMI, although relatively few in number, were often at the sharp end of intelligence gathering for the Inspectorate and the Office about street-level, community-based activity designed to ameliorate problems affecting young people, including unemployment. Such activity often went well beyond the responsive capacity of most formal educational institutions, whether schools or FE. It was, potentially, a major task for the country's YS with its diverse, if unbiddable, organisations. The voluntary youth organisa-tions in particular used the government schemes creatively to carry out a great deal of valuable work, as for instance in John Ewen's invention, at NAYC (rather than during his important work as HMI), of Community Industry.

YW itself had little national policy direction for most of the 1970s. As indicated earlier, the Milson–Fairbairn Report (*Youth and Community Work in the 1970s*) had lacked the authority of Albemarle. It was, moreover, an uneasy and often contradictory compromise document stitched together from two separate texts. It landed on the desk of the incoming Secretary of State, Margaret Thatcher, was eventually rejected and (more seriously) the YSDC itself was disbanded. However, while awaiting her decision a number of LEAs, and HE institutions engaged in professional training, anticipated a favourable outcome. They accepted the vague 'philosophy' of the Report, re-titled their services and courses, and even re-structured them as amalgams of youth and community work, often even including adult education with them (see pp 98–100).

Neither the Office nor HMI favoured these developments, and such localised, often idiosyncratic decision making intensified the difficulty caused by the absence of a national policy rudder. These arrangements may well have resulted from LEA (and even DES) administrators cobbling together disparate bits of activity outside formal schooling and FE to save a post here and there. Elsewhere it may have been a case of YW colonising an even weaker area (in terms of staffing and union muscle) when it realised that agendas such as 'the enabling of clients', which it increasingly espoused for the young, could be the answer for some vulnerable adults. Moreover, the youth workers' national professional body also had community centre wardens within its remit. It was therefore no great problem for LEAs and training institutions to sweep all post-school work into 'Youth and Community'.

Misapplied concepts taken from community development theories – as in *Youth and Community Work in the 1970s* – also played a part in the thinking of some LEAs and among DES architects working with schools HMI. The resulting confusions were paralleled in French work on *animation socio-culturelle*. The links and the distinctions between these areas of work were clear to OFE specialist HMI across the board; they did their best to discourage rash policy changes in the field, though not always successfully. In the process some maintained their interest across all three main areas of OFE, while some AE specialists seemed content to shed their responsibility for community development on to YW colleagues.

Various parliamentary attempts to clarify the statutory basis and role of the YS eventually smoked out of the DES a commitment to review the Service. Inevitably, it established a review group, chaired by a recently retired DES Deputy Secretary, Alan Thompson, with the customary secretariat and support from serving and recently retired HMI, including Edwin Sims who had remained active on the national and international scenes following his retirement as SI for the YS. In 1982 the review group produced a thoughtful, humane and integrally coherent document in the best tradition. The Department, however, cherry-picked its recommendations. Some useful initiatives were set in train, but the most important needs of the YS identified by Thompson – notably for a clearer statutory basis – were not addressed. In due course the agenda of the formal education bureaucracy reasserted itself.

Meanwhile renewed fears raised by major social disturbances had created new demands. They were reflected in an increase to 14 of the cadre of HMI with substantial YW assignments. However, this change also reflected in no small measure the sympathy and recognition of Eric Bolton, soon to become

SCI, for the contribution of youth specialists to the overall work of the Inspectorate. Some non-specialist HMI also continued to take an interest in youth provision within their districts, just as youth specialists were expected to contribute to the generality of FE inspection. The new HMI youth team members had substantial backgrounds in youth and community work, and SI leadership passed unequivocally into a notable succession of specialist hands. As after Albemarle, the Office and the leadership of HMI reacted constructively to social disturbance by means of the leadership they provided and the quality and amount of staffing. Their treatment of AE was the diametrical opposite.

For the wider educational world the arrival of Sir Keith Joseph as Secretary of State for Education in 1981 had marked an important change of gear in matters other than his eventual curt dismissal of the key elements in the Thompson Report. As Eric Bolton (1998) later observed:

> As the arch-monetarist, less government, more self-help guru of what was beginning to be called Thatcherism, his agenda was to reduce public expenditure on education and minimise the influence of bureaucrats and professionals. He also wanted to raise levels of achievement and make what went on in education at all levels more relevant and useful to the worlds of making and spending; and generally to bring the education service more into line with a market place characterised by informed consumers choosing among competing providers.

Publish and be damned?

Sir Keith also set about a review of HMI as a whole. There were fears about its survival but, in the event, decisions on this scrutiny concluded that the Secretary of State regarded its work as indispensable to the process of making educational policy. Furthermore, the emerging concept of a market in education, sustained by informed consumer choice, also underlined in ministers' view the need for HMIs' reports, both on individual institutions and on broad educational themes, to be published. He decided that they would be from 1 January 1983 (see also p 106, 123).

At first an unwelcome demand to some HMI, this sharpened the role and raised the profile of youth and community specialists. They were drawn into inspecting and contributing evaluative paragraphs about youth services to published reports on the overall work of LEAs (eg on Coventry, Sheffield and Cornwall); to thematic reports, including an earlier example *The Response of the Education Service to the Young Unemployed*; Health Education, and also to the annual reports on LEA expenditure. They brought a YW perspective to inspections of FE colleges and of young offender institutions. However, attempts to work on school inspections were less successful, generally because of the dominance of subject specialisms in the school context.

The traditional mode of HMI inspection and reporting in preceding decades was of the individual school or college or, by extension, youth club or centre, though inspections of the YS in LEAs as a whole or in parts of their territories were not uncommon. The reports were often widely leaked by recipients. Officially, however, they were only available to the professionals involved, their governing bodies, the LEA for the area, and of course the Ministry or Department. In the early days of published reporting a few YS reports continued the tradition; one of the first, for example, was highly critical of work in three Lambeth youth clubs.

There was no prospect of HMI ever providing reporting inspections of all schools, still less of all youth projects. In any event, the primary purpose of formal reporting after full inspections (as opposed to informal evaluation and discussion after pastoral visits) was to inform the Office about standards. Accordingly, the national youth team soon decided it was not worthwhile to concentrate on publications about individual youth centres or projects. Instead it deployed its limited resources on inspecting and reporting on the overall YS provision made by a particular LEA, a national voluntary organisation, or a specific form of YW. Such reports – over 50 of them by the end of the 1980s – still based their judgements on work observed by HMI in particular clubs or projects. However, by working co-operatively and thus on a larger scale it was hoped to inform policy, respond to the field more widely, and disseminate good practice. Inspection also focused on training, especially initial qualifying training for youth and community work. This was reflected in a series of reports on HE courses. As a pattern of work this was, in effect, a re-invention of the OFE remits of the 1950s and 1960s.

HMI thus inspected YW in the mushrooming variety of settings and projects, on the streets as well as in buildings, in the voluntary as well as the maintained sector. Such inspection activities challenged, widened and deepened their inspection methodology: how were judgements to be reached of street-based or outdoor education, of crime prevention programmes, of the totality of an authority's youth provision? The honing of collective judgements and a greater measure of 'inter-rater reliability' became imperative as reports were now public documents and, properly, open to critical comment. One early external commentary on the first half dozen or so published YS reports had identified some apparent differences of emphasis between inspection teams. It had also suggested that HMI were eternally disappointed with the quality of the YW practice they observed! In the days before they codified their criteria for judgement and made them publicly explicit, the strength and weaknesses of HMI's approach lay in collegiality, the testing out of perception and judgement with colleagues who brought a range of nation-wide inspection experience into the evaluation of a service or a particular area of work.

The growing diversification of YW across the country, and its targeting of specific groups of young people according to their needs, was captured in a series of published reports. There was the seminal report on *Effective Youth Work* of 1987 in the series *Education Observed*. This sought to characterise the distinctive values and educational methods of YW. It emphasised personal and social development as its principal *raison d'être* and, in a set of case studies, exemplified how various activities could be used to this end. More specifically, there were reports on, eg, the National Federation of Young Farmers' Clubs, Youth Work on Urban Housing Estates, Youth Work Responses to Unemployment and, more controversially, 'to the needs of girls and young women'. Under the new dispensation not all of these passed straightforwardly through the Inspectorate's editorial command: some senior colleagues with FE college backgrounds found it difficult to understand that HMI were reporting on the work of an education service with young prostitutes or young drug users, as they did in *Developmental Approaches to Youth Work in Wirral* in 1988 and in *Responsive Youth Work* in 1990. But most reports made it into print, albeit with tempered messages.

Reporting was complemented by specialist courses within the Department's Short Course Programme, by HMI support for a variety of field-based networks and by acting as assessors to national bodies such as the NYB and CETYCW. HMI contributed their national perspective and inspection evidence to all of these, possibly more effectively at times than through publications which had to run the gauntlet of senior non-specialist HMI and, less often, the Office which was less timid than CI(FE). In the absence of any policy direction from Government, and lacking a professional institute, these relatively loose arrangements often helped to sustain, however imperfectly, a sense of agreed purpose in a diverse field of work. They also contributed to the development of a profession whose members were often isolated, structurally and temperamentally, within LEA departments.

International links

British experience of YW gained and always retained international interest from the 1950s on, especially within Europe. The Council of Europe's Committee on Cultural Co-operation established a misleadingly named 'European Youth Centre' (a conference and training venue); successive SI served on its governing body and ran courses, symposia, study tours and other events which were organised by it and, later, by what was then the EEC, UNESCO, OECD and the Commonwealth Youth Affairs Council. EJ Sidebottom, Edwin Sims and JA Simpson were especially involved in the creative phase of these activities. However, youth services had their own extensive networks of international contacts and activities, since many youth organisations are international in character. In 1985 the Council of Europe began to develop a pattern of European Youth Ministers' Conferences. HMI attended, accompanying the successive junior ministers holding the portfolio. These were, by and large, rhetorical events with little practical outcome, and in this as in other fields DES briefing encouraged ministers in their natural inclination to be defensive. The Department's line was thus rarely in tune with UK youth interests, not least in resisting any opening of links with Eastern Europe, which was pioneered by several British youth bodies. Not for the first time DES policy struggled to keep up with the innovative practice of youth organisations and thus failed to gain credit in European youth circles for the quality and enterprise of British youth work. More productive work was done behind the scenes where specialist HMI were allowed, probably without the knowledge of superiors or the Office, to get on with the business of helping to re-shape the roles and functioning of the Council of Europe's youth bodies, and to play a part in developing some transnational associations, for example for youth information services.

The smack of firm government?

The command of what went for policy on YW remained with the Department. Here it was anchored in the shifting sands of ministerial and official interest. Some initiatives pressed by HMI captured political support. One such was the YW apprenticeship scheme crafted by Janet Paraskeva, then an HMI, and sold by senior HMI to the then Secretary of State. It was designed to bring a new, younger, cohort of peer educators into YW practice. The Thompson Report, too, had identified various possibilities for action, including the creation of the Council for Education and Training in Youth and Community Work (CETYCW) and of a National Advisory Council for Youth Service (NACYS). Specialist HMI invariably supported such bodies as giving the possibility of greater field influence on policy-making. Departmental officials generally disliked them for the same reason. The time needed to build consensus in such a diverse field generally ensured a slow start and thus offered a good excuse to terminate developments at a convenient moment. Moreover, if these were genuinely representative of the YW field, they could be relied upon to be critical of government policy towards young people and youth services. So it proved again with NACYS: a departmental official, against HMI advice, bundled it into touch just when it was getting into its stride with a series of useful reports.

In any event the Department now had other ambitions for the governance of the YS. These were expressed in three major administrative actions. The grant scheme for national voluntary youth organisations (a monument to the efforts of HMI in the 1970s to achieve a principled and even-handed effectiveness) was re-cast to tie funding to specific, normally short-term, programmes which would be closer to Government priorities. Some HMI jibbed at this, but it was hardly exceptional given the climate of the times; in a version of their earlier Victorian task (*viz* 'payment by results') they continued to assess the work of these bodies against the overt grant criteria.

Second, in 1990 the Department decided to withdraw its funding from the National Youth Bureau, from CETYWC, from the British Youth Council and the National Council of Voluntary Youth Services. Instead it would create a National Youth Agency (NYA) as the central focus for YW in England. In its grand design this proposal was far-sighted, but the details and administration were flawed. At the heart of the difficulty was the decision to create the NYA as a non-departmental public body (ie, a 'quango') with a membership appointed by the Secretary of State, and activities and services largely determined by the Department, on pain of withdrawal of the grant on which the NYA would depend for its existence. HMI counselled against this model, the Office pressed on, a prominent YS specialist HMI became the first director. But both the British Youth Council and the National Council of Voluntary Youth Services were determined to maintain an independent voice for their constituencies. They sought funds from elsewhere and survived independently, to await a turning DES tide.

The third and most ambitious of the Department's initiatives by the late 1980s was an attempt to identify a 'core curriculum' for the YS. This had echoes of the National Curriculum for the schools set out in the 1988 Education Reform Act. As with the creation of the NYA, the Department's goals were not wholly misguided. The cold climate for public expenditure required services of all kinds to be clearer about outcomes and benefits, and the sprawling YS was particularly vulnerable. HMI agreed with the Department's analysis – indeed their reports contributed to it.

However, the attempt to produce 'curricular consensus' across the wide field of LEA and voluntary endeavour, and in a form which would be genuinely useful, was doomed from the start. In the view of HMI, considering themselves guardians of educational principle, it was made worse by the failure to offer clarity about the meaning of the very word *curriculum*. The Department's great project was also handicapped by the generally hamfisted management, by an alliance of the Office and the newly formed NYA, of a tortuous process involving a series of ministerial conferences. Since HMI were known to be sceptical they were kept at a distance. The result pleased no-one. The Department blamed the field for its failure to answer the questions correctly, and an incoming official ordered full speed astern and changed the compass from *dirigisme* to *laisser faire*.

The end of involvement

By this time it was becoming clear that HMI's specialist knowledge, advice and professional judgment were welcomed on specific matters such as the Department's grants to, now, over 70 national voluntary youth organisations, on grant programmes for inservice training, or on the development of specific initiatives such as the YW apprenticeships in the inner cities. It was less welcome when

HMI raised questions about the Department's overall stewardship of YW and, in particular, its unwillingness to give unequivocal statutory underpinning and a consistent policy framework to a diversifying sector. The much enhanced inspection activity, both across the country and across the range of needs which the YS was endeavouring to meet, had exposed the feebleness of Government policy and funding for YW. This was not a comfortable message for HMI to convey. More reporting, involvement as the Department's assessors on a range of national youth-related bodies, the short course programme and willingness to speak, as in duty bound, however judiciously and on professional matters, on public platforms, heightened HMI's profile in the field. All this risked illuminating tensions between the Department and the professional advice its inspectorate offered on policy development, or its absence.

Yet HMI's relationships with ministers and DES officials in the youth field were only a small part of a much larger picture. As the 1990s opened, HMI was publicly and heavily involved in inspecting, reporting and advising on policy and its implementation across the whole education service. As Eric Bolton (1998), now SCI, was later to comment, it:

> had become accepted that all that inspection effort would lead to publication and, given HMI's remit to report without fear or favour, there were many tensions with ministers and officials, opposition spokesmen on education, local politicians, chief education officers, heads' and teachers' associations and unions, as well as with the heads and staff of individual institutions. In short, almost everything that was concerning the education service in the late 1980s stemmed from Government policy and its implementation. While that meant that the Government and its officials were increasingly dependent on inspection-based information and advice about the effectiveness of their policies, they were becoming increasingly irritated that most of it went public, especially as some was very critical, and little, if any, ever wholly congratulatory.

In such a context the relatively minor, if emblematic, flurries of disagreement between the Office and YW specialist HMI were, by 1992, to be swamped by the political waves which would overwhelm the Inspectorate as a whole. Fortunately individual HMI, both those already retired but still very active throughout the 1970s and 1980s (pre-eminently Edwin Sims), and those who resigned at that time or soon after in the light of subsequent experience, like Tom Wylie (who had led the team during much of its last dynamic phase) and other leading specialists, continued to play an active part in constructive developments. As the 1980s progressed, and subsequently, this part was to become increasingly as independent of the Department, and even more substantial than had been the case earlier with their adult education colleagues. Youth work started without HMI. It may be justly claimed that it flourished and outlasted the inspectorate because it colonised a small but important part of it, and retained these active experts into a new era. Youth service HMI cannot be accused of having gone out 'with a whimper'.

Notes

1. Dr Mark Abraham's Survey of Consumer Spending estimated it at 5 per cent of the national total as early as 1959.
2. A fear often expressed but never (so far) justified.
3. An HMI youth specialist's marginal note: 'Seems quaint now! Unrealistic then. Jewish Y. Work was outstanding!'
4. Developments in YS provision and working can be traced in detail in *Youth Service* which was published by the Ministry from 1960.
5. Such encouragement to Local Authorities to help the YS was followed in 1965 by the setting up of a Sports Council to advise them on matters relevant to the development of amateur sport and physical recreation services, and to foster co-operation. The SI for physical education and his team, almost all of whom had OFE responsibilities, were heavily involved in this development and worked closely with the Council subsequently. When the Council in 1972 became a non-departmental public body (a 'Quango') with a royal charter, an OFE SI was appointed as a formal assessor to it.

6   Careers education and guidance

Such efforts as had been made in the 1930s to help young people secure suitable employment had resulted in a patchwork of provision. The Ministry of Labour had a long-standing interest in the welfare of young people who were in employment. It and a number of LEAs were the major providers of a 'Juvenile Employment Service'. However, this was not universal, and generally speaking it was concerned only with those who left school at the statutory minimum age. The main concern was to find jobs for fourteen year-olds rather than with advice or guidance; no comprehensive information about career opportunities and their various requirements was collected or disseminated. Many areas with substantial populations had no provision at all. In some the Ministry of Labour also ran a restricted service until 1952 for voluntary associations of grammar schools; public schools, too, had an advisory organisation. They, and a number of other schools individually provided some sort of careers service through nominated careers teachers. These mostly saw their role as job-finding. The basis of information on which it rested was often very slender, except where their advice related to higher and, more rarely, to further education.[1] There was no co-ordination between such concerned organisations as existed.

A number of voluntary organisations contributed useful careers information. Most important was the National Institute of Industrial Psychology. This also provided a careers advisory service to young people on a fee paying basis, and it was responsible for much early work on the technical aspects of effective careers guidance.

Early post-war development

In 1944 the Ministry of Labour set up a committee under the chairmanship of Sir Godfrey Ince (lately its Permanent Secretary), with Dr AE Morgan, the leading academic expert of the time on the problems and needs of young people, as its secretary. Both the Board of Education and the Scottish Education Department were represented. The most comprehensive account (Hegginbotham, 1951) of the committee's work makes no reference to HMI, but stresses the importance of the pioneering work being done by some LEAs.

The Employment and Training Act 1948 resulted partly from the committee's work. It variously re-organised, rationalised and universalised provision to give modest help at least to all those who were leaving school at the minimum legal age. It established a unique inter-departmental unit, the Central Youth Employment Executive (CYEE), to run the service. This was now to be provided by all the LEAs which chose to assume the responsibility, but it would be financed through the Ministry of Labour. In the event, 144 of the then 189 LEAs in Great Britain, covering 80 per cent of school leavers, opted to run the service. Many of them had not previously had this responsibility. The minority of LEAs were obliged by the Act to facilitate the work of a similar service organised by the Ministry of Labour, with nominated staff working to the new CYEE.

In practice the CYEE was part of the Ministry of Labour, which was responsible for the general direction of policy, the style of the service, and its administration as the Youth Employment Service (YES). However, two HMI (one of them from the Scottish Education Department) were seconded to be members of the executive committee running the service. Its chairman was an assistant secretary from the Ministry of Labour, which also provided the other members of the Executive. These included officers responsible for administration and finance (including LEA expenditures), the chief of an inspection team, a member in charge of producing an increasing volume of information about careers, and one of the Ministry's occupational psychologists, a group whose work had developed enormously during the war years. All the subordinate staff were from the Ministry. A National Advisory Council represented the LEAs and the increasingly influential professional association of LEA Youth Employment Officers which later developed into the Institute of Careers Guidance.

Growing educational influence

RD Salter Davies joined the CYEE as its English HMI member, and he played a major part in setting up the new system. Like his successors he devoted most of his time during that posting to CYEE work, including the training of Ministry of Labour staff for the work. The Scottish HMI member worked in a more part-time capacity, though in the early stages of development an Anglo-Scottish group had been formed to assist in planning. Subsequently Scottish HMI as well as the Employment Department's CYEE Chief Inspector were members of the HMI sub-panel which met regularly to consider the needs of the developing service. Its work was based in the usual way on the findings of pastoral visits and the full inspections undertaken. For these, OFE HMI were always the reporting inspectors; the inspection teams always included the schools HMI concerned as well as a CYEE inspector. In the early years of the new service OFE HMI ran a number of courses both for HMI themselves and for staff of LEAs and their schools, to introduce them to their new responsibilities. Salter Davies took over SI responsibility for both the YES and the Youth Service and was replaced by R Field in 1949.

The structure of the new service was always dominated by the Ministry of Labour (later Department of Employment) which financed it. Staff operating the LEA services, however, saw themselves as belonging to the LEA service and working to its standards while meeting the Ministry of Labour requirements. One of them remembers HMI as their 'principal friends in the work context'. Policy was increasingly affected by the outcome of the inspections conducted by HMI with a CYEE inspector, leading to the regular issue of DES-style reports. The OFE inspectorate assumed a leading role in evaluating the careers education and guidance work of the youth employment officers in the schools, as well as the schools' own contribution to the work.

It may seem anomalous that careers education and guidance should have been made, and remained for 30 years, the responsibility of the OFE inspectorate rather than secondary schools HMI. Its relationship to life after school may have been one reason. The main one was probably the presumed relationship to the ill-founded expectation of universal day release to county colleges. Many OFE HMI had, of course, considerable schools experience, and all had some. Schools general inspectors spent varying amounts of time contributing to the inspections and reports, and schools insights were thus available to the sub-panel which kept the service under review. It also included TCA HMI to bring in vocational education expertise, and CYEE representation.

The inspecting expertise brought by HMI to the reporting process was a significant factor in the steady improvement in the quality of careers education and guidance throughout the 1950s and 1960s. The inspections were essential in sorting out problems which often stemmed from aspects of the unaccustomed relationship of the LEAs with the Department of Employment. HMI certainly were influential, too, in improving local YES practice. However, up to the end of the 1970s only two HMI had had previous professional experience in the Careers Service, and one, who came in later and from the mid 1970s took over the staff inspector responsibility, had been a respected careers master. Owing to this limitation, and because of the weakness they identified in the system, HMI tended to emphasise the role of school staff in careers guidance rather than that of the Youth Employment Service.

In both LEA and Department of Employment-provided services, the organisation had started out primarily as a service aiming to place particularly the less able school leavers into jobs. With some notable exceptions this had led to the recruitment of staff at a level which could not really cope with the sort of long-term individual and group-based education and guidance, based on comprehensive information, which became recognised as the prime need of all pupils. Moreover, the service as a whole was split into its two distinct sections for 'statutory' and 'older' school leavers. Prior to the Local Government reforms of the 1970s, it was fragmented into far too many, often inefficiently small units. As a result the number and level of senior posts available was very restricted. The service, in consequence, attracted few really able entrants, although the high level of job satisfaction attracted and held many devoted and hardworking youth employment officers. The LEA staff professional association, later to become the Institute of Careers Guidance, played an unusually important role in the development of the service. From the outset it was responsible for the award of professional qualifications as well as publishing the only journal which dealt with professional problems, and thinking about careers work, up to the mid-1960s.

Impact on training and on the LEAs

Individual HMI played an important part in improving training facilities for officers employed in both the Ministry and LEA services. They gave substantial formal help to the Percy Committee which, in 1950, planned and secured improvements in the training of youth employment staff. These further stimulated the pioneering work of the Kent LEA, whose college at Swanley provided a one year course of training for LEA careers work staff from 1949. The Manchester LEA established a similar course soon after for the North of England. Much shorter courses, for which the HMI Executive member was primarily responsible, continued to furnish a less satisfactory preparation for the Employment Department staff.

The most important source of HMI influence was, however, as usual their ability, in co-operation with the CYEE inspectorate, to bring to the LEAs and those who worked in the service advice on its needs and development. It was, as ever, advice rooted in detailed knowledge of actual operations, which they acquired in their visits to Youth Employment Service offices and to the schools, where they observed the officers' interviews and talks. This was always done in close co-operation with a CYEE inspector, and extended as necessary to a scrutiny of record keeping and the officers' own industrial visits. The weight which HMI carried with LEAs was a most important factor, and tribute was paid to their role, notably by the LCC and its successor in education, the ILEA. Alone among LEAs, this employed a very substantial and pioneering careers staff which later included an inspector appointed to monitor its service. She became a major professional influence on development, wrote extensively on its problems (Avent, 1997) and co-operated closely with HMI in the development of careers education, which is considered below.

Training for careers work improved significantly after the establishment of the Local Government Training Board in 1964, and with it concern for improving the standard of local authority services generally. University interest in training for careers work also grew, and subsequently research. Professor Alec Rodger's activity at the National Institute of Industrial Psychology and, later, at Birkbeck College, provided a much needed intellectual as well as practical stimulus to developing professional practice. Later Professor Dobbinson at the University of Reading became a major influence towards developing a much more client-centred and educationally oriented approach to careers work.

All these developments offered the prospect of major changes, but these were not easy to secure. The YES had started as a low-cost mechanism for placing less able statutory leavers in jobs, and its officers were expected to cope with anything from 500 to 1,000 individuals each year. Poor resourcing continued to affect adversely both attitudes and practices in the new service which developed after the 1948 Act. Pupils were talked to, encouraged to think before running blindly into jobs, interviewed and offered 'placing interviews'. However, the system was still very rigid and its approach to meeting the needs of young people in planning their future careers sadly limited.

Field, and HE Edwards who succeeded him in 1960 as the English HMI seconded to the CYEE, undoubtedly played a part in a general improvement of the service in the 1950s and 1960s, but had less obvious influence on its development than their predecessor was able to exert when it was being created. However, the growing number of trained staff rapidly made a favourable impact. CYEE published more and steadily improving information about career possibilities. Under its influence, too, the minimal information statutorily provided by the schools about the educational potential of those leaving at the minimum age was supplemented and then superseded by better general practice. In all this the Institute of Careers Officers played an important part.

Nevertheless the careers service still concentrated on talent matching by placement, and failed to give any real attention to helping school leavers to understand, let alone prepare themselves for, the career possibilities which the world of employment offered. The precise weight of the HMI contribution to general improvement of the organisation and practice of the Careers Service (as the YES came to be called) is unclear. What remained to be understood and acted upon was the potential contribution of the schools.

A radical new approach

HMI's contribution to the development of careers work within the schools is better documented. It began quite simply. HES Marks, who joined HMI in 1950 from AE, was based in the West Riding. As part of his training he had to learn rapidly about schools. In the process he found himself upset by what he saw as an *educational* failure, to inform young people about the world of work, to use this obvious interest on their part to illuminate the standard subjects of the curriculum, to help them to discover their own career interests and potential, and thus to make a really informed career choice. This led to discussions with (Sir) Alec Clegg, the Chief Education Officer, and the conviction that a careers concern needed to be developed within the schools as part of the normal curriculum and pastoral care. What was new was the idea that education about the world of work and its possibilities, and reflection about oneself as an individual person and the discovery of one's own interests and potential, should be seen as an important objective throughout the standard curriculum and over a period of years.

Careers teachers had, of course, long been in post in independent and later in some other secondary schools. However, their role was usually limited to placement, in which they often worked devotedly but without the skill and resources available to the careers service, and sometimes more to the advantage of local employers than of pupils. The development of an educational role for careers teachers in all secondary schools seemed as essential a key to progress as the improvement of the statutorily based YES. A first experimental course for school careers staff was organised by HMI with the West Riding LEA in 1953. OFE HMI interest in the possibilities and in the improvement of the work of careers education, guidance and advice generally, continued and intensified as the pioneer work in the West Riding fed through to the HMI YES Sub-panel.

An important breakthrough in the recognition of the development of careers education and guidance work in schools came with the running of a first DES national short course for careers teachers in December 1960,[2] which was followed annually by others. The movement to develop careers education was, later, given considerable impetus by the publication of the Newsom Report in August 1963 (Ministry of Education, 1963), which echoed HMI's original concern by advocating careers education as an essential and pervasive feature of the curriculum. It should involve a team of teachers, and a deliber-ately outgoing programme during the last years, rather than weeks, of schooling. Significantly, both Clegg and Catherine Avent were members of the committee.

The YES Sub-Panel of HMI had now recognised the need to disseminate information about careers education and its chairman, Geoffrey Petter (now a DI, with substantial OFE experience in addition to his secondary roots) wrote a pamphlet on Careers Guidance which was published by the DES in 1965. As commonly with DES publications, it was based on a series of inspection visits, described existing good practice in different kinds of secondary schools, and analysed the role of the careers teacher. *Trends*, the Department's quarterly journal (October 1966) also contributed to what was as near a campaign as HMI could contemplate, with an article on 'Team Work in Vocational Guid-ance' by Salter Davies, now Chief Inspector OFE. Others followed.

It was realised, however, that neither the pamphlet nor an annual short course could be expected to make the large-scale impact on every secondary school in the country which was needed. The Sub-panel now adopted the cascading methods in which OFE specialists had been engaged to make a similar large-scale impact on youth service leadership. The scheme began with a sequence of three national advanced courses for selected groups of leading practitioners from each region, intended to turn them into trainers. This resulted in the creation of regional training teams of HMI and LEA staff, which spawned hosts of local and regional courses organised by the LEAs and HMI. The scale of this vital development is indicated by figures which show that in 1970–71 alone (five years after the first trainers' course) 800 teachers attended basic careers teachers' courses and 100 were members of follow-up courses mainly intended to produce staff for further short courses. Some of the regional courses successfully used the cachet of HMI's active involvement in overcoming head teachers' resistance to giving time and resources to careers work. They were invited to join their own careers teachers and participate actively in the culminating final day of courses. Several chief education officers, including Sir Alec Clegg, set an example by joining in.

Recognition of the need for development of careers advisory work in schools and colleges had been greatly helped by the import from the United States of thinking about counselling, both client-centred and vocational. The first English training courses for counsellors were established at Keele (directed by Professor Gilbert Wren from the University of Minnesota, assisted by a recently retired Chief Inspector (CJ Gill), and at Reading. A Careers Research and Advisory Centre had been established in 1964 as a private organisation. Its courses and publications became increasingly influential and, as the National Institute for Careers Education and Counselling, it continues to be a major influence.

Teachers' unions also began gradually to take an active interest in careers work. Commercial interests realised the possibilities in relation to their own recruitment needs. Even more importantly, they started providing information and later counselling services on a commercial basis, like those of the National Institute of Industrial Psychology. Careers exhibitions and conventions became common features of the educational landscape. A specialised one term training course for school careers staff was established first at Edge Hill College, and extended to a full year in 1971. The interest of the teacher members of DES careers short courses, encouraged by HMI, led by 1969 to the foundation of a National Association of Careers Teachers. Trailing perhaps behind other areas of counselling, careers work gradually gained a fair level of acceptance as part of educational provision.

Effect on the CYEE

Securing improvement in the style and effectiveness of the work of the YES was inevitably slow. HMI influence towards change was, perhaps unfortunately, not radical in the period. It developed steadily in scope and authority, but never tackled effectively the major problem of the proper relationship between the careers teacher and the careers officer, calling for team style co-operation but leaving detail to be worked out in each individual situation. However, Marks now took over the English HMI post at the CYEE from 1969 to 1971. With the crucial aid of a sympathetic Chairman he was able to influence the Executive towards policy changes which took increasing account of the development of careers education and relevant counselling within the schools, and recognised the case for much longer-term careers guidance. Other OFE HMI helped increasingly also with the training of Department of Employment Careers Officers, for which he was responsible.

Drawing upon the output from so many courses in addition to inspection reports and visits, the YES sub-panel of HMI was now able to provide a stream of detailed advice on the conduct of careers education, on co-operation with the YES and its officers, and on the creation and equipment of careers rooms and other resources in schools. However, further progress on these lines also depended on YEOs having time for these further duties, and this must involve more expenditure on the service. The need for more and better training for all YES staff was also constantly emphasised.

Obtaining additional funds was a source of difficulty. On the other hand the raising of the school leaving age and the trend for more pupils to stay on beyond that age allowed HMI to exert pressure for a better careers service and for more and better careers teaching. The best provision for older school leavers was a helpful model, as were the careers teams in schools, which were increasingly emerging from the joint training teams' efforts.

By 1975 a new Employment and Training Act had put an end to the unique and imaginative cross-departmental control of the careers service, but it also ended, at last, the dual provision. All LEAs were now obliged to run the service in their schools with Department of Employment finance and control. The Act also allowed them to offer an adult vocational guidance service if they wished. They made increasing use of this, particularly for students in FE colleges. A new 'Careers Branch' in the Department of Employment was given powers to run a general adult careers guidance service, and took advantage of them. The Branch provided schools with a steadily improving flow of more comprehensive careers information. Following further published surveys of school practice, team work involving careers officers and school careers staff in providing longer term guidance including an educational element was further pressed upon schools by the DES, and now became the accepted pattern.

Transfer of responsibility

After 1975 primary responsibility in the DES rested with a secondary schools SI who had experience as a leading careers master. He presided over a Careers Sub-panel (now more prosaically named a committee) which included high level FE inspectors as well as some who survived from OFE days, and representation from the Department of Employment. The old pattern of joint inspection continued at the beginning of the new era, though with growing demands on HMI time their help with inspection on the ground diminished. By 1983–84 the Department of Employment Careers Branch Annual Report noted that HMI participated in less than half the formal inspections, and that by no means all the DES Divisions still had concerned committees. While the

HMI function survived, however, they continued to run training courses for careers teachers.

From being a very minor concern of the DES hierarchy, however, careers education became from the 1980s onwards increasingly a matter of high-level government interest. As early as 1977 the DES publication *Educating our Children*, linked with growing worries about comparative educational standards, identified careers education as 'one of the fixed points in the curriculum'. Though this was for a time dropped from policy statements, from the early 1980s the spectacular growth of unemployment among young people gave further impetus to high-level government interest. Careers work gained again, too, from the appointment of a Secretary of State in 1983 who urged the need for development in the schools of a positive and co-operative attitude towards industry. This chimed with the Thatcherite years' enthusiastic development of the general trend towards the 'new vocationalism' as central to educational planning, and an increased recognition of the importance of industrial training. The improvement in provision was halted from time to time, or even forced into retreat by demands for economy. Provision also suffered from the growing passion for constant organisational change, including privatisation and efforts to introduce competition into education. Whether even the long-delayed amalgamation of the Education and Employment Departments will lead to improvements in careers assistance to young people remains to be seen.

A large number of publications now testifies to the increased significance of careers education. Among them the most recent account of the work and its problems (Watts *et al*, 1996) comments that the problem of the relationship between careers education and professional vocational guidance remains unsolved and 'the (careers) service probably faces a future with as many if not more uncertainties than at any time since its establishment'. What is clear is that, starting in the 1950s and reaching its peak during that and the following decade, OFE inspectors were primarily responsible for the major development in English education which has been outlined in this chapter. They also bequeathed to it problems which they had recognised, but which they had not the power to solve.

Notes

1. 'Sir, I would rather see one of my girls serving behind a shop counter', shuddered a grammar school headmistress to HMI, 'than allow her to go to the Tech'.
2. The editor, then a recent HMI, recalls his own and fellow course members' excitement at what seemed a revolution in what could, and was beginning to, happen in this, to him, new field of endeavour.

7 Liberal and general studies in Further Education

Until the mid-1950s a major part of post-school technical, commercial and art (TCA) education was provided in part-time evening courses. Some, primarily at more advanced levels, took place in separate further education institutions or in secondary technical schools which changed their name to 'institutes' in the evening. A very large proportion, however, was housed in school buildings – especially the evening institutes which provided the bulk of preparatory (lower level) general, technical and commercial courses. These part-time courses were mostly taught by part-time staff, some of whom were school teachers though many were employed during the day in industry and commerce.

Attendance, though sometimes encouraged by employers, was voluntary and spread over two or three evenings a week. In such a time-constrained context courses were strictly technical in content and contained no separately defined 'liberal' or 'general' ingredient. Where a language element was specified it was defined as 'secretarial English', a curious linguistic monster; otherwise there could simply be a requirement to have passed matriculation or the general certificate examination in English before Chartered status in the technologies or some equivalent would be conferred. English as a form of general education was made a compulsory part of the course in the rare exceptions where day release FE had been introduced by enlightened employers such as the Post Office and the chocolate manufacturers, or in areas where survivals lingered of the Fisher Act's intention to start day continuation schools, or of intended county colleges. One of the authors has vivid memories of teaching it from 4 to 5 pm on Friday afternoons in 1950 to butchers' and tailors' apprentices in the cellars of what is now one of London's universities. Some academic roots go deep.

Inspection of whatever was perceived as, or derived from, county college work, and of the evening institutes as such, was the responsibility of OFE HMI. However, where TCA work 'proper' was concerned there was no identifiably 'liberal' element to inspect. No specialist inspectors as distinct from those qualified and experienced in technical and commercial subjects were sought or appointed. The technical, commercial and art specialists appeared in a separate TCA column of the handbook of HMI duties ('List 6'), with their own hierarchy headed by a CI with an appropriate complement of SIs and basic grade HMI, with subject and geographical assignments matching, though separate from, those of the schools or OFE inspectorates. Only rarely did TCA inspectors have schools assignments, and then mainly in secondary technical or 'central' schools. The number of these schools shrank rapidly as they were absorbed into the newly formed comprehensives, or became the day time components of technical colleges or institutes when these developed day provision.

Origins

Changes to the organisation of TCA provision, its curriculum and the manner of its delivery proceeded with increasing momentum from the mid-50s, driven particularly by the White Paper, *Technical Education*, of February 1956. They affected all levels of the FE curriculum and context in the public sector and stimulated the promotion of liberal and general studies as a desirable feature of vocational education.

A number of influences had contributed to this. The most important was almost certainly the publication of *Liberal Education in a Technical Age* (NIAE, 1955). This was the report of a committee of enquiry set up by the NIAE with the additional sponsorship of the Association of Principals of Technical Institutions and the Association of Technical Institutions. Its chairman was Sir Robert Wood, who had played such an important part in the creation of OFE and its inspectorate, and by then retired from the permanent secretaryship of the Ministry. The Ministry's assessors were F Bray of the Office, Sir Ben Bowen Thomas who was personally much involved with Welsh AE, and WR Elliott, then SI for AE. Boris Ford (later of the University of Sussex), who had been involved in army education, was the secretary, and evidence was taken from every conceivable source, including OFE HMI.

The report took its inception from the NIAE's 1952 report on *Social Aspects of Further Education*, and its enquiry into what was then being done to 'encourage ... students ... to widen their cultural interests and help to develop their sense of social responsibility'. The report continues: 'It is a question which has been much debated in recent years as part of the larger problem of reconciling liberal and cultural values with the technical and specialist skills needed in contemporary society.' To pursue the question the NIAE set up the new enquiry in 1953; its report (NIAE, 1955) was published to much acclaim in 1955. According to the librarian of a technical teachers' training college the report had the temporary distinction of being stolen even more frequently than engineering textbooks.

CP Snow's famous article, 'The Two Cultures' (Snow, 1956) and its detailed expansion and passionate peroration in his Rede Lecture (Snow, 1959) provoked enormous publicity. Together with the NIAE report it stimulated a rapid response in the form of DES Circular 323 of 1957, on *Liberal Studies in Technical Colleges*. The circular's immediate purpose was to suggest the broadening of the curricula for the new full-time Diploma in Technology then being pioneered by the developing Colleges of Advanced Technology. It gave voice to Ministry awareness of the growing opinion in higher education circles that such advanced courses of full-time study should be broader in concept and content than had been feasible in part-time technical education.

Ministry and HMI reaction

The drafting of the Circular was largely the work of the TCA SIs for Engineering and Business Studies; there is little evidence that the members of their respective HMI panels, or the Art specialists, were significantly involved or in sympathy with its recommendations. It should, however, be borne in mind that the role and mode of working of TCA HMI differed greatly from those of serving OFE and Schools HMI. At this time their major responsibility was control over the distribution and validation of courses leading to the, then, core of technical and business education qualifications, the National Certificates and Diplomas in all the main technologies. The Minister of Education was joint signatory to each of these, and therefore a guarantor of their quality and national recognition. Nearly all of the legwork and monitoring of the courses leading to these qualifications was a major task of TCA HMI. To these quasi-administrative duties was added the monitoring, in co-operation with the LEAs, of the design, buildings and equipment of the new and expanding FE Colleges at all levels.

It is therefore hardly surprising that, at first, Circular 323 had only a limited impact on the TCA inspectorate, or indeed on the inspectorate as a whole. After all, liberal and general studies could not be identified as the territory of any existing business or technical subject specialist HMI specifically appointed and assigned to inspect them, nor were they examined. There were, however, a number of HMI already in post and designated as FE, albeit 'Other' FE, whose principal concern was the so-called 'non-vocational' education and personal development of post-school young people and adults. OFE HMI operated in the statutory and voluntary youth service or in the great variety of AE in university or WEA classes, LEA evening institutes, educational centres, community centres, women's guilds and institutes, and many other concerns. This relatively small group of HMI had all been appointed with relevant experience and qualifications in one or more sectors of this wide field. They were headed by a CI for OFE who, prior to his promotion, had been on secondment to the CYEE with its overarching concern for careers guidance in school, further education and transition to employment.

It was to these latter HMI that the Ministry, the SCI and the CI for TCA were to look increasingly for information and guidance based on first hand inspection of developments in liberal and general studies in FE. It would be comforting to record that all this was the result of clear and conscious decision, but it would be misleading to do so. It was rather a *post hoc* reaction by the inspectorate to a particular aspect of the much wider changes afoot in FE as a whole. The significant milestones were the Crowther Report, *15–18*, in 1959 and the White Paper *Better Opportunities in Technical Education* in 1961, whose impact on AE in evening institutes has been mentioned earlier (p 54). The former had recommended that part-time (ie, mainly day-release) courses for craftsmen and technicians should be lengthened to 330 hours per year, and that time given to English and general studies be proportionately included.

The Advisory Committee and the pamphlet

This recommendation was taken up in the 1961 White Paper, which went on to refer to the need for 'experiments in the form in which general studies [*sic*] can best be introduced into courses for this type of student, and into the best methods of teaching them'. On the recommendation of the Working Party on the Reorganisation of Part-time Technical Courses, the Ministry set up an advisory committee on general studies, whose members were nominated by national and regional examining bodies, relevant teachers' associations, industry, the TUC and the BBC. It thus brought together people with a wide variety of teaching experience in FE and industrial training under the chairmanship of the CI for technical education. Two HMI OFE specialists with AE backgrounds supported him. SI Ted Parkinson was able to report on HMI experience of inspecting English and general studies in county college-type courses. The other, Eric Sudale, was subsequently promoted to be the first SI for general education, with specific responsibility for general and liberal studies in FE.

The Working Party was asked to 'draft notes' for the guidance of FE colleges on the arrangements for and treatment of general studies when part-time technical courses were lengthened, 'to make approximately 90 hours per year available for them'. The immediate context of its observations and suggestions was the new General Course in engineering. The Committee, however, encouraged by its chairman, did not hesitate to point out that they were equally relevant to part-time courses for technicians and craftsmen in other technologies. It added that its recommendations were 'based on the assumption that two and a half to three hours per week are available for these studies'. 'Where this allocation is not yet possible [they] may be helpful to colleges making provision for general studies on a more limited scale both within and outside the curriculum.'

The Working Party noted that it was aware of a widespread lack of experience in the field, as well as among its own members. This prevented any subsequent fleshing out of Circular 323, and they continued modestly that their immediate purpose was to 'suggest material and treatment for general studies in lower level technical courses (though) its findings may also stimulate constructive thinking about the possible forms in which these studies might play their part in more advanced courses.'

The Working Party's findings were published as a Ministry of Education Pamphlet, *General Studies in Technical Colleges*, in July 1962 with a commendatory foreword by the then Minister, Sir Edward Boyle. The final draft was the work of Fred Flower, the Principal of the LCC's Kingsway Day College, and Parkinson.

The pamphlet went much further than was usual with Ministry publications of the kind at the time, in not only suggesting lines of approach to the content of general studies but also the actual subject matter in which they might be embodied to provide a coherent teaching and learning strategy. It offered guidance on how such an approach might be deliberately planned so as to enhance the students' performance in both the spoken and the written word, to link their studies in college with their experience in their jobs, to indicate sources and materials which could be drawn on, and how the effectiveness of these studies and the students' reaction to them might be assessed.

Because of the working party's widely representative membership, valuably reinforced indeed from its City and Guilds host and by HMI, the pamphlet went further still and added an appendix offering detailed suggestions as to how its general lines of approach might be embodied in specific themes such as Communities and Relationships, A Study of Commercial Television, Trades Unions and Industrial Relationships, and Personal Relationships. All four treatments were based on experimental programmes of general studies being pioneered in actual colleges at the time.

For a 23-page HMSO pamphlet, costing two shillings, its effects, both in the short and long term, were remarkable. It rapidly went to the top of the HMSO best seller list of Ministry of Education pamphlets and was still selling well in the 1970s. It was a basic text in the courses leading to the FE Teachers' Certificate in the Colleges of Education (Technical). These colleges became the major sources of recruitment of staff for the newly formed and rapidly expanding departments of Liberal/General Studies in the FE colleges at large. Last and by no means least, the pamphlet gave substance, purpose and definition to a new and often challenging element in FE curricula at all levels, which had been supported by the Ministry from Circular 323 onwards. As such it was clearly an important area of concern for HMI in their routine inspection of the work.

Field response and co-operation

The Office and HMI in particular had thus been active not just in pressing innovation but assisting it practically. Even before the pamphlet was published, the field responded constructively with the foundation of a new professional body, the Association for Liberal Education (ALE), which merits a special note both for its own sake and because, unfashionably, its main preoccupation throughout was the improvement of professional practice. Its inaugural conference in April 1961 was chaired by the principal of a Polytechnic and addressed by the chief education officer of what was then still the LCC, by the director of education of United Steel, the principal of a college of technology and a senior university lecturer in physics. A key role both in the organisation of this conference and of the Association's subsequent annual conferences was played by the assistant secretary of the Cambridge University Board of Extra-Mural Studies, Denis Raymond, later to become HMI. Offered annually until at least the end of the 1970s, these conferences were essentially teachers' courses, and much appreciated as such. At field level, ALE was strongly supported by OFE HMI who had been assigned to general studies in FE; most of them joined or at least attended meetings of ALE's local or regional branches.

Throughout the period from 1960 to 1980 the Association made a significant contribution to the broadening of the scope and vision of FE at all levels. As HMI sought new members with experience appropriate to match the growth of general and liberal studies in the colleges, it is hardly surprising that at least three of these were former officers of ALE. From then on, at any rate until the introduction of Ofsted and new arrangements for the inspection of FE, the ALE and HMI general education specialists maintained close contact. For several years, indeed, ALE's officers had an annual meeting with the SCI.

The advent of general studies in FE was intertwined with two other developments. One was the rapid increase in the 1960s and accelerating beyond, in the number of 16-year-old school leavers who chose to attend O and A level courses at FE colleges rather than school, or re-sit them there after initial failure. The other was the eventually spectacular growth in the number of mature students returning to study and taking the same courses as 'second chance' education. Together they quickly made up a sizeable body of work and required a corresponding proportion of college staff.

The 1960s saw a proportionate increase in the recruitment of OFE HMI whose experience in teaching and management matched the whole of this area of work in FE. Each territorial division had its named specialist HMI for 'general education in FE', of whom a rapidly growing proportion had relevant experience. These specialists formed the substantial core of a national panel or committee chaired by the SI (Parkinson) who had been a co-author of the General Studies pamphlet and a member of the committee which produced it. He was succeeded on his retirement by EW Sudale.

Problems and conflict over curriculum and organisation

Circular 323 had suggested two ways of broadening technical curricula, by adding further subjects to them or by the more liberal approach to the technical subjects themselves which, as has been noted (see p. 62f) HMI was pressing upon the whole of LEA adult education as well, especially so in craft and language subjects and the arts. For a variety of reasons, deriving most powerfully from the departmental structure of the colleges and the points mechanism of determining staffing levels, it had been the additive approach with its lower salary bill which tended to make the running. The teaching of the additional subject matter was serviced by staff with, mostly, a humanities background whose numbers rose gradually to form general/liberal studies departments.

In many colleges this had produced something of a culture clash. From the heads of department down, the staffs of the dominant engineering and construction departments had in many cases left school at 14, 15 or 16, begun work in industry as apprentices, and had gained their technical qualifications through long, arduous and strictly focused part-time study on three or four evenings a week over a number of years. The typical general studies teacher on the other hand tended to be a product of full-time, often university, education, qualified in English, the humanities or the social sciences, with scant if any experience of industry. He, or she, was frequently in tune with, if not actually involved in, the turbulent anti-nuclear and other anti-establishment causes of the time. They were not uncommonly suspicious of, if not directly hostile to, their technical colleagues' image of the industries in which their students worked.

Many of them brought a missionary zeal to their teaching, often to be rebuffed by the suspicion, indifference or downright hostility which they met from their students. This was especially the case with day release students who could spend anything up to twelve hours a week on their courses. In order to fit in all their subjects, this sometimes entailed having to return to, or remain in, college for an evening session. Liberal studies were frequently allocated to these twilight or evening periods. Day release students were often critical of the subjects and topics which had 'to be fitted in'; they were 'too theoretical' or 'too remote' from the jobs they did during their working weeks.

In this context liberal and general studies were particularly open to criticism since neither the students, nor many of their technical or business teachers, nor their employers sympathised or even understood their purpose. One, then recently joined, HMI vividly remembers, at the end of a day inspecting liberal studies classes, being told by the principal of the college, 'Of course, most of my heads of department, and I agree with them, consider liberal studies to be a load of rubbish.' The tyro HMI replied, 'Well, Principal, in your college they are', and then with horror realised that this was not how he had been taught by his mentor to proceed. Fortunately the principal took the riposte good-naturedly, and he and the inspector were able to carry on more fruitfully to discuss instances, in his and other colleges, where such studies were not rubbish.

For many a young day release student, general studies did, however, provide opportunities to discuss and sometimes learn more about topics like human relationships, multiracial societies, and law and order in a more or less controlled atmosphere. But it was all too easy for even sympathetic participants and specators to satirise the sort of classroom scenes which could result. In the novel, *Wilt*, published in 1976 with nostalgic hindsight, its author, Tom Sharpe, a sometime liberal studies lecturer himself, set his eponymous hero in a fairly typical FE college and tracked him through various encounters with day release students. In a class of apprentice butchers (Meat 1 on his teaching timetable) Wilt, having had a bruising time trying to interest them in Golding's novel *Lord of the Flies*, 'sat and listened as the class ranged far and wide about vasectomy and the coil, and Indians getting free transistors, and the plane that landed at Audley End with a lot of illegal immigrants, and what somebody's brother who was a policeman said about blacks, and how the Irish were just as bad, and bombs, and back to Catholics and birth control, and who'd want to live in Ireland where you couldn't even buy French letters, and so back to the pill'. It took teachers of exceptional charisma, patience, skill and motivation to sustain such a teaching programme for any length of time. It was hardly surprising that even the enthusiasts sometimes succumbed to the attractions of GCSE O and A level class teaching and other work with full-time students – which, moreover, attracted more 'points' and therefore a higher salary.

In short, the burgeoning liberal/general studies scene provided more than its fair share of interest for OFE HMI in the classroom, in negotiation with college administrations, with the LEAs concerned, and with HMI technical and commercial colleagues who, after all, shared the career and personal backgrounds of senior staff in the colleges. Through their first-hand observation in the course of both routine and reporting inspection, OFE HMI with general studies assignments were well aware of the chronic tensions inherent in the 'additive' approach to the task. Many of their technical specialist colleagues were similarly aware of the shortcomings of the occasional attempts by teachers in these departments at 'broadening' the treatment of the technical subjects themselves. The teachers' qualifications for doing so could be rather frail, and they were perhaps understandably prone, as the examination season approached, to use general studies time to add a final revisionary polish to the technical components of the course.

Further changes

By the early 1970s, major changes in the educational and training system were afoot. Many of them sprang from the growing body of opinion that the existing structures of vocational education and training were meeting the needs of only a minority of young workers, and that many of those identified by the Newsom Committee as the *other* half were ill-suited to the existing academically oriented and examination directed school curricula and modes of teaching. Even after the raising of the school leaving age to 16 in 1973, many still left school with no examination 'qualifications', or relevant vocational guidance.

Because the 1970s were a period of virtually full employment, most of these young people were able to find unskilled or semi-skilled jobs. However, they (especially girls) were often ill catered for by an inadequate and obsolescent system of industrial training, and ill-suited to an economy which was already experiencing an accelerated pace of technical change. The advent of the Technical and Business Education Councils and the qualifications they promoted stimulated major changes in the structure and content of technical and commercial examinations, while the Training Services Agency and its successor, the Manpower Services Commission, promised a major expansion of the coverage and constituency of vocational training.

This was also the context for the changes in the structure of the inspectorate. The OFE label disappeared and at both divisional and national levels there was now a single FE inspectorate. Separate meetings and conferences were replaced by single joint ones. Most of the HMI panels or committees for the major technologies and business studies came to include a representative of the general education committee, and there was reciprocal cross-representation.

Effects of changing HMI organisation

There were marked changes, too, in the working pattern of individual HMI. As district inspectors for the whole of FE, the former OFE specialists now found themselves as general inspectors, in most cases, of all the FE colleges in their integral LEA districts in addition to their former OFE (and sometimes school) loads, which included specialist responsibility for inspecting and advising on general studies throughout their territorial divisions. General studies departments were by now well on the way to becoming the largest departments of most FE colleges. Moreover, former OFE HMI brought with them the concept of a general inspector having responsibility for observing the teaching, and doing so right across all departments of an institution. It was clear that in institutions as large and complex as a majority of FE colleges this duty could only be discharged on a very modest sampling basis. Nonetheless, it appeared that few colleges had previously experienced even this reduced level of pastoral visiting by their general inspectors. After some initial surprise it was welcomed and appreciated as a useful 'new' service by HMI.

For former OFE HMI the increased assignments and their traditional concept of a general inspector's role meant greatly increased loads. If the colleges concerned received more educational attention than they had been used to, this could only be achieved by reducing that which had previously been paid to the AE, Youth and other components of these HMIs' assignments. The deficit was not made up from what may have been other, balancing, reductions. Former TCA – now FE – HMI retained (as did most FE colleges) their traditional structure of separate departments based on separate and specific technologies or subjects. However, they were progressively freed from their monitoring of the former National Certificate and Diploma courses and qualifications. These were now re-shaped and became the responsibility of the Technical and Business Education Councils and the Council for National Academic Awards. The SIs for the major technologies acted as the Department's assessors to their specialist committees.

Among these complexities and the net growth of FE it was perhaps inevitable that HMI's detailed knowledge of work on the ground should gradually become diluted, and with it their capacity for influencing it. Locally their most effective means of informing themselves and, where possible, giving educational assistance was through meetings of the ALE and similar gatherings. Nationally there had always been a sizeable section aimed at general and liberal studies lecturers at the annual OFE Salisbury course (see p 38). With the advent of the Technical and Business Education Councils and their assumption of the major responsibilities for both curricula and awards, there was a growing feeling in the inspectorate that change was needed. It was decided that the annual programme of HMI short courses for FE teachers should include at least one which was specifically focused on the general and communication studies components of courses for the TEC Certificate and Diploma courses in the context of the Councils' overall curriculum policy.

New concepts and related training

Such a course was accordingly mounted at the University of York in January 1976, planned and largely staffed by the general education in FE committee of HMI, and directed by EW Sudale. It brought together some 70 invited members of college staff drawn from each major region of England and Wales. Most of the colleges represented had accepted the course director's invitation to send two members of staff, both actively engaged in the planning and teaching of TEC courses but representing different disciplines. There was, therefore, an almost equal balance between the general and technical aspects of the curriculum. Both the principal speakers and the full-time HMI staff of the course had a matching diversity of specialist interest and teaching experience. The Manpower Services Commission, industry and the Technician Education Council were also represented.

In both conception and execution this course marked a crucial stage in the changing role of the general component of many FE curricula. There is no doubt that it moved in the direction of an integrationist rather than an additive approach: it looked towards the teaching of vocational subjects in their total context and meaning, rather than decorating them with cultural icing. Both had been suggested in Circular 323 in 1957, but it was the additive which had so far been most influential. The 1976 course and its successors embodied HMI's experience as well as that of leading practitioners, and gave general studies a decisive steer in the other direction, which it has maintained ever since.

There was a further and more general respect in which the amalgamation of the two FE inspectorates influenced the whole of FE and not just general studies. Following the publication in 1972 of the James Report on *Teacher Education and Training*, an Advisory Committee on the Supply and Training of Teachers (ACSTT) was set up, and this in turn created an FE Sub-Committee which became known as ACSTT(FE). Its First Report ('ACSTT 1'), on the training of full-time teachers in FE colleges, met with ministerial approval and was published in 1976. The Sub-Committee then settled down to consider training for the huge total of part-time teachers employed in vocational and especially in OFE, and the small number of full-time AE staff. The sub-committee's assessor was the SI for FE teacher training, J Maitland-Edwards, a biologist whose open-minded sympathies were later to make important contributions at a European level. He was anxious to make the findings of HMI inspection of FE training available, and to transfer into TCA practice the developments in training methodology which had characterised OFE over the years. He therefore secured the addition of SI for AE (HES Marks) and HMI responsible for AE training and research (KT Elsdon) to the team of assessors, and the addition of some experienced AE trainers to the Sub-Committee. The resulting Second Report ('ACSTT 2'), its immediate effects and eventual fate, have been described in Chapter 3 (p 64–67). However, Maitland-Edwards went on to organise a new annual inservice course on methods of teacher training and inservice training generally for FE staff. Former OFE and particularly interested former TCA HMI formed the course team under Maitland-Edwards's direction. The two ACSTT(FE) reports (the second of them for as much as two years before it was eventually published), *Explorations*, and some of the AE training papers became important texts for these courses, and they did much to introduce more recent thinking and practice into the field.

As early as 1967 two recently joined HMI were startled to hear themselves referred to as 'a new type of animal'. They soon discovered that they were to be the first newly recruited HMI with experience in OFE fields to take full FE responsibilities, including being general inspectors of technical and art colleges, within their LEA districts. In the event the OFE terminology did not die out for over a decade, since so many of the colleagues with whom they worked, including their mentors, had been recruited and still considered themselves, as OFE inspectors primarily, rather than as FE inspectors with an OFE specialism.

From General Education to General Certificates and NVQs

By 1980, however, the term OFE was rarely heard, and never in the General Education in FE committee. Within that committee, after Sudale's retirement as SI and chairman, there were still vigorous discussions about the development and practice of liberal studies. However, there was no chance in terms of inspecting hours available, or of an interested audience within the inspectorate or the Office, of mounting a formal inspection or survey of their provision. In many FE establishments also there was an increasing emphasis on examinable English and communication studies, often at the expense, at least in terms of curriculum development, of general or liberal studies. A few members of the General Education in FE committee had specialist assignments in AE, but the majority were concerned only as FE general and district inspectors with what had been OFE affairs.

From 1985 there was a faint echo of the 1960s and 1970s, when the SI for General Studies, David Short, became one of the two CI for FE. He took over responsibility, among other matters, for the area of work which had been OFE. From the late 1980s, however, both he and his fellow CI were more and more involved in arrangements to ease the passing of the established form of the inspectorate. What remained of liberal and general studies passed with it into the new educational forms and approaches that had come into favour.

8 Epilogue

In our introduction to this study we explained that this chapter differs from its predecessors in both purpose and content. It is even more of a composite than the rest; its amalgam of verbatim quotations and general or linking text is intended to convey something of the variety of personal attitudes and experience of OFE HMI and those who observed, worked and lived with them. It may assist readers if they remember that passages in inverted commas (both within the linking text and the longer indented sections) are verbatim quotations.

Different origins – different HMI

Adult education, youth work and community centres at any rate, the most clearly defining constituents of OFE, originated mostly from voluntary movements and wholly from services rather than long established and universally accepted institutional structures such as schools and colleges. Their very nature, as well as their relatively recent establishment, made them essentially dynamic and experimental in their concern to develop social, cultural and personal 'goods'. These had no conveniently measurable outputs, such as examination successes. It was HMI Bill Blake who, in 1969, 'disturbed the stagnant pool of the annual conference of all FE HMI by asserting that adult education was about love.' Most OFE HMI would have known what he meant.

Schools and colleges, by contrast, had relatively standard and mostly predictable tasks even if individual approaches to them differed. OFE had to meet widely differing local needs, could never be standard: every centre, club, or organisation had to invent itself in relation to its own particular (and frequently changing) context. However diluted, the sense of a movement, of vocation – and the legal and financial insecurity of being *other* – coloured work and workers to a greater or lesser extent: OFE was other in origin and remained other in all these respects; so, necessarily, was the self-concept of full-time workers in its various fields, if not all the part-time force.

Once a decision had been made to create a section of the inspectorate to have the care of this area of work, various consequences followed inevitably. It would have to be recruited from among those who were already expert in one or more of the disciplines covered by the acronym. This much was normal for HMI recruitment. What differed was that no-one doubted that schools and colleges should exist and be resourced. This was never true of OFE. Because of its peculiar nature, expertise here meant not only high competence and innovation; OFE experts also had to be developers, organisers, advocates and missionaries in and for their field; very often they had to defend its very existence. What may, perhaps, have been unexpected was that, as HMI, their attitudes and their approach to the task would have to reflect this peculiarity and its differences from the work and attitudes of their schools and TCA colleagues; they and their work would be regarded and valued accordingly. OFE inspectors and inspection had to reflect their field no less than their colleagues had to reflect schools, or colleges. 'X [who] never gets any dinner' (see p 155) illustrates the surprise to at least some established colleagues caused by the new arrival's enforced lifestyle.

Nevertheless all HMI were caught up in the hopeful ferment of reconstruction and educational development after the end of war in 1945. OFE duties were never intended to be a solely specialist task and especially in the first decade numbers of schools colleagues and a few from TCA were active members of the OFE team and often much committed to the work. They included some of the 'housecraft' or 'women's subjects' and many of the physical education specialists. These and other subject specialists continued to play an important part in OFE inspection.

Thus, in 1951 72 HMI had substantial OFE assignments. Of these only ten had been recruited as primarily OFE specialists, while 55 schools HMI (about one-sixth of the schools strength) had OFE duties and many were active in them. OFE HMI reached their maximum strength of 38 main specialist appointments (including CI and four SIs) in the mid-1960s; almost all had substantial professional experience in the field. A firmer leadership core had been formed; on the other hand the contribution of schools HMI as substantial general and district inspectors of OFE had, by then, shrunk to, perhaps, no more than some 20 really active contributors. The specialist core reflected inevitably and increasingly the educational environment from which HMI were drawn, an environment which differed greatly from that of schools and colleges, and changed far less over time, remaining insecure and subject to continual change.

For these reasons, and more than in schools and colleges, leading OFE staff were all overwhelmingly conscious of a vocation, of being part of a movement. They knew that their whole service was one that had yet to be developed. Moreover, all this had to be achieved against a background of widespread educational indifference, often of hostility, within severe financial constraints and repeated threats of extinction, and with all the penalties of being characterised as 'other' in origin. Their situation was unique to OFE. It inevitably coloured the outlook, if in varying degrees, of those who carried major responsibility within it. OFE HMI were drawn from among these.

Structures and relationships

The characteristics of the field had a further consequence for the relationships between HMI and those employed in it. All OFE provision shared a characteristic professional structure which differed diametrically from the rest of education, where very large numbers of full-time and an exiguous proportion of part-time (more accurately, *spare-time*) staff are employed. Thus schools and colleges had, and have, much steeper and more hierarchical structures of staffing and government. In OFE a tiny number of full time workers organised, controlled and sometimes trained a vast army of part-time professional staff. In the YS in particular these part-timers were overwhelmingly volunteers, though growing numbers of them received training, and over the years some passed from lay to professional and even trainer status. There were no, or next to no support staff. The pattern of few full-time staff, and enormous numbers of part-timers, voluntary, paid or unpaid, trained or untrained, professional or lay, was infinitely varied, and created structures which often found mutual understanding and co-operation difficult. The role of fostering these rested on OFE HMI, because their duty of care and knowledge, and their believed status, made them the only reference point which was universally accessible to the whole range of work and its organisations.

AE (including the universities and WEA districts, with much more generous staffing ratios than the LEAs) was better off than community and worse than the YS; it may serve to illustrate the point. There, at the time when the OFE HMI section was being built up to its eventual complement of 38, the overall proportion of full-time to part-time organising and teaching staff was 1:468. Later it briefly rose but then dropped steeply. OFE thus had an extremely horizontal structure; it was and remained distinctly democratic and egalitarian.

When specialist OFE HMI first came to be appointed they were necessarily drawn from among the full-time members of their emerging professions. Because there were so few of these, those recruited to HMI represented a disproportionate part of these tiny full-time cadres.[1] The element of selectivity was, of course, equally true of schools HMI, but these formed a minute proportion of a vast and established profession. The OFE specialists' numerical relationship to their field thus differed from that of HMI in schools and colleges. Because of this relationship their former colleagues continued to regard them as part, and leading members of, their profession and the movements from which they came, not as outsiders; not uncommonly they were re-absorbed by them on retirement. Meanwhile they tended to be regarded by their late colleagues still labouring in the field as being responsible to the vision which the 1944 Act presented, and for the Department's brief as it had been foreshadowed in that Act and the Ministry's early pronouncements. Subsequent changes in Ministry policy had not, after all, been propounded to the public with equal conviction. OFE HMIs' status and relationships *vis-à-vis* their field, as well as their own view of their role, thus differed again from that of HMI concerned with schools and colleges. An early OFE appointee recalls a carpeting from a chief inspector for publicly criticising ministerial policy aimed at reducing expenditure on AE classes. He learned that discretion was essential in the exercise of developmental activity: HMI independence, though guaranteed by Parliament in regard to reporting, had considerable if undefined limits elsewhere. In OFE even more than elsewhere words had to be selected with considerable art to ensure the publication of reports.

The field's perception of HMI was coloured further by the informality and collegiality typical of OFE work. When DES courses for YS staff and housecraft teachers shared a venue, a brief exchange was overheard: 'I heard one of your people call an HMI by his first name.' 'We usually do.' '… Kinky!' Both the bonds and the influence were stronger and more intimate because HMI and their peers holding the few full-time posts in the field were working in an overall educational environment which was at best neutral and sometimes hostile to their role. They depended on each other's expertise, support and, often, personal friendship.

It was rare, but possible for the pressures and relationships to cocoon HMI in their original or acquired approaches to their professional specialism or, more insidiously, in the practice of a given territory. The perennial policy of posting HMI to different parts of the country and varying the balance of their assignments was sound, necessary, and mostly sustained.

On the horns of a dilemma

OFE HMI were of the field but also of the Department. The field's expectations were that the Department would implement the Act and thus enable it to carry out its mission. The Department set up OFE HMI with the same end in view, only to be forced into reverse after a disappointingly short period. HMI were thus caught in the tension between, on the one hand, the developmental brief implicit in the Act, the policy brief with which they had been called into being and their personal sense of mission, and, on the other, the restrictive policies of the Department. Intended to report objectively to Ministers, but also to act on the field as advisers, catalysts, helpers and honest brokers, many felt themselves to be impaled on the horns of conflicting roles.

For some at least this added yet another element to their sense of distinctness from long established, seemingly secure and self-possessed schools colleagues and apparently power-conscious and managerial TCA brethren. 'Joining HMI from the free and easy collegiality of AE was stressful', writes a 1960s recruit. Another, facing his first residential Divisional Conference (with SCI and all CIs at the table) within months of joining, had been advised by his mentor to hide at the back and keep his mouth shut, only to be instructed by his DI to present the Division's OFE report. He recalls that the night before doing so he dreamt that he had to drive a newly painted red bus round an exhibition of antiques with CI for OFE and the regional OFE SI as his passengers.

The otherness of OFE inspection is nicely illustrated by Verner's (1959) classic theory of the marginality of AE as compared with the main body of education, but also points to its partial inadequacy. Marginal activities do indeed pay obvious penalties due to their remoteness from structural and political centres. However, marginality also places work and workers on the periphery, and this is where constructive and innovatory interaction with the environment can most easily take place. All OFE HMI and especially the core drawn directly from service in the field, were more directly in touch and often actively engaged with all forms of development than others, often leading it indirectly and sometimes even directly as in training courses and through research.

Work patterns and habits involved in all OFE inspection necessarily differed from those of other HMI; some consequences were noted in Chapter 2 (p. 34ff). However, what was it like, what did it 'feel like' to be, (as quoted there) one of that 'powerful and committed group' living and working among its peculiar institutions and in a manner somewhat different from other HMI? As might be expected from the nature of the job, and from their exceedingly varied backgrounds, the OFE group was a collection of individuals so diverse, so heterogeneous, so idiosyncratic, as to be an endless source of amazement, delight and sometimes vexation to its members as well as their colleagues. Their personal attitudes, and relationships with each other and with other sections of HMI, varied according to personality and outlook. They were also coloured by the great changes in the inspectorate generally and in departmental policies over the 30-odd years of the OFE inspectorate which this study endeavours to describe in some detail. Some of the subsequent developments up to 1992 only affected a later generation. Conditions also varied in the different territorial Divisions. Even the strength of commitment which characterised the background and the ethos of the group as a whole varied individually, and took different forms.

Nevertheless, because they were so few, because of their sense of being *other*, and proponents and defenders of a faith, however each of them might see it, their personal heterogeneity became a source of strength, and often the cement of friendship. Some of the 'little flock' may have felt permanently insecure, but generally they sensed that they shared a kingdom of their own. No generally valid picture is possible, but a mosaic may be attempted with the help of a number of colleagues' individual accounts of what it meant to them to belong.[2]

Personal experience

It is at least possible that, in addition to the personal there may have been generational differences within the group. Later recruits tended to add more pieces to the mosaic. This lends weight to the long account with which we

open. The writer, recruited in 1950 as an adult educator, 'recalls being introduced by the formidable CI for secondary schools to breakfast colleagues at his
first divisional conference: "this is X; he never gets any dinner"'. The style of
such a superficial remark may serve to illustrate a number of characteristics of
the inspectorate he joined in 1950:

> The feeling was of being admitted to a somewhat old-fashioned brother-
> hood, membership and feeling part of which I enormously enjoyed over
> nearly thirty years. It was a brotherhood with a common 'club' culture
> spread over all its sections ... This was the result of a deliberate post-war
> effort to create a more unified and egalitarian as well as teacher-friendly
> body to take the place of the more hierarchical, class-bound and (in
> many schools) feared inspectorate of the past. Membership of the broth-
> erhood brought for me, and I think fairly generally, a network of good
> friends, access to insights and wisdom and sources of specialist knowl-
> edge on almost every conceivable subject – a valued feature of
> inspectorate life.

> Brotherhood was an appropriate descriptor in the fifties, in that sex
> equality was still to be fully achieved. Early recruitment for OFE of a
> number of able women practitioners may have been an element in its
> speedy achievement. Independence of thought and action, including
> freedom to plan most of one's own daily activity with the freely accorded
> help of one's colleagues, were other aspects of the club culture. Freedom
> to organise one's own time also, of course, allowed professional indolence.
> Being both freer and 'marginal', OFE HMI may have been more at risk,
> but it was fortunately rare, if sometimes serious in its consequences.

> A genuine atmosphere of equality among at least potential equals was
> deliberately fostered. In my earliest days the sense of equality was main-
> tained by the relative absence of rank-based pay differentials and by a
> linked deliberate discouragement of ambition for promotion. Pay equality
> was brought to an end ... with some return of hierarchy and increased
> interest in promotion. Ability to plan one's own work was largely eroded
> for schools inspection by the 1970s, with mixed results for the impact and
> effectiveness of HMI influence, which it had been designed to
> strengthen. For OFE HMI it continued longer in some degree at least, to
> be one of the great attractions of the job, but amalgamation into a unified
> FE section of the inspectorate involved conforming to a pattern of work
> much more fully dictated by a variety of external influences. One major
> aspect of the common club-like culture which changed little over the
> years in spite of increasing work pressures, lay in the courtesy and restraint
> which marked our dealings with each other. It was reflected in the
> genuine friendliness and helpfulness of our mutual relations. A certain
> formality in relationships which survived rather longer in the inspectorate

than in other occupations was probably of some help in securing smooth team working; conflicts were almost unknown.

Regardless of the widely varying intensity and scope of working, amicable team work was one of the great strengths as well as the pleasures of inspectoral life. It provided a feeling of mutual support and was a source of constantly available friendly but usefully critical comment. It bettered the quality of my writing ... [helped] greatly towards sounder and relatively unbiased conclusions, towards an essential effort to deal with problems in the round and to discount individual prejudice ... it was an important factor in giving HMI reports and other pronouncements what authority they commanded. Whether the coded language and restrained expression of criticism ... were carried to excess is open to question. The inspectoral passion for confidentiality in relation to reports too long diminished their impact ... Teamwork was essential to our enjoyment of a job which was by its nature highly stressful, marked by considerable influence but without any executive power, dependent on persuasive abilities and the gaining of voluntary agreement. Empathy with the 'inspected', with HMI still retaining a certain sense of distance and even authoritative knowledge, had to be the basis of that relationship too, as has been suggested already. Perhaps it came more easily to OFE inspectors, but was also in some ways more difficult to sustain for them than ... for others. That I can recall very few incidents of unpleasant tension, let alone of angry confrontation, with those in the field I was trying to help should perhaps be a reason for some self-criticism. The deep-rooted conviction and insistence of inspectoral culture on keeping up friendly relationships with the inspected, if at all possible, was perhaps carried further than was warranted, particularly in OFE, where it was strengthened by a keen appreciation of the difficult problems its experimental nature posed to workers who were often volunteers, and generally poorly trained. Whether its deliberate abandonment overall with the reorganisation of the old inspectoral arrangements in 1992 produced better outcomes for educational provision seems to the writer to be doubtful. There may well be further changes, even incorporating some older models, as well as further fresh thinking.

In the decade following the 1944 Act, but decreasingly thereafter, HMI efforts to develop the extent and quality of OFE provision, depended to a considerable extent on the help of schools HMI. This co-operation reflected another aspect of inspectoral culture, then deliberately fostered through recruitment policy and involving a two year probationary period after joining. This was devoted in considerable measure to familiarising tyro HMI with the rich variety of educational provision as well as inspection of their field of special interest; it was conducted largely by sitting by a variety of Nellies, and later helping them in their work. This long probationary period provided a time of great interest for many, but it was also resented as keeping new HMI, including myself to some extent, in an unaccustomed pupillage too long and stopping them from making full use of what they felt to be the contribution they had joined to make. All had, of course, been selected because of their enthusiasm and imaginative approach to some aspect of education. In my case, due to the particular fortunate circumstances, the hasty posting of my mentor and the disinterest of my DI, the 'training period' was reduced and its intensity modified.

A related comment from another source notes 'the flexibility with which even probation was handled, while maintaining its forms, was typical of the way in which inspectorate practice varied endlessly according to "the needs of the service", the characteristics or the needs of individuals.'

The previous writer continues:

War-time experience and general post-war social optimism, combined with what they learned of the new OFE area, helped many schools inspectors to a lasting concern for OFE or some aspect of it, and OFE development in its early stages owed much to these relative amateurs. Of lasting importance too was the effective inspectoral influence ... of subject specialist HMI ... The considerable amount of time I spent, especially in my first fifteen years as an HMI, in introducing colleagues to the, for them, usually strange world of OFE provision, was a generally very enjoyable aspect of the job; it often 'paid off' in engendering a lasting interest.

Joining later and from the more turbulent worlds of youth work and community development, another colleague asks:

What drove us? Salter Davies's vision for a start ... the post-war dream of reconstruction; the idea of a new structure of society; in the war-time reports which blue-printed its possible nature, and which built on inter-war experiment to include a hefty element of community education/settlement/youth work. Salter's recruits' background reflects this. We had a natural impetus to bond, not only because of our separate label, but also because of the aggressive separateness of TCA, and the monolithic impermeability of P&S. We also had the impetus of a dream largely shared, and the freedom of HMI to roam, to see and to share. There was an immediate post-war intake, Charles Harvey, Simpson, and others, who brought a pre-war experience I can only guess at. Our group, I suppose, had been lucky to work in the immediate post-war years, when anything seemed possible, and experiment was welcome. The sixties, when there seemed to be a new flowering, were ideal for welding us together.

... The strength of the OFE team was implicit in its membership and circumstance. What of its impact? I think it did affect the thinking

and action of the inspectorate, partly through some effective writing –
the Community Working Party papers, *Explorations*; partly joint working
with TCA and P&S – eg, area surveys, and not least the concept of
everyone having an OFE assignment however little they did. Perhaps the
main effect was merely to force a different viewpoint based not within
but without the education service, but there was also challenge to
accepted views and hallowed practice.

... Was there any influence beyond the inspectorate? Was it sufficiently
affected to pass the influence on to the Office or the system? Doubtfully
and slight in my view, but I think there was substantial influence outside
the inspectorate and the established channels. In the field I suspect OFE
HMI had a direct influence on practitioners and practice much stronger,
or at least more effective than that of colleagues in schools and TCA. This
was partly because the world of OFE was itself less understood by main-
stream, and therefore by circumstance as well as nature more open to
reasoned outside influence, but partly also because from Salter on we all
held to a more informal discussion among equals rather than a hierarchical relationship ...

That egalitarianism was illustrated more than once by accounts of CI Mr Salter
Davies, such as his almost timid offer of his services to a very junior HMI course
director who had to fill an unexpected gap in his course team at short notice.

Another colleague describes his expectations:

My previous experience had given me the satisfaction of shaping and
developing institutions and met my need for the exercise of power. It had
also taught me that, to continue in such positions, I had to accept all the
much more humdrum responsibilities of maintenance. I had had my fill
of power and was glad to be rid of it, and of the bumph that is its inevitable accompaniment. Responsibility, on the other hand, and a sense of
service to others and to a cause is something I have always craved. It was
clear that I could look forward to both.

There was another reason why I felt reassured by the prospect. I knew
I was continually learning about various aspects of my profession and
contributing to discovery and innovation in it. But I was also afraid that a
time would come when I would run out of ideas, when my teaching
might become repetitive, and my administration mere maintenance. The
inspectorate promised to keep me and my knowledge and practice bright
through vicarious learning even if my own should run out of steam.

Women, men and families

If men HMI felt positive, even privileged, their wives and families were mostly
less than enthusiastic. There were positive aspects. The job was secure once

probation was passed, and the pay good. Much of the information husbands brought home and some of their enthusiasms were stimulating and led wives into new avenues and even new careers. The disruption of postings, however sensitively they were handled most of the time, was the same for all HMI families. OFE HMI had something of an advantage in that they almost certainly knew and were friendly with some main field professionals in the new area.

However, the negative side was more pronounced:

> For me it meant many anxious late nights when I knew the best thing to do was just to go to bed, but I nevertheless waited until I saw the car turning into the drive, and tried not to appear too relieved.

> Coming home after absence he was usually tired and overwrought.

> Our joint social life suffered. We couldn't commit ourselves to go to anything regularly together because we never knew what calls there would be on his time. But this also caused me to take initiatives to set up activities of my own.

> I felt increasingly isolated from my husband's life. In his previous work I felt involved because I knew the people with whom he was working and participated in the social activities. When he came home and talked about work I could take an interest. Now it was different. I rarely met the people with whom he worked; I could not take an active interest in the innumerable names and voices on the telephone. In later years and under less stress I have met and learned to know and love many of the far-scattered colleagues who were mere names in the past.

> The effect on children was less than beneficial, and doing his 'O' at home was a nuisance to them.

And, in sum: 'A good organisation, very committed, with good personal relationships, but a little hard to live with as an outsider.'

If wives of men HMI bore unfair burdens, many women HMI carried yet more than their share. The (universal) history of unequal pay ended in the 1950s for HMI; it left few traces, and briefly. More seriously, some of the older and especially pre-war HMI were not at ease with women and did not like working with them. Moreover, the style and manner of some of the older women craft specialists (as well as others) did little, maybe in response to their pre-war second-class treatment, to ease relationships or to welcome a new and different generation of women into their ranks. This confirmed what can only be called a degree of chauvinism common among TCA inspectors with their predominantly industrial engineering and construction background. It tended to shore up undesirable attitudes after they had disappeared from P&S, and which had had no chance of establishing themselves in the newly created OFE team.

In these circumstances it could and, indeed, did happen that the personal and home problems of women – both those with families and the single – were given less consideration than those of men HMI, especially if these had children of school age. To this must be added the perennial difficulty of recruiting women to the inspectorate. They were badly needed in their own right. In addition, while there were no HMI responsibilities a woman could not discharge, there were some which men could, or did not. There was a strong tendency consequently for women to be overloaded – especially if they were good at the job and perceived to be especially helpful. For a woman with major personal responsibilities OFE inspection was clearly more demanding than for most men: 'it was only after I retired that I realised I had friends and relations whom I had neglected … any sort of social life was practically ruled out.'

Finding enough women OFE specialists was thus specially difficult. Until the 1970s they were even more seriously under-represented in senior OFE field posts than elsewhere in education. This absolute shortage and the special characteristics of OFE assignments meant that few would contemplate applying. The close relationships with the panel dealing with domestic subjects helped: it was from its members that men HMI learned some of the specialist skills needed for their work as general inspectors in AE: 'I was always particularly well received by the very great majority of OFE colleagues with whom I worked closely, not least because they were so glad to have someone to help them with … expert knowledge on the women's craft side.' There were other skills, too. 'It was clear to me', writes a male HMI, 'that only a woman, and one with the intelligent sensitivity but unshakeable persistence of a Joan Sumner-Smith, could have persuaded X (a previously impenetrable LEA) to transform its OFE. Her engineer RSI used to maintain she was a lunatic; now he called her a witch for her pains.'

However, what was it like to *be* a woman in the OFE context as it evolved? How you reacted and managed as a woman, in the view of one colleague, had much more to do with individual personality than with the fact of sex. This colleague was always very happy with the OFE work, partly because OFE colleagues shared her attitude of enthusiasm and were themselves a more welcoming sort of team than a TCA group tended to be. 'I liked my work in OFE', another confirms, 'and I liked my OFE colleagues. I got on well with people in both FE and OFE, with very few exceptions.' The first colleague reports that she 'never had any trouble from being a woman with the people I inspected, who were always so memorably appreciative of the help HMI were trying to give.[3] The worst of OFE work were the endless long night journeys it involved.'

There were no problems, then, among OFE colleagues, though, one woman remembers, one could come across the rare male colleague who innocently assumed that one would *want* 'the little room' or to 'be mother' when the tea tray arrived. But generally speaking, among OFE colleagues equality of expectations no less than of status was so much taken for granted that the question did not arise. The few who could not call upon a major 'subject' qualification in addition to their rich and varied 'phase' experience could be exposed to experiences which their similarly qualified Primary specialist colleagues escaped, but this affected men no less than women. It was a different matter working with former TCA colleagues after amalgamation, when patronage was commonly added to their widespread dismissal of the validity of general studies. 'How I longed for the inspectorate to last just long enough to appoint a female engineer – did they ever?'

What was it like, how did it feel?

A voice from the early 1960s generation of HMI illustrates some causes of family stress, and also the way in which the unconsciously class-oriented 'club' feeling was being leavened by sometimes incandescent professional passions. 'Brotherhood' was taking on a different meaning:

> Not long after I had been told that I would be assigned to the X Division I received a postcard which began 'Welcome to the brotherhood' and asked me to meet the writer, my mentor, on my first morning. In the light of experience there turned out to be, as everywhere, rare individuals who did not seem to measure up to expectations. But a brotherhood it was in the sense that there was a kind of unquestioning trust in each other, and also the bond of generalised caring. Its essential ethos was more like that of an order, because its members imposed higher standards upon themselves than they expected from the profession at large. In that sense they were also an élite in intention and more often than not in practice. I mean an élite in the proper, not the jargon sense, as a group defined by freely accepted responsibility rather than privilege. It perceives itself as being *privileged to serve*, and its source of pride is the fulfilment of duty. This seems to me to have been the fundamental ethos of the OFE inspectorate and its attitude to its work and its place in society. It offered endless challenges, and a sense of being stretched to one's potential stature, to be used, and all this as one of a group bonded together in friendship as well as common purpose. For me, the inspectorate, or at least its OFE branch, was such an élite, and I rejoiced in it.
>
> Moreover, it was fun – and hardly ever boring. In over 20 years I cannot recall a day when the morning's stack of manilla envelopes did not contain something that interested and stimulated me.

A striking unanimity about the sense of service to a cause, of coherence and belonging emerges from the many comments of former colleagues, quite regardless of their varied specialisms. Perhaps we should therefore re-consider the nature of OFE in that light. Was it indeed a ragbag of activities which nobody knew what to call, and which were therefore lumped into the common anonymity of *otherness*? Was it mere chance or inspired foresight that linked together a range of endeavours which turned out to share a fundamental unity, and which reinforced a sense of that unity in their proponents?

Where lies the difference?

One colleague sees all OFE activities and most work done in OFE as second-choice or second chance, a retrieval of what has been missed, of failure, of incompleteness or dissatisfaction. Most obvious in penal education, youth work, Access education, liberal and general studies, he sees it as inherent also in the bulk of adult education. Another colleague points out its connection with community centres, community education and community development. OFE HMI, in sharing the hurt, worked not just at healing but at creating and strengthening the opportunities for fulfilment that were so often missed. They included creative activity of all kinds, extending and broadening enjoyment of a richer cultural life, and widened participation in civic education, active citizenship and social intercourse.

'We may accept the realities of that experience', comments another, 'but prefer not to see "The whole earth [as] our hospital". Is there an alternative interpretation?' Most colleagues' responses pointed to the contrast between the informality of what was OFE, compared to the institutional structures of schools and TCA. Institutions have their own tasks and their own momentum; however caring or person-oriented, their purposes are prescribed and their effectiveness is generally measured in terms of criteria such as pre-determined knowledge or skill acquired, examinations passed, qualifications won. They and their standards are subject to the imposition from outside of objectives, curricula, methods and policies.

Almost all the activities which sailed under the flag of OFE (one colleague points out that careers guidance may be considered in some degree an exception) had in common a number of radically contrasting characteristics most of which, indeed, constituted fundamental principles. The first of these was that OFE activities sought to discover the potential, whatever it was, within individuals, groups or indeed a community at large and the society of which it was part, and endeavoured to help them, by whatever means, to approach as near as possible to its fulfilment. The second was a corollary of the first, namely that the objectives and standards of every form of OFE were internal to that activity, arising from the characteristics and the potential within those who were involved in it, and not externally imposed, nor intended to serve external purposes. A third arose from the second. If objectives and standards arose from within, then the degree to which they were being achieved was, substantially, a measure of the distance that had been travelled from where the process had started in each individual instance, and the appropriateness of the direction of travel. The commonality here goes far to explain the sense of one-ness in OFE, and the bonds that united HMI who served it. So, a colleague points out, does the degree to which the efforts involved constant experiment and innovation, and were felt by some to be in the admired tradition of social and political emancipation through community educational activity.

OFE could never hope, nor was it intended, to increase the number of diplomas and certificates on the nation's walls, though it did, incidentally, do so to important effect in 'night school' and in the many youth organisations which operated 'badge' schemes to widespread family and client satisfaction. It could, and did, increase the nation's capacity for physical and spiritual health, for creativity and innovation, for critical thought, for imagination and for active citizenship. Governments which increasingly saw continuing education as solely aimed at the accumulation of formal qualifications could not be expected to support OFE except when (as some HMI believed) they saw some aspects of it as a means of countering the risk of social unrest.

The insecurity of OFE

The Youth Service, indeed, succeeded in maintaining itself, as did some aspects of OFE which were not subject to the Department, or had been hived off to Schools and to vocational FE. Everything else suffered, and the attitudes and reasoning are best illustrated in relation to AE. The view so clearly expressed by the later Lord Eccles (see p 61) was widely shared in the Department but also by many HMI, especially in schools and TCA, and sadly even by a few OFE specialists, who would have preferred to see what they dubbed 'a middle-class subsidy' transferred to what they regarded as more deserving beneficiaries. In its purely materialistic form, as worded by Eccles, it quite simply illustrates ignorance of the economic condition of the majority of the population – namely those who simply do not have the disposable income required to pay class fees which posed (and pose to-day) no problems for the minority. At the time of Eccles' minute a workman on national average wages, or his wife, could still 'buy' a course of 24 two-hour class meetings for five shillings, rarely more. Allowing for the cost of public transport, this was still practicable expenditure. Only a few years later the real cost which Eccles and others wanted students to meet would have been not around 2.5 (new) pence per hour but 21.8 pence (Hutchinson, 1959). This was simply beyond the purse of the great majority; so is its 1999 equivalent of 301.25 pence.

Were OFE HMI doomed to fail?

AE continued under attack for attracting mainly the middle classes. Yet it was known ever since the first publication of Trenaman's (1957) research that willingness to participate in demanding or cultural activity in adult life relates to the duration of initial education. As the 'children of the Fisher Act' reached the stage in their lives when they had spare time for adult education, they created the post-war boom of 1946–51 in new enrolments. So did those of the Butler Act in the 1960s and early 1970s. Throughout the period, participation in AE was steadily penetrating down through the class structure of society. When fee increases at multiples of the rate of inflation were imposed this development was reversed. Writing in the mid-1970s Wiltshire (Mee and Wiltshire, 1978) pointed out that British AE was rapidly approaching a condition in which only the affluent and the conspicuously deprived could afford to participate. Daines *et al* (1982) produced the evidence, as did a number of HMI full inspection reports. In effect, Wiltshire's prophecy had become fact by the time of its publication. The critics who described AE as a middle-class ghetto had themselves created it by pricing participation beyond the purses of anyone not very comfortably off. In so far as helping to bring AE to the people of England and Wales was OFE HMIs' duty, they had failed to overcome the resistance of successive governments, of the Office, and of their own colleagues in other sections of HMI.

A concerned woman colleague has pressed the editor to include comment on the consequences. He does so regardless of this section's balance, if only to recall AE's contribution to the life of this society before its cost to adult learners rose to current levels: this in order, as the Office calculated long ago (see p 60), to reduce educational expenditure by a percentage so minuscule that it could not benefit any other items in the budget. We have referred to the former mature state scholarships, to the few hundred students at a time in long-term residential colleges, to those in second chance courses in FE and those who prepare for them in Access courses. All these, and the large proportion of mature students in higher education (including the Open University) represent what was and remains a minority, namely those for most of whom these forms of AE are routes to career change. Yet they represent no more than a fraction of the number of those who *used to attend* ordinary, non-qualifying AE classes, however provided, before these were priced beyond the reach of most ordinary people. We should never forget that literally millions of them (two thirds women, whose need is greatest) in any one year did so to the enrichment of their lives, their personalities, and those with whom they came into contact. We need to remember the enhancement of their capacities for learning, of their judgement and of their sense of civic coherence contributed to society at large and, directly or at least indirectly, to the economy. When in doubt, it may be as well to recall Mrs A, the South Yorkshire miner's illiterate wife. She came, distraught, to a dressmaking class to find comfort and support, and help out the family budget. Over years of part-time study in an AE centre she became confident, an enthusiastic craftswoman, an excellent designer, a student at ease with print and number, took subject qualifications, trained as a teacher, and finished up as a lecturer in craft and design. Nor has the writer of these lines forgotten that it was the WEA which led him from the factory bench to university and work in AE. Neither his present-day equivalent nor Mrs A's can afford present-day class fees for AE. The very offer of NVQs and credits, and the conditions for acquiring them, would convince both that such classes are not for them: the drive for formal qualifications no less than fee levels, has destroyed AE's relevance to the lives of all but a minority. The attack was briefly staved off by Churchill's intervention (*cf* p 46), but in the long run the Philistines from Florence Horsbrugh and Eccles to Callaghan, Thatcher and the present incumbent have had their way, and the country has lost more than it can yet surmise.

At a much earlier stage HMI and others' concentration (based on then trusted research) on the geographical neighbourhood as the only proper basis for community provision, rather than narrower propinquities or the wide variety of interest groupings, was singularly unfortunate. Other mistakes supported or unopposed by OFE HMI will have occurred to readers of our account. The benefit of hindsight will discover legions of sins of omission. Many would agree that the failure to press on to a quick completion and publication of the Russell Report, before it could fall victim to political change following the defeat of the first Wilson government, was the most serious of all.

Other problems arose from the inspectorate's own structure, although by no means unknown elsewhere. A former DI generalises an earlier reference: 'some HMI were simply idle'. This may mean no more than saying that a few weeds may turn up in the tidiest garden. However, like other 'establishment' groupings, HMI – however selective – made mistakes and did not always succeed in ridding itself of them. Moreover, the law of gravitation applied. 'As in all bureaucratic organisations' one colleague comments 'those who were barely competent at their work but good at not offending powerful interests, had a way of rising irresistibly, and had then to be found a niche where they could do least harm. In accordance with the class structure of education generally the inspectorate tended to "hide" them not uncommonly by promotion to, or in, OFE and especially AE. Consequently the leadership of OFE was weakened as its number diminished.' The overall hierarchy of the inspectorate was drawn from schools and technical branches, and not overly imbued with ideas about the need to carry out the Act's intentions for OFE, nor HMI's duty to work, and speak independently, to that end. During the second half of our period at least (as in Matthew Arnold's day), those who did were as likely to sink as the compliant were to rise. 'Was AE seen as inessential cargo to jettison in order to save the foundering inspectorate ship?' asks one cynical colleague.

Two contrasting passages remain for the conclusion of this epilogue. One mirrors some of the measured reasonableness of HMI's way of conducting themselves in public writing, the other the passion that drove OFE HMI. Both are from primarily AE specialists; both are true and command the assent of both authors, depending on their mood. The editor must shoulder responsibility for the order of their appearance.

Looking back on my 20 years' service, I recall them as happy and generally optimistic, productive for their time as well as for the future, in spite of constant frustration and disappointment at slow progress and checks to improving provision. During my years of service post-war economic difficulties appeared to me a temporary if exaggerated reason for holding back from a fuller and more rapid implementation of the 1944 Act's ideals. AE then expanded remarkably fast through the 1960s, particularly perhaps in the areas in which I had most interest and personal responsibility, as elsewhere in good measure. So did other aspects of OFE provision, even if the search for economy became an increasing threat. It was not until the shelving of the Russell Report that major hopes faded, and even then possibilities of future political change gave some hope for the future of OFE and, particularly, for AE, for which a possible relatively rosy future had now been mapped out, while the YS continued in favour.

Happily even the later rush to narrow vocationalism in education, the passion for privatisation, the curbing of local government as well as the elevation of restricted public expenditure generally as a major 'good', the encouragement of commercial provision without thought for the likely effect on standards and quality, and the enormous growth of the entertainment industry with its own very different standards from those expressed in the 1944 Act − even all these have not entirely wiped out developments to which the OFE inspectorate made a modest contribution. Arts educational activities, the Open University which reflects so many AE values, the general acceptance of the need for lifelong continuing education (even if apparently often restricted to work leading to qualifications and alleged direct economic value), together with widened demand for liberal education from those who can afford it, give some hope that OFE HMI influence may in some areas continue and even strengthen. Careers education and other activity directed in a multiplicity of ways to young people's welfare and problems, as well as various types of community work, many of them concentrating on fundamental and long recognised social problems, also owe much to OFE deceased.

The other colleague writes:

The OFE inspectorate was one of many outcomes of the 1944 Act and its assembly of the apparent ragbag of educational activities, concerns, movements − most of them already existing in some form, a few yet to be created − which did not fit comfortably into the traditional, normal and popularly accepted categories of formal schooling. Neither OFE nor its inspectorate ever succeeded in persuading either the education profession at large, or a majority of other HMI, or more than a few exceptional politicians and civil servants, or a sufficiently large and vocal public, of the validity of OFE's educational, social, and even its economic claims. The evidence it was able to adduce was strong but it never overcame the blind assumption that monolithic institutions for the young and qualifications directly related to potential income are capable of delivering what is claimed for them, and sufficient for the health of an *adult* nation.

The loss of a system of inspection which rested upon detailed and continuous independent evaluation deprived formal education and those who govern and deliver it of a unique source of thoroughly grounded, unbiased and undoctrinaire evidence and advice. That of so much of OFE and, particularly, of a modern system of general adult education available to *all,* to 'the people of England and Wales', goes deeper. That loss amounts to the denial of values concerning the whole quality of life and of democratic citizenship. It is a denial of educational rights to the people at large as opposed to the young only, and of that broadly exploratory education which fulfils potential and delivers both mature responsibility and innovation, rather than mere completion of examinable modules. In midst of that cultural catastrophe, OFE and its inspectorate could not claim to be more than a very small piglet in the herd at Gadara, but it turned its snout uphill. It was trampled underfoot for its pains, yet its memory lingers.

Notes

1. For example, as late as the early 60s there were only 192 full-time LEA adult educators in England and Wales.
2. We would remind readers that all text in inverted commas is quoted verbatim from personal contributions.
3. Has she forgotten her first visit to the meat department of a nameless college, which quickly ceased trying to be superior after she taught them how to sharpen their own knives? (ed.)

Appendix 1: HM Inspectorate of Schools

The Inspectorate began to change significantly (as it had done in 1945) from about 1972, soon after the time when its Other Further Education group was amalgamated with the larger Technical, Commercial and Art section. The reasons for this are outside the brief of this volume; in any case experienced OFE specialist HMI who remained tended to maintain their commitments as far as practicable though their numbers were rapidly eroded by retirement, and new policies governed such replacements as were made. Compared with any other country, and with the arrangements which followed the end of its original form and role, HM Inspectorate of Schools was unique because its major role was evaluation, support and advice as opposed to monitoring and control. No other country has ever had such a service or a body of people providing it with that particular role or the degree of independence which made it practicable.

The function of HMI as a whole was to have a deep and wide knowledge of the state of education in all its institutions and services throughout the country, and to advise the Minister of its state, of its needs and of the practical and policy implications. Having this knowledge and expertise also enabled them to advise and support all those in the field who had the task of providing and administering the service, whether they were individual classroom teachers, heads of institutions or of whole services, such as the chief education officers of LEAs. The following outline of the inspectorate';s organisation and structure may seem formal, but in reality the service was highly flexible.

Every HMI had some of the generic functions just mentioned, though in different proportions. They were individually deployed to carry both territorial and specialist responsibilities. Specialism was a matter of both phase (eg, primary or secondary schools, the whole post-school sector or particular aspects such as technical or adult education) and of subject specialism. Territorial responsibility could cover greater or smaller areas depending on the overall geographical and specialist balance of individual assignments. Territorial responsibility also involved HMI acting as a trusted and well informed link between the Department and the LEAs. Divisional Inspectors (DI) were responsible for the organisation and oversight of the whole of this network in a large region; Regional Staff Inspectors (RSI) had administrative responsibilities in vocational Further Education. Staff Inspectors (SI) carried national responsibility for a subject or phase. Committees of HMI for each phase or subject focused their experience and advice nationally and made it available to Department, Minister and the field. This was done more particularly through the small group of Chief Inspectors (CI) and the Senior Chief Inspector (SCI) in one direction, and through courses and publications in the other.

Within their personal assignments for the time being HMI were responsible for building up, by regular visiting over a period of years, their knowledge of the institutions and services to which they were assigned as 'general inspectors'. All visits were recorded in informal notes which were deposited in an institutional file, and, together with all other information, built up a continuous evaluative account of every school or college or youth club or county education service, and so on, over the years. Visiting specialist HMIs' notes were added to the collection. Until government replaced the original inspection arrangements and set up Ofsted, inspection was thus a frequent and continuous process. Excepting some of the innumerable small institutions in the OFE remit, all were covered in this way until the latter years, when much HMI time was diverted into other tasks. Full, or Reporting Inspections took place at long intervals. Their aim was to focus the continuous informal process with the help of a team of specialists who worked with their local generalist colleague to create an all-embracing and intensively searching portrait. This depicted most often a single institution, but could also adopt the form of a 'survey' of a geographical area or a type of work, structure or content, thus throwing light on more generic problems or patterns. However, even such surveys, prior to later changes, rested on continuous inspectoral visiting and secure knowledge. The individual files on every institution, organisation or service throughout the whole of education formed a unique and vast source of knowledge which could have been of inestimable value to historians no less than educators. It is understood that, at the time of reorganisation, they and many other irreplaceable records were destroyed instead of being deposited in the PRO.

One essential characteristic of the Inspectorate was thus that *it knew* the state and the needs of the field with a thoroughness and intimacy which began to be unattainable as continuous personal knowledge based on intensive regular visiting was replaced by broad surveys, and eventually by the present system of periodic spot checks. HMI was responsible for having and continuously updating their knowledge, and for making it, and its implications for action in the field and policy at the centre, known without fear or favour. It was also responsible for ensuring that its knowledge of best practice was made available to the field through individual advice, through the provision of courses, and by means of publications.

The other equally essential characteristic was that HMI had *unlimited responsibility within their assignments, but no power whatsoever.* The only important exception to this was the power of TCA inspectors over the allocation of course provision and building programmes, both of which inevitably affected their relationships with the field in ways which other HMI would have regretted. In general, however, nobody could stop HMI presenting evidence and giving advice, whether centrally or locally, but nobody was obliged to take any notice of it: influence had to be earned. Not only did HMI make no appointments or promotions; they were not permitted to give testimonials or act as referees. Since nobody's career depended on HMI, people could and did trust them, and came to them with problems and difficulties in a way they could not approach their superiors or local inspectors and advisers. HMI's job was to discover the potential in people, institutions and services, and then to stimulate and enable them to meet it *in their own way,* not HMI's.

All this meant that certain qualities and characteristics were required in people who were going to be effective in such an unusual role. Those choosing among applicants for the service looked for people who were expert and innovatory, at the growing edge of their particular discipline and field of work, and who appeared to have the vitality and creative energy to remain there. They looked for senior administrative or organising experience – the kind of people whose experience enabled them to advise and entitled them to the respect of chief education officers, principals and the like. They looked for appropriate personal qualities and, of course, for a constitution that could stand the pace of work and the psychological demands.

The demands were great. There was always far more work than could be done. Certainly one of the main sources of stress was the need to decide priorities in the knowledge that important work would be neglected. Not all newly appointed HMI found it easy to come to terms with having responsibility but no power, and the temptations open to excellent and experienced practitioners to exceed their brief or even throw their weight around were real. They were not always resisted, but (thanks mainly to careful selection among very large numbers of well qualified applicants, and a very long probationary period) lapses and outright failures were rare.

Finally, it must be stressed again that this apparently formal service was extraordinarily flexible. There were always exceptions to any generalisation that could be made about HMI – including those in this note.

Appendix 2: A Note on the Historical Context

This book records events which took place during the professional lifetimes of authors born in the first and early second quarters of the 20th century. The events happened mainly in the third quarter, though our account overlaps necessarily and sometimes substantially both its past and future. It is published in the 21st century. The general social and political context of our story, and its significance for the out-of-school education of adults and young people, may thus be no longer equally familiar to all readers, and deserves recalling for some.

World War I (1914–18) spelled the end of an epoch in many ways but also encouraged people to look towards a better future. The Fisher Education Act of 1918 raised the minimum school leaving age to 14 and proposed the intro-duction of compulsory day release to part-time schooling, although few of its day continuation schools materialised. It was followed in 1919 by the *Final Report of the Adult Education Committee of the Ministry of Reconstruction* (re-printed in Wiltshire *et al*, 1980), which has had a lasting influence far beyond Britain on thought about the need for and aims of liberal, cultural and socio-political education of adults. In British practice, however, it led only to minimal increases in RB provision and some expansion of adult and youth social education by a few LEAs.

This lack of action was due partly to the economic aftermath of war, greatly exacerbated from 1929 by world depression. Continuing gross primary poverty was reflected in housing conditions and living standards generally for the mass of the population, which suffered additionally from large scale unemployment and inadequate welfare provision. These factors further stimulated an already wide-spread and deep-rooted surge of social, political and economic re-thinking.

The threat of new war led to some amelioration of economic conditions. When World War II (1939–45) erupted it had a much more widespread and socio-economically significant impact than World War I: it involved virtually everyone personally in various ways, as well as whole communities and their development. War purposes were clearer, more rational, far-reaching and idealistic. Above all, great efforts were made to educate the whole nation about war problems and the complex socio-political changes necessary if the problems which had been widely recognised before the war in health, housing and education in particular were to be rectified. A new and all-embracing educational framework to embody these aims was enacted by the National (*all party*) Government in 1944, and a surge of other major legislative developments followed after hostilities ended in 1945.

The new Labour government with its large majority was committed to the developments proposed in the war-time government's Education Act as well as to other reforms, including especially the National Health Service. Those who were involved in the creation and development of the Education Act's great innovation, Other Further Education – the theme of our book – shared in the passionate enthusiasm and devotion to the task of creating the new world which was foreshadowed in these massive and all-embracing aspirations.

However, compared with 1918, the conclusion of the war left Britain not just with this wider agenda of social improvement, but with a more daunting task of physical reconstruction. Both tasks had to be attempted with the country in an increasingly serious economic and financial situation due to the enormous costs of war and the fundamental and continuing change in the international position of its economy.

Thus in the two decades immediately after the war all educational development was seriously hampered by the building industry's inadequacy to meet the enormous demands of reconstruction, renewal, and improvement of housing standards. To this incubus were added variably intense but persistent financial problems. It became quickly clear that in such circumstances OFE would suffer disproportionately, and so it proved. The enthusiasm for lifelong social and cultural education was widely shared in education, including among top Board of Education officials before and during the war, though but few officials or ministers, none of them senior, shared it afterwards. The expectation had been that it would now be backed by willingness to provide resources. The reality proved to be that it was now much attenuated: priority was to be given to schools, formal further education and universities, and the preceding text details the process by which this viewpoint, joined to recurring economic and financial crises and other social and political developments, led to slowed growth and in many cases final decline of aspects of OFE.

Social and political developments included growing fears of social disorder at some stages, which led to the unusual result of loosening the purse strings, at any rate for youth work. An increasingly multi-ethnic society had more varied effects, including a belief in the efficacy of adult literacy education, seen first as of major social importance, but later as part of education for direct economic vocational ends, and accorded absolute priority.

This narrow viewpoint became dominant. It stemmed from other influences, too, and especially from growing dissatisfaction with what was seen by some as a result of a 'failing school system' which needed to be re-organised to raise standards. This trend, initiated by the 'Black Papers' group, was given wider currency by a speech of the Prime Minister, Callaghan, rather curiously at Ruskin College Oxford, in 1975. Growing youth unemployment fuelled the concern, which variously affected all aspects of OFE, and linked with mounting calls for education at all levels to be directed to securing improved economic performance.

The virtual ending of gross primary poverty due to unequal but general rises in the standard of living and the development of the welfare state was of less obvious but long-term importance to the fortunes of OFE in the decades our study covers. Public perceptions of social need changed greatly as social inequality diminished, until the major reversals of public policy stemming from political change in the 1980s. Other major changes, which diminished support for various aspects of OFE, were the growth of a huge commercial entertainment industry, public support for various cultural developments, and the decline of trade union power and their support for liberal education as a route to social emancipation. Other and more recent factors influencing a decline in OFE provision mostly stem from changed government policies from the mid-1980s on. They include a growing belief in the overriding value of competition and private enterprise, the elevation of reduced public expenditure to the status of a major policy objective, and the centralising tendency which has reduced local government's ability to meet the general social and educational needs of adults and young people, even where it still has the power to do so.

It is clear, however, that changes in the balance of political power were not major factors in the chequered history of post-war OFE. The negative developments initiated in the 1970s and exacerbated from the mid-1980s have been maintained by the present administration. It can be argued that the decline of concern and provision was rather due to the prevailing of a narrow view of the purposes proper to state-assisted education. This, moreover, seems to derive from an underlying philistinism which Matthew Arnold had identified in the latter part of the nineteenth century, and which has prevailed over the ideals and practices out of which OFE (and much else of value) was born.

Bibliography

Note: All substantial publications to which the text makes more than passing reference are listed here. Minor items such as lesser reports, circulars, memoranda, etc, are referred to and identified as necessary in the text. Unpublished materials and personal texts or statements (in inverted commas where verbatim) referred to in the text are not listed.

ACSTT 2 (Advisory Committee on the Supply and Training of Teachers, FE Sub-Committee), (1978) *Second Report*, London, the Committee.

Adam, Sir R (1945) 'Adult Education in the Forces', *Adult Education*, vol 18, no 2.

Adkins, G (1981) *The Arts and Adult Education*, Leicester, ACACE.

Army Education, vol VII, no 1, Sept 1943 (an account of Bendall's approach to army education as set out in *Education in the War Time Army*, issued in Sept 1940).

Avent, C (1997) 'Looking Back', *Newscheck*, vol 8, no 3.

Banks, F (1958) *Teach Them to Live*, London, Parrish.

Batten, TR (1957) *Communities and their Development*, London, Oxford University Press.

Baxendale, AS (1993) 'Maurice Lyndon Wallis and Prison Education', in Neale, K (ed), *Prison Service People*, vol 1, Wakefield, Prison Service College.

Bolton, E (1998) 'HMI – The Thatcher Years', *Oxford Review of Education*, vol 24, no 1.

Central Advisory Council for Education (England) (1959) *15–18* (The Crowther Report), London, HMSO.

Clarke, R (1990) *Enterprising Neighbours*, London, National Federation of Community Organisations and Community Projects Foundation.

Council of Europe, Council for Cultural Co-operation (1971) *Permanent Education*, Strasbourg, the Council.

Daines, J *et al* (1982) *Changes in Student Participation in Adult Education*, Nottingham, Nottingham University, Department of Adult Education.

Deakin, Sir N (1996) *Meeting the Challenge of Change*, Report of the Commission on the Future of the Voluntary Sector, London, NCVO.

Directorate of Army Education (1944) *The British Way and Purpose*, the Directorate.

Dunford, JE (1998) *Her Majesty's Inspectorate of Schools since 1944*, London and Portland, Oregon, Woburn Press.

Education and Science, Dept of (1970) *Explorations in Adult Learning and Training for Adult Education*, London, DES (and various other editions).

Education and Science, Dept of (1972) *Teacher Education and Training* (the James Report), London, HMSO.

Education and Science, Dept of (1973) *Adult Education: a Plan for Development* (The Russell Report), London, HMSO.

Education, Board of, Youth Advisory Council (1943) *Youth Service after the War*, London, HMSO.

Education, Ministry of (1944) *Community Centres* ('The Red Book'), London, HMSO (reprinted 1946, 1950).

Education, Ministry of (1947) *Further Education* (Pamphlet no 8), London, HMSO.

Education, Ministry of (1954) *The Organisation and Finance of Adult Education in England and Wales*, London, HMSO.

Education, Ministry of (1956) *Evening Institutes*, London, HMSO.

Education, Ministry of (1958) *The Youth Service in England and Wales* (the Albemarle Report), London, HMSO.

Education, Ministry of (1962) *General Studies in Technical Colleges*, London, HMSO.

Education, Ministry of (1963) *Half our Future* (the Newsom Report), London, HMSO.

Edwards, HJ (1961) *The Evening Institute: Its Place in the Educational System of England and Wales*, London, NIAE.

Elsdon, KT (1962) *Centres for Adult Education*, London, NIAE.

Elsdon, KT (1975) *Training for Adult Education*, Nottingham, NIACE and University of Nottingham.

Elsdon, KT (1984) *The Training of Trainers*, Cambridge, Huntington Publishers.

Evans, WM (1965) *Young People in Society*, Oxford, Blackwell.

Ferguson, J (1981) *Christianity, Societies and Education*, London, SPCK.

Fieldhouse, R (ed) (1996) *The History of Modern British Adult Education*, Leicester, NIACE.

Forster, W (ed) (1981) *Prison Education in England and Wales*, see ch. 5 (Edmonds, R) and ch. 4 (Birkie, W), Leicester, NIACE.

Fox, L (1952) *The English Prison and Borstal System*, London, RKP.

Hastings, K (1998) *In a Right State*, the Book Guild.

Hegginbotham, H (1951) *The Youth Employment Service*, London, Methuen.

Hutchinson, EM (1959) 'Some Questions of Cost', *Adult Education*, vol 32, no 1.

Jennings, B (ed) (ND/1980) *Community Colleges in England and Wales*, Leicester, NIAE.

Kekewitch, GW (1920) *The Education Department and After*, London, Constable.

MacLure, JS (2001) *The Inspectors' Calling – HMI and the Shaping of Educational Policy, England & Wales, 1945–1992*, London, Hodder and Stoughton Educational.

Marks, HES (1949) *Community Centres and Adult Education*, London, National Council of Social Service.

Marriott, S (1998) 'The Board of Education and Policy for Adult Education up to the Second World War', *History of Education*, vol 27, no 4.

May Committee (1980) *Report of the Committee of Enquiry into the UK Prison System*, London, HMSO.

Mee, G and Wiltshire, HC (1978) *Structure and Performance in Adult Education,* London, Longman.

Morgan, AE (1935) *The Needs of Youth*, London, King George's Jubilee Trust.

NACRO (1980) *Bridging the Gap*, London, National Association for the Care and Resettlement of Offenders.

National Institute of Adult Education (1955) *Liberal Education in a Technical Age*, London, Max Parrish.

Pflüger, A (1978) *Training and Retraining of Adult Educators*, Strasbourg, Council of Cultural Co-operation, Council of Europe.

Ritchie, KJ (1958) 'Memo. of Reflections on his Work Prepared by KJR on His Retirement as Staff Inspector, for Sir Lionel Fox and the Commission, PRO, ED Box 2.

Select Committee on Education, Science and the Arts (1990, 1991/2) *Reports on Prison Education*, London, HMSO.

Simpson, JA (1972) *To-day and To-morrow in European Adult Education*, Strasbourg, Council of Europe.

Snow, CP (1956) 'The Two Cultures', *New Statesman*, 6 October.

Snow, CP (1959) *The Two Cultures and the Scientific Revolution*, Cambridge, Cambridge University Press.

Tight, M (1982) *Part time Degree Students in the UK*, Leicester, NIACE.

Trenaman, J (1957) 'Education in the Adult Population', *Adult Education*, vol 30, no 3; reprinted vol 34, no 5 (1962).

Verner, C (1959) 'Conceptual Framework for the Identification and Classification of Process for Adult Education; Preliminary Working Paper Prepared for the Annual Seminar of the Professors of Adult Education', Madison, Florida State University.

Watts, AG *et al* (1996) *Rethinking Careers Education and Guidance, their Practice and Policy,* London, Routledge.

White, ACT (1963) *The Story of Army Education, 1643–1946,* London, Harrap.

Wilson, NS, (1948) *Education in HM Forces, 1939–46; the Civilian Contribution.*

Wiltshire, HC and Bailiss, F (?1965) *Teaching through Television,* London, NIAE.

Wiltshire, HC *et al* (eds) (1980) *The 1919 Report, the Final and Interim Reports of the Adult Education Committee of the Ministry of Reconstruction, 1918–1919,* Nottingham, Nottingham University, Department of Adult Education.

Glossary

ABCA Army Bureau of Current Affairs
ABE Adult Basic Education
ACACE Advisory Council on Adult and Continuing Education
ACSTT Advisory Committee on the Supply and Training of Teachers
ACSTT (FE) ACSTT's FE sub-committee
AE Adult Education
AEC Army Education Corps (later RAEC)
ALBSU Adult Literacy and Basic Skills Unit
ALE Association for Liberal Education
Board, (the Board of Education) – see DES
CEO Chief Education Officer (sometimes entitled Director of Education)
CETYCW Council for Education and Training in Youth and Community Work
CI Chief Inspector (CI OFE; CI for OFE, etc.)
CSV Community Service Volunteers
CYEE Central Youth Employment Executive
DES Department of Education and Science (previously Board, then Ministry of Education, and subsequently Department for Education and Employment)
DI Divisional Inspector
EI Evening Institute
FE Further Education
HMI Her/His Majesty's Inspector (Inspectorate) of Schools
ILEA Inner London Education Authority (Successor to LCC Education Dept.)
LCC London County Council (and especially its Education Department)
LEA Local Education Authority
Ministry, The Ministry of Education (see DES)
NABC National Association of Boys' Clubs
NACRO National Association for the Care and Resettlement of Offenders
NACYS National Advisory Council for the Youth Service
NAYC National Association of Youth Clubs
NAYSO National Association of Youth Service Officers
NCSS National Council of Social Service (now NC of Voluntary Organisations)
NFCA National Federation of Community Associations, now Community Matters
NIA(C)E National Institute of Adult (Continuing) Education
NYA National Youth Agency
NYB National Youth Bureau (previously YSIC)
OFE Other Further Education
Office, the headquarters organisation of the DES and its predecessors
P&S Primary and Secondary (schools, education, HMI)
PRO Public Record Office
RB Responsible Body (mostly the adult education departments of universities and the Workers' Educational Association)
RSI Regional Staff Inspector
SCNVYO Standing Conference of National Voluntary Youth Organisations
SI Staff Inspector
SCI Senior Chief Inspector
T Branch pre-1944 term for HMI serving TCA (qv) institutions

TCA Technical, Commercial and Art (education, specialist HMI)
UGC University Grants Committee
VO Voluntary organisations
VSO Voluntary Service Overseas
WEA Workers' Educational Association
YES Youth Employment Service
YS Youth Service
YSDC Youth Service Development Council
YSIC Youth Service Information Centre, later NYB
YVFF Young Volunteer Force Foundation
YW Youth Work

Index

Abbreviations will be used as shown in the Glossary